Irish

427.415

taobh**tíre**

A BETTER LIBRARY SERVICE FOR RURAL AREAS

Tá an leabhar seo fá do choinnese. Thig leat leabhair a fháil ar iasacht ón chnuasach seo chomh minic agus is mian leat. Nuair a bheidh tú réidh leis, tabhair ar ais é, le do thoil, le go mbeidh deis ag daoine eile sult a bhaint as. This book is for you. You may borrow from this collection as often as you like. When finished, please return the book for others to enjoy.

Fuair mé an leabhar seo ar iasacht ar an:
I borrowed this book on:

Ar thaitin an leabhar seo leat? Buail isteach i suíomh idirlín Leabharlann Chontae Dhún na nGall go bhfeicfidh tú na mílte leabhar maith.
Did you enjoy this book? Check the Donegal County Library website for thousands of good books.

www.donegallibrary.ie

Irish

Phrases, Terms and Epithets
beginning with the word 'Irish'

THORNTON B. EDWARDS

MERCIER PRESS

First published in 2004 by Mercier Press
Douglas Village, Cork
Email: books@mercierpress.ie
Website: www.mercierpress.ie

Trade enquiries to CMD Distribution
55A Spruce Avenue
Stillorgan Industrial Park
Blackrock, County Dublin
Tel: (01) 294 2560; Fax: (01) 294 2564
E-mail: cmd@columba.ie

© Thornton B. Edwards, 2004

ISBN 1 85635 420 2
10 9 8 7 6 5 4 3 2 1

A CIP record for this title is available
from the British Library

Cover design by mercier vision

Printed in Ireland by ColourBooks,
Baldoyle Industrial Estate, Dublin 13

CONTENTS

Introduction

Most people are aware that the word 'Irish' has sometimes been used as a derisive prefix. For instance, an *Irish screwdriver* is a hammer and *Irish lace* (apart from referring to a unique form of Irish embroidery and rare flower hybrid) also means cobwebs. Yet it is amazing how many other types of phrases and expressions feature the word 'Irish', most of which are flattering and even poetic, rather than mocking. My intention in compiling this dictionary was not to provide a list of trite anti-Irish insults, but to present the first ever collection of expressions beginning with the word 'Irish', which reflect both the richness and beauty of Ireland and Irish culture. The result is a comprehensive volume containing well over a thousand fascinating entries ranging from the *Irish Achilles* to the *Irish Zorro*.

We have all heard of *Irish coffee* (which is also, incidentally, a variety of narcissus) and *Irish stew,* but how many of us know what an *Irish cluster* is? The *Irish canary* is not a bird, but what is it? Similarly, the *Irish salmon* is not a fish but a rare species of plant. What is meant by *Irish blight*? And what is an *Irish clubhouse*? Many will probably be able to guess who the *Irish Caruso* was, but who was the *Irish Mussolini* or the *Irish Solomon*? Which group of Irishmen have the reputation for being the *Irish Gascons*? And where could we find the *Irish Flanders*, the *Irish Thebaid* or the *Irish Riviera*?

Irish contains a rich hoard of literally hundreds of words and phrases containing the word 'Irish' which relate to food, drink, folklore, mythology, crafts, dances, music, tools, leisure, fine arts, flora and fauna, personal epithets, toponyms, history, weapons, education, religion and rhyming slang.

Whenever an entry, such as *wild Irishman*, has more than one meaning (i.e. a train and a type of plant), I have indicated this by numbering the different connotations or usages. As an aid to the reader, I have added cross-references to most entries.

Some entries appear under the word 'Irishman' rather than 'Irish'; these include an *Irishman's cutting* (a cutting from a plant with part of the root attached) and an *Irishman's friend* (the potato). A few entries can be used with either the word 'Irish' or 'Irishman' (*Irish or Irishman's hurricane*), in which case they usually appear under the word 'Irish' in the main part of this dictionary. Entries which are only used with the word 'Irishman' can be found in Appendix 3.

As far as possible I have tried to present faithfully only those phrases including the word 'Irish' that have entered oral tradition or have been coined by certain (usually Irish) writers. In most cases I have endeavoured to locate the source for each entry. Where the origin is untraceable, I have at least tried to identify other references to a particular phrase. A bibliography for almost all such references cited has been included. I have also made use of internet facilities, the sources of which are noted within each entry. Material taken from newspapers and magazines is likewise acknowledged in the text rather than in the bibliography.

I have also supplied six appendices: Appendix 1 analyses the various meanings of the word 'Irish'. Appendix 2 contains the meanings of the word 'Irishman'. Appendix 3 lists phrases that feature the word 'Irishman' (as opposed to 'Irish') and is divided into two sections, which relate to phrases beginning with 'Irishman's' (*Irishman's harvest* and *Irishman's pocket)*; and phrases where 'Irishman' is preceded by another word (*smoked* or *sunburned Irishman* and even a variety of cactus called *red-headed Irishman*). Appendix 4 provides some phrases in which the word 'Irish' is the second or last element (*black Irish, Mediterranean Irish, mere Irish, two-hand Irish* and *Turkey Irish*). Appendix 5 contains a list of phrases where the word 'Paddy' is used. In several instances the words 'Paddy' and 'Irish' are interchangeable (*Irish* or *Paddy's apple, Irish* or *Paddy's hurricane,* and *Irish* or *Paddy's toothache*). Finally, Appendix 6 provides a list of names of cocktails which contain the words 'Irish', 'Irishman' or 'Paddy'.

It is perhaps to be expected that only very few of the phrases in this dictionary retain the word 'Irish' (i.e. *'Gaelach'* or *'Éireannach'*) when translated into the Irish language (*caife Gaelach = Irish coffee* and *iúr Éireannach = Irish yew*). For Irish people, when referring to something that is essentially their own, the prefix 'Irish' seems redundant. Hence the *Irish hare,* for example, is called simply *'giorria'* or just 'hare'. There is only a need to be explicit when referring to the non-endemic species common elsewhere, i.e. the 'plain' hare, which is called *'giorria gallda',* or 'English/foreign hare'. By adding the suffix *'Gaelach'* in Irish, i.e. *'ghiarrfhia Gaelach'* (Thomson's aspirated spelling, 1982), it becomes *Irish hare* in the sense of 'hare cooked Irish style'.

In a few cases, the word 'Irish' is replaced by a synonym, for example 'Hibernian' is used in phrases or epithets like the *Hibernian prima donna* or derivatives thereof, such as *Hiberno-jazz*. In such cases, I have tentatively listed the main heading as 'Irish', with inverted commas, but have acknowledged that 'Hibernian' is the true form of the phrase. Moreover, the Latin form of this word, *hibernica,* can be seen in many scientific names of animals or plants which are translated as 'Irish' (*sorbus Hibernica,* or the *Irish whitebeam,* a species of tree). I have not been able in this limited space, however, to include the dozens of obscure species and subspecies of flora and fauna which have no common name (let alone the name 'Irish' something or other) but include the Latin word *'hibernica'*.

Similarly, 'Gaelic' is sometimes used, as for instance in *Gaelic football* (also more rarely called *Irish football).* Likewise, 'green' can be used to mean 'Irish' (the legendary Green Army, for which see *Irish national colour),* as can 'emerald', (the *Emerald Tiger).* The pejorative prefix 'bog' is used in a few cases as a synonym of 'Irish' (bog orange, for which see *Irish apple);* most such phrases can be found in the entry *Irish bog-trotters.* Ironically, some of these phrases come from the mouths of the Irish themselves. For instance, 'the jackeens' (please forgive the term), often refer to the very Irish sport of Gaelic football as bog-ball since it is played in the heartlands of Ireland (and is thus associated with the stereotypical Irishmen whom the former dub 'culchies').

I have also used inverted commas in a few instances where the word 'Irish' was not strictly used (the *'Irish' Athens* and the *'Irish' Canterbury* for what are really called 'the Athens of Ireland' and 'the Canterbury of Ireland'. Occasionally, a place can be known by two forms of the same epithet (Knock has been dubbed both the *Irish Lourdes* and the Lourdes of Ireland).

For entirely different reasons, non-Irish people have also sometimes deliberately refrained from using the word 'Irish'. With reference to the prejudices of the late seventeenth and eighteenth centuries, Connolly (1998) writes: 'The term "Irish" continued to have strong negative associations ... writers were prepared to employ an astonishing range of circumlocutions in order to avoid the terms "Ireland" and "Irish".'

Today, however, the word 'Irish' is almost as rich in meanings as the culture to which it belongs. This is why it is added to give a special 'colour' to the names of beautiful floral hybrids like *Irish blue* and *Irish spring*, not to mention more than a dozen rose varieties, including one called *Irish harmony*. To misquote Shakespeare's *Romeo and Juliet*, a rose by any other name would not smell as sweet – nor sound as sweet! As we can see from the wide variety of phrases in which it is used, the word 'Irish' almost always conjures up images of beauty, magic, mystery, warmth, charm and a great wealth of life and tradition.

Thornton B. Edwards

Abbreviations

Amer.	American (American English)
A.Mx	Anglo-Manx
Aust.	Australian (Australian English)
Bret.	Breton
Brewer's	*Brewer's Dictionary of Phrase and Fable*
BWA	*Bulletin of the Welsh Academy*
CGG	Celtic Gods and Goddesses (webpage in site www.geocities.com)
Chambers	*Chambers Twentieth-Century Dictionary*
Corn.	Cornish
Dan.	Danish
Encycl. Amer.	*Encyclopedia Americana*
Encycl. Brit.	*Encyclopaedia Britannica*
ESGP	*Encyclopaedia of Sports, Games and Pastimes*
Fr.	French
Gael.	Gaelic (refers to the Gaelic of Scotland)
GPC	*Geiriadur Prifysgol Cymru* (a dictionary of the Welsh Language)
Gk	Greek
Ir.	Irish
It.	Italian
Mx	Manx
NAR	National Apple Register of the UK (see Smith, M. W. G. in Bibliography)
nd	no date
NZ	New Zealand (New Zealand English)
O.Ir.	Old Irish
OED	*Oxford English Dictionary*
RDGED	*Readers Digest Great Encyclopaedic Dictionary*
Scot.	Scottish
Sl.	slang
Sp.	Spanish
Tk.	Turkish
Webster's	*Webster's 3rd New International Dictionary*
W.	Welsh
W.E.	Welsh English
W.I.	West Indies (West Indian English)

A

'Irish' Acapulco, the With reference to the popular Mexican resort, Ó Muirithe (1999) writes that the holiday area near Skibbereen, Co. Cork, has been described in a brochure as 'the Acapulco of the South'. See also *Irish Riviera*.

Irish Achilles, the 1 Epithet of Cúchulainn used by Alfred Nutt ('Cúchulainn, the Irish Achilles' in *Popular Studies*, No. 8, 1900). Cúchulainn defended Ulster single-handed and is perhaps the greatest hero in Irish mythology. Like Achilles, he was a tragic hero and was invulnerable except for one weak point. He could only be killed when tied to the Pillar Stone. He has also been called the Irish Hercules. **2** Ailill Dubh-dedach, the 'black-toothed' warrior who, as Ellis (1992) observes, 'like Achilles ... could be harmed by no weapon and yet had a weak spot'. He was thus slain by Art. Just as Achilles' heel was not dipped into the River Styx, so in sixteenth-century Ireland 'the right arm of the male child was left "pagan" (unbaptised) so that it might strike harder blows' (Leach, 1949). See also *'Irish' Atlantis, 'Irish' Camelot, Irish Elysium, Irish Odyssey*. Not to be confused with *Achill Irish* (Appendix 4).

Irish acre A unique Irish unit of measurement. Evans (1957) wrote that 'a crack hooksman' could reap and tie fifty twelve-sheaf stooks a day, or say an Irish acre (one and two-thirds English acres). Elsewhere, an Irish acre is given as 'seven yards to the perch (whereas the statute acre is five and a half yards to a perch)' (Macafee, 1996). Connolly (1998) states that 'the "Irish" or "plantation" acre was 1.62 statute acres, as opposed to the Cunningham acre (used in Ulster) of 1.29 statute acres'. A Scots acre was 1.3 statute acres (Robinson, 1985); a Welsh acre was 2 statute acres (Edwards, 1998) and a Cornish acre was 120 statute acres. See also *Irish mile, Irish spirits measure, 'Irish' yard*.

Irish Act of Uniformity The Act of Uniformity, often prefixed by 'Irish' (for instance by Connolly, 1998), really refers to two Acts: **1** The 1560 Act forcing Irish clergymen to use the English Prayer Book of 1559 (which was not translated into Irish until 1608). **2** The Act of 1666, adopting the revised English Prayer Book of 1662.

Irish adventurers 1 As the colonists of the so-called *'Irish'*
plantations have sometimes been called (Dodd, 1972). **2** A
synonym of *Irish rogues* (Ó Ciosáin, 1998).

Irish Afterglow A unique variety of soft pink rose (Brett, nd).

Irish Agitator, the As Daniel O'Connell was dubbed (*Brewer's*),
for whom see *Irish Dan*. See also *Irish king, uncrowned*.

Irish Agrarian Rebellion J. Donnelly's phrase in an article of
the same title on the Whiteboys' activities (in *Proceedings of
the Royal Irish Academy* 183, 1983). The Whiteboys (Ir. *Buac-
haillí bána*), so-called because of their white shirts, opposed
tithes, enclosures and other agricultural injustices. The movement began in Co. Tipperary in 1761 and soon spread to
other counties.

Irish Agreement, Anglo- 1 1938, between Éamon de Valera and
Neville Chamberlain to conclude the Economic War. **2** 15
November 1985, signed by Taoiseach Garret Fitzgerald and
British prime minister Margaret Thatcher, agreeing that the
Irish republic would have a consultative role in Northern
Ireland.

Irish ague A disease prevalent in the sixteenth and seventeenth
centuries and marked by headache, aching bones, weak-
ness and loss of sleep and appetite. It was difficult to cure
and may have been typhus or malaria; it was common in
bogland areas (Connolly, 1998). See also *Irish fever, Irish Plague,
the*. Few epidemics or diseases contain the word 'Irish'; the
Irish nicknamed this one the English 'bug', 'bugs having,
as it is said, been introduced into Ireland by the English'
(Share, 1997).

Irish air demons So the Genity Glinne are called (CGG). They
helped the Ulstermen in battle by confusing Medb's army.

Irish alphabet 1 The ancient ogham alphabet was used in Ireland and Wales and each letter (named after a tree) consist-
ed of different strokes (*Webster's*). **2** There is also an alphabet of eighteen letters for the Irish language; the letters in
this alphabet have both a roman and a beautiful Gaelic
form. Some Gaelic letters, such as 'g' and 's', are very different from the standard roman letters, making various shop
signs and other notices almost indecipherable to the un-
initiated. To aspirate, where the roman alphabet adds 'h',
the Gaelic alphabet adds a dot above the letter. See also

Irish manuscript lettering, Irish typeface.

Irish American soda bread Like *Irish soda bread* but with added caraway seeds and cardamom, as well as citron peel and raisins (Campbell, 1997). See also *Irish brown soda bread.*

Irish amulet An eighteenth-century misspelling of Irish omelette (Fitzgibbon, 1983).

'half Irish and all American' Refers to an Irish-American who has become more American than Irish. (Frank Capra described John Ford thus.) See also *Irish than the Irish, more.*

Irish and Country or 'Country and Irish'. Country-and-western-style Irish music. See also *Irish Athabaskan, Irish Cajun, Irish music.*

Irish Anglo-Saxon With reference to ecclesiastical music, 'the term "Irish Anglo-Saxon" neume-type was coined by ... Peter Wagner' (Encycl. Brit., Vol. 15).

Irish annulet A very rare variety of moth officially listed as *odontognophos dumetata hibernica.* It is a subspecies of a type seen only in the Mediterranean until the late Peter Forder discovered it in the Burren in 1991. For the so-called 'white moths', see also *Irish Tinkers* and *'Irish' pug.*

Irish answer An evasive one. To give an Irish answer is similar to answering 'Scotch fashion' (Partridge, 1937), i.e. to reply to a question with another question, conforming to stereotypical *stage Irish* expectations. 'I imagined that I should have nothing to drink in Ireland but whiskey, that I should have nothing to eat but potatoes, that I should sleep in mud-walled cabins, and that I should know nothing but the Irish howl, the *Irish brogue,* Irish answers and *Irish bull'* (quoted by Kiberd, 1991).

Irish Anthony Morton (1961) writes that the early Irish Christian community 'even possessed an Irish St Anthony, in St Kevin, whose legend it is that he pushed his temptress – a lovely girl named Kathleen, of course – into the lake'. St Anthony is known for suppressing his own passionate urges, and legend says that he once put nails inside his shoes for this purpose. See also *'Irish' Mary, Irish patron saint.*

'Irish Apostle' Or 'the Apostle of Ireland' (Edwards, 1995) was St Patrick, for whom, see the *Irish patron saint.* Irish bishop James Louis O'Donnell (1738–1811) was called 'the Apostle of Newfoundland' (Boylan, 1998). 'The Apostles' was also

the name of Michael Collins' twelve-man squad. See also
Irish Temperance, Apostle of.

Irish apple A potato (Green, 1996; Share, 1997) which is called
in NZ slang *Paddy's apple* (see Appendix 5). The Irish connection between apples and potatoes can also be seen in
terms like potato apple or pirrie-apple-pie (which in Ulster
means 'potato bread with apple', Macafee, 1996). Synonyms
include *Irish apricot, Irish football, Irish gem, Irish grape, Irish
lemon, 'Irish' navigators, Irish plum, Irish root* and *Irishman's
friend* (Appendix 3). See also *Irish apple sauce, Irish cherry,
Irish cobbler, Irish peach, Irish potato* and *Irish queen.*

Irish apple bannock Irish recipe for oatflake bannock (a round
flat loaf) and apple, served warm with cream or cold with
butter (Ross, 1997).

Irish apple cake A special Irish dessert with cloves and cinnamon added to apples (Cole, 1973). Campbell (1997) recommends that, like barmbrack, it is 'especially well suited to
Hallowe'en'. The top must be crunchy and, if warm, the
cake can be eaten with cream or custard.

Irish apple potato cake Unique Irish recipe of mashed potatoes, parsley and stewed apples made into patties and then
sautéed in butter (Johnson, 1995). It is supposed to be served with wild rabbit cider stew.

Irish apple sauce In American slang of the 1960s, this meant
mashed potatoes (Green, 1998). See also *Irish apple.*

Irish apricot A potato. First recorded by Grose in 1785 (cited in
OED). Also called Munster plum or bog orange (Green,
1996), yet distinct from an *Irish orange.* See *Irish apple* for
more synonyms.

Irish aqua vitae So *Irish whiskey* has been called (Magee, 1980;
Logan, 1986; Booth, 1995; Mahon, 1991). Etymologically,
both the Latin *aqua vitae* and the Irish *uisce beatha* (which
both mean whiskey) mean literally 'water of life'. Note
also 'vodka' (from Russian *voda* = water). In the mid-nineteenth century, 'water of life' meant whiskey (Green, 1998).
Yet Partridge (1937) said that in the 1820s, 'water of life'
was applied to gin, whereas the identical meaning in French,
eau de vie, referred to brandy. In Shakespeare's *The Merry
Wives of Windsor,* Ford, a gentleman in disguise, says of
trusting his wife: 'I will rather trust a Fleming with butter,

Parson Hugh the Welshman with my cheese, an Irishman with my aqua-vit [*sic*] bottle'. See also *Irish poteen, Irish Russian, Irish wine.*

Irish archeology, the father of George Petrie (1790–1866), famous for his records of early Christian antiquities in Ireland as well as his study of the *Irish round tower* in Rahee Island, Co. Down, and Tara, Co. Meath.

Irish ard A primitive form of plough about which there are few details (see Evans, 1957). See also *Irish foot-plough, Irish plough, Irish spade.*

'Irish' armchair Form of armchair taken by Irish settlers to Australia and Upper Canada. Kinmouth writes that it is a 'distinctly Irish form of armchair, with its interlocked armrest and corner spindle, and its lack of stretchers' (1993). See also *Irish chair, Irish Chippendale, Irish Windsor chair.*

Irish arms 1 Thick legs. Similarly, a Mullingar or Munster heifer was nineteenth-century Anglo-Irish slang for a girl with thick ankles (Partridge, 1937). Note also Scotch pegs = legs. The confusion of arms with legs is also seen, for example, in the word *crubeen* (Wall, 1995), which refers to a pig's foot but in jocular usage is a hand. Indeed, *Irish arms* can also be referred to as *Irish legs.* **2** The arms of Ireland – azure – a harp in stringed argent (silver). Not to be confused with *Irish coat of arms.*

Irish arse, kiss my royal (KMRIA) An expletive and play on MRIA (member of the Royal Irish Academy), according to Share (1997). No relation to the 'Erse-hole', which was how Behan dubbed the *fáinne* (the ring-shaped badge worn by *Gaeilgeoirí,* or Irish speakers) (quoted by Kiberd, 1991). Similarly, the word 'pogue' (see also *Irish Charles Bukowski* for reference to the Pogues) is used by Americans as a nickname for an Irishman. The term may be the result of the American host repeating the Irishman's unintelligible insult, *'póg mo thón',* meaning ' kiss my arse'. On the same anatomical lines, the Irish-sounding phrase 'have a Murphy' refers to 'having one's underwear caught between the buttocks' (Green, 1998).

Irish Articles The Hundred and Four Articles of Faith proposed by Archbishop Ussher in 1615. These articles were more Calvinistic than the Anglican Thirty-nine Articles and were accepted in Ireland in 1635 (Livingstone, 1977). See also *'Irish' Canterbury*.

Irish as Paddy Murphy's pig, as Very Irish indeed (Rawson, 1991; Green, 1996). There was also the phrase 'as poor as Paddy Murphy's pig' and the NZ equivalent 'ignorant as Paddy's pig' (Green, 1996). Similarly, 'Murphy's countenance' or 'Murphy's face' once meant a pig's head (Partridge, 1937). Yet the true Irish expression should be *'Chomh Gaelach le muca Dhroichead Atha'*, i.e. *'As Irish as the pigs of Drogheda'* (Rosenstock, 1993). See also *Irish bacon, Irish cattle, Irish grazier, Irish greyhound, Irish landrace, Irish pig, pig in the parlour Irish* (Appendix 4) and *Paddy Ward's pig* or *Paddy's pig* (Appendix 5).

Irish assurance 'Bold forward assurance' (Partridge, 1937) and thus 'shamelessness' (Green, 1996). Similarly, Green informs us that in Czech there is the term *irska samolibost*, which translates as 'Irish assurance' and means 'boasting'. The nineteenth-century expression 'dipped in the Shannon' referred to someone who is 'shameless or devoid of shyness' (Green, 1996). See also *Irish Gascons* and *Fighting Irish* (Appendix 4)

Irish Athabaskan Musical term used by some Irish-music experts (Ó hAllmhuráin, 1998; Vallely, 1999) to refer to the blending of the similar styles of *Irish music* with the music of the Irish and other settlers of Alaska. See also *Irish Cajun*.

Irish atheist John P. Mahaffy says that 'an Irish atheist is one who wishes to God he could believe in God'. Similarly, Dave Allen confesses 'I am an atheist, thank God' (both quoted by MacHale, nd). Eagleton (1999) records the story of a tourist in Belfast who, to play safe, told a 'drunken sectarian mob' that he was an atheist. They demanded: 'But are you a Protestant atheist or a Catholic atheist?'

'Irish' Athens or **the Athens of Ireland 1** Belfast (*Brewer's*) **2** Cork – due to its thriving literary activity in the nineteenth century (Share, 1997). See also *Irish Bath, the; Irish capital; Irish Flanders; Irish Harrogate; 'Irish' Normandy; Irish Salisbury; Irish Siberia; 'Irish' Sodom*.

'Irish' Atlantis *Hy Brasail* or *I Bhreasuil*, an *Irish Otherworld* believed to be in the Atlantic, and named after King Breasal. It was visible only every seven years, and if a person saw it,

he or she would die. Many writers have identified it with
Atlantis (Wall, 1995; McMahon, 1997). Kavanagh (1959) explains that under Lough Neagh 'is a city inhabited by fairies'
which fishermen can see in fine weather. Irish folklore is
extremely rich in stories of sunken islands (such as *Fin-
chory* or *Fianchuibhe*, from which the sons of Tuireann were
asked to fetch a spit). See also *Irish Elysium*.

Irish attack Opening move in chess 1.Nc3 e5 2.f4. See also *Irish
gambit*. (www.geocities.com).

Irish Aubrac Either the imported cattle breed from France,
which is Irish-reared, or the cross-breeds of the French
Aubrac with native Irish cattle for beef. 'Straws were taken
from the best (Aubrac bulls) ... and used on dairy and
suckler cows, mostly in the west Cork region' (see www.
tasc.ie). Apart from its usual meaning, a 'straw' is also a
container of bull's semen for artificial insemination – in the
case above, with native Irish cows. See also *Irish cow, old*.

'Irish' Augustus Turloch Mor O'Conor, king of Connacht and
High King of Ireland in the twelfth century who was called
'the Augustus of the West of Europe' (Killanin, 1962).

Irish authors, father of James Joyce (1882–1941), novelist. He is
called this by Crotty (1992). Kinsella called him 'father of
authors' (Crotty, 1992). See also *Irish Ulysses, The*.

Irish aviation, father of As Ron Kirwan dubs Dr Brendan
O'Regan, founder of Shannon International Airport. O'Regan
also established the airport restaurant at Foynes (see the
internet newsletter the *Limerick Leader*, 27 July 2002).

B

Irish babu A West Briton. The word 'babu' (or 'baboo') is an
honorific title for a Hindu gentleman. In the Anglo-Indian
slang of the British Raj, babu came to mean a 'clerk, half-
anglicised Hindu' (Hawkins, 1984). By extension, Paul
Dunne writes with reference to a 'half-anglicised Irishman'
that 'A West Brit or West Briton is one term applied to an
Irish babu ... the West Brit is characterised by their attempt
to ape English manners, customs, games, accent, etc.' (See
website *A History of Ireland in Song*). See also *Irish Gandhi,
Irish hooley* and *Irish soma* for other Hiberno-Indian connections.

Irish baby buggy American miners' and loggers' slang for a wheelbarrow (Blevins, 1993). A synonym of *Irish baby carriage, Irish buggy, Irish chariot, Irish local* and *Irish pluggy*. For other gardening equipment and tools, see *Irish banjo, Irish combine, Irish screwdriver* and *Irish toothpick*.

Irish baby carriage A wheelbarrow (Green, 1996).

'Irish' backgammon According to Halliwell (1847), the word 'Irish' referred to 'An old game, similar to backgammon, but more complicated.' Yet according to MacHale (1979), 'backgammon ... is a sort of rasher.' See also *Two-hand Irish* (Appendix 4), *Irish checkers, 'Irish' chess, Irish gambit, Irish loo, Irish poker, Irish quarters, Irish roulette* and *Irish whist*.

Irish backsword 'The French *estoc*, the German *Katzbalger* and the Irish backsword' were preferred to the rapier as the 'shorter, heavier cut-and-trust weapon' of choice of sixteenth-century warfare. (See website www.latourdulac.com)

Irish bacon Distinct form of bacon, produced from native locally bred Irish breeds and processed by pump-injecting the brine into the meat, thereby improving its taste in the curing process (Connolly, 1998). In the nineteenth century, Irish bacon curing was a greater industry even than the Danish. Bluett (1994) cautions that 'Irish bacon is very salty and has to be soaked overnight just before eating.' Since this type of bacon is of exceptional quality, the Irish did not like what they called 'American lad', i.e. fatty bacon imported from America (Share, 1997). See also *Irish cattle, Irish grazier, Irish greyhound, Irish landrace* and *Irish pig*.

Irish bagpipes In Ireland there was a mouth-blown bagpipe comprising a bladder and pipes analogous to those used in Scotland and on the continent. However, owing to eighteenth century prohibitions (see Vallely, 1999), possibly owing to its use in war, it very soon became replaced by the *'Irish' uilleann pipes*. Today, this latter form of elbow-blown pipes, while very distinct, are often referred to as an Irish bagpipe (see Baines, 1992). Apparently, one method of discovering a changeling (a baby of the fairies, left by them in place of a real baby – called in Irish *iarlais, síofra* or *fágálach*) was to place *Irish bagpipes* near the cot, as the changeling cannot resist the temptation of the bagpipes. See also *Irish bouzouki, Irish harp, Irish tambourine*.

Irish Balzac 1 George Moore is 'sometimes called the Irish Balzac' (Honoré de Balzac was a famous French novelist [1799–1850]) according to Brian Blood in his internet article 'The Dolmetsch Story' (www.dolemtsch.com). **2** 'Benedict Kiely is the Irish Balzac' as Heinrich Boll said (quoted on the *Wolfhound Press homepage*). **3** Canon Sheehan has also been called the Irish Balzac (www.dun garvanmuseum.org).

Irish bandit Christensen's term for the *Irish rapparee* (1996). Yet, as Ó Ciosáin (1998) suggests, ' *"bandit"* means literally "banished", in other words, an outlaw'; thus etymologically it applies to his social status rather than to any illegal activities. He has also been called the Irish bandit-hero (Ó Ciosáin, 1998). See also *Irish bushranger, Irish pikeman, Irish rogues*.

Irish banjo A shovel (Rawson, 1991; Green, 1996). For other jocular names for a spade, see *Irish fan, Irish harp* and *Irish spoon,* and for other tools see *Irish combine, Irish screwdriver* and *Irish toothpick*. See also *Irish spade*.

Irish bank A rhyming-slang phrase for masturbation, derived from 'Allied Irish Bank' or 'Irish bank' (the word 'bank' is often omitted) (Share, 1997). See also the parallel British slang phrases 'Barclay's bank' and 'Yorkshire penny bank' (Green, 1998), as well as the more common phrase 'merchant banker'. For similar meanings, see *Irish promotion* and *Irish wedding*. For other examples of rhyming slang, see *Irish lasses, Irish rose, Irish stew*.

Irish barmbrack The 'Irish' is sometimes prefixed, but usually it is called simply *barmbrack* (from Ir. *bairín* = 'loaf' and *breac* = 'speckled', since it is speckled with currants). Barmbrack is a fruit loaf which contains a variety of objects: a ring (to represent marriage), a thimble (spinsterhood), a coin (wealth), a button (bachelorhood), a chip of wood (a married life during which one partner would be beaten by the other) and a rag (poverty) (see Danaher, 1972). Barmbrack – like colcannon (mashed potatoes and cabbage) – is made especially for Hallowe'en.

'Irish baronies' Petty kingdoms or subdivisions thereof during the English occupation of Ireland (Evans, 1957). See also *Irish fifth*.

Irish bath Evans (1957) refers to 'the *tigh'n allais,* or the stone sweat-house, the Irish version of the Turkish bath, which the Germans indeed call the Irish bath'. It could also be described as an Irish sauna or Irish sweathouse. Joyce (1910) refers to it as 'sweating house' which conveys the actual meaning of the Irish (*tigh/teach* which is house and *allais* which is the genitive of *allas* or sweat, perspiration).

Irish Bath, the Mallow, Co. Cork. Connolly (1998) writes that 'Mallow's warm springs were promoted as a cure for consumption from 1738, and led to the town being dubbed the Irish Bath'. Bath, in the west of England, is one of the few towns to be described as a spa, indicating the presence of spring water there. For other toponyms, see *'Irish' Athens, Irish Bay of Naples*.

Irish Battalion of St Patrick The group of Irish soldiers led by Major Myles O'Reilly, who served Pope Pius IX in resisting Italian nationalists in 1860. See also *'Irish' greenfinch*.

Irish battleship In nineteenth- and twentieth-century naval slang, a barge (Partridge, 1937). A synonym of *Irish man-of-war*.

Irish Bay of Naples Area around Killiney Castle in Co. Dublin. Killiney homeowner, Paddy Fitzpatrick said: 'The estate took in the Hill of Dalkey and the Hill of Killiney, and went down to the famous Vicker Road, which is described as the Irish Bay of Naples' (quoted by Cole, 1973). This analogy had already been made by Morton (1930), who – fortunate with good weather – described the Connemara sky as being 'blue as the Bay of Naples'. See also *'Irish' Athens*.

Irish beauty 1 Woman with two black eyes (Partridge, 1937; Rawson, 1991). The phrase may be intended to stereotype the supposedly violent Irishman – yet even the roughest Irishman would never hit a lady! It is possible that the phrase (like the song 'Spanish Eyes', or perhaps more appropriately 'When Irish Eyes Are Smiling') derives from the dark (often glistening blue) eyes of the *Irish colleen*, who is indeed renowned for her beauty. Ó Faoláin (1941) was also unclear about the meaning when he alluded to 'the miners and their girls, both black-eyed (for different reasons)'. See also *Irish coat of arms, Irish wedding, to have danced at an.* **2** Variety of white rose (Brett, nd).

Irish beef stew *Irish stew* with beef rather than lamb or mutton. This particular recipe has turnips, carrots and parsley as well (Cole, 1973).

Irish beef tea A beverage for medicinal purposes consisting of steak boiled in salted water without the usual onions and herbs (Sheridan, 1996).

Irish beehive hut (Ir. *clochán*). Hut shaped like a beehive and built by early hermits. See also *Irishmen's cottages*.

Irish Belgian Blue The imported Belgian Blue cow (for which see websites of the Belgian Blue Cattle of Ireland). Although the Irish-reared cattle were referred to as Irish Belgian Blue, this appellation would seem appropriate only for those calves successfully produced as a result of cross-breeding this breed with native Irish cows (as in the case of the *Irish Aubrac* or *Irish Blonde d'Aquitaine*). See also *Irish cow, old*.

Irish bell house See *Irish round tower*.

Irish bender tent Round wagon-frame tent supported by bent sticks used by the *Irish Travellers*. While Share (1997) provides us with an Ulster meaning of 'tent' – to notice or pay attention, as in 'take tent' – according to Green (1998), the word 'tent' is Anglo-Irish for 'umbrella'. This is not as unlikely as it may seem: take, for instance, the Persian *chador* (a Muslim woman's veiled cloak), from which the Turks took the word *çadir*, for 'tent' (borrowed by the Greeks as *tsadiri*, meaning an exclusively Gypsy tent). Yet in Bulgarian, *chadur* means 'umbrella'. See also *Irish caravan*.

Irish Bigfoot The 'Shanneyganock' is, according to the Newfoundland music site www.tidespoint.com, 'a creature of the night, an Irish Bigfoot. Some also know the Shanneyganock as a Newfoundland spelling of "Shanachie", an Irish storyteller.'

Irish bird (W. *aderyn Gwyddelig*) A Welsh name for the seagull (GPC).

Irish bird goddess The epithet of the goddess *Uairebhuidhe* (CGG), about whom we know very little. For more on birds, see the *Irish goddess of beauty, Irish goddess of healing and pleasure* and *Irish war goddess*.

Irish birth, English of A post-Reformation term for the Old English Catholic settlers or those who assimilated into the native population. Mostly relates to Anglo-Normans in Dublin, Galway and the Pale who considered themselves to be Irish (Thomas and Thomas, 1997). See also *Irish Pale; Irish* *than the Irish, more; English Irish* (Appendix 4).

Irish bitch The female of an Irish hound, i.e. the *Irish wolfhound*.

Irish black moss In north-east Canada, *Irish moss* harvested but not yet bleached. See also *Irish bleached moss*, *'Irish' rake moss*, *'Irish' shore moss*, *Irish spring moss*.

Irish Blackbottom A name for a dance, and particularly the song for this dance written by Louis Armstrong to accompany it, combining swing with Irish material. It was sung by Ella Fitzgerald.

Irish blackguard In eighteenth-century usage, a brand of tobacco or snuff (Green, 1996).

Irish Blacks The Irish Black cattle which are bred in the US. As with all introduced breeds, the legitimacy of the prefix 'Irish' would depend on whether the breed has native Irish blood (see Webpage on *Breeding Cattle*). No relation to *Black Irish* (Appendix 4). See *Irish cow, old*.

Irish bladderwort (Ir. *lus an bhorraigh Gaelach*) A native plant also called intermediate bladderwort. In Latin it is known as *utricularia intermedia*. See also *Irish broom, Irish furze, Irish lady's tresses, Irish rose, Irish saxifrage, Irish spurge, Irish yew*.

Irish blanket chest A tall chest with bas-relief at sides and two drawers underneath, made in Co. Kilkenny (Shaw-Smith, 1984).

Irish blarney Eloquence. When the expression is used by a British speaker, it is not generally applied to a fellow Briton but refers to an Irishman's unique brand of eloquence: a combination of Irish charm, sometimes flattery and perhaps an amusing use of genuine *Irish logic*. The phrase derives from the Blarney Stone in Blarney Castle, Co. Cork, which is kissed upside down for this gift. (The stone itself is named after the rhetoric of the castle's owner, MacCarthy, who Elizabeth I called 'All Blarney').

Irish bleached moss (North-east Canada) *Irish moss* that is bleached in the first step for extracting carrageen (see *Irish moss*) for food purposes. For other 'Irish moss' terms, see *Irish black moss*.

Irish blight A late blight in the potato harvest (*Webster's*).

Irish Blonde d'Aquitaine The Blonde d'Aquitaine is a French beef-cattle breed. The name refers either to those pure Irish-reared herds or 'the cross between Irish dairy breeds and

French breeds' (see webpage of the *Irish Blonde d'Aquitaine
Cattle Breed Society*). See also *Irish cow, old.*

Irish blondies Type of biscuit containing walnuts and (Carolan's) *Irish cream* (Johnson, 1995).

Irish Bloody Mary A cocktail of Bailey's and Bloody Mary mix
(tomato juice, vodka and spices) (see www.*webtender.com*).
The 'Bloody Mary', not called after the '*Irish*' *Mary* but the
English Queen Mary I (1516–58), who persecuted religious
dissenters, usually by having them burned. Her half-sister
Elizabeth (who succeeded her) was just as hateful, giving
orders to 'hang the harpers wherever found' (see *Irish
harper*). The word 'blood' is also used in another Irish drink
'Beetle's Blood', which is Anglo-Irish for *Irish stout* (Green,
1998).

'Irish' Bloody Sunday (By analogy to the Russian Bloody Sunday, 22 Jan 1905, when over a hundred people were killed
in St Petersburg.) **1** 13 November 1887. British police and
lifeguards dispersed a meeting held by the Social Demo-
cratic Federation for the release of nationalist Irish MP William O'Brien. Two were killed and more than a hundred
injured. **2** 21 November 1920. IRA men killed fourteen and
injured four (mostly British intelligence agents) in Dublin;
and later three IRA men were killed at Dublin Castle and
twelve civilians were killed in Croke Park by Auxiliaries. **3**
10 July 1921. Fifteen people were killed, sixty-eight injured,
and 161 Catholic homes razed by Orange factions and RUC
Special Constabulary during the Belfast Boycott. **4** 30 January 1972. Thirteen people killed by British paratroopers in
Derry.

Irish blowers Makers of Irish glass, especially in its initial forming through blowing (Brady, 2000). No relation to the 'Kerryman glass blower' mentioned by MacHale (1979), who in-
haled instead of blowing and 'got a pane in the stomach'.

Irish blue Type of geranium with pale blue flowers originally
found in Ireland in 1947 (see www.geraniaceae.com). This
flower was especially popular as the colour of St Patrick
was once blue (see *Irish national colour*).

Irish blue blouse Female supporters or wives of the *Irish Blueshirts.*

Irish Blue Cross (Or sometimes just 'Blue Cross'). A pet charity that has mobile clinics in Dublin. See also *Irish Cross*.

Irish Blueshirts A fascist group that was formed in 1932 and, from 1933, was led by Eoin O'Duffy. Like the *Irish Christian Front*, the Blueshirts supported Franco in the Spanish Civil War. See also *Irish Brigade*.

'Irish Bluestockings' Jeffery's (nd) term for 'the Ladies of Llangollen', Eleanor Butler (1729–1829) and Sarah Ponsonby (1755–1831), two eccentric aristocrats who left Ireland to set up home at Plas Newydd, Llangollen, where they entertained various distinguished guests.

Irish blue terrier (Ir. *brocaire gorm*) Also called the Kerry blue terrier or blue terrier. See also *Irish Glen of Imaal terrier, Irish springer spaniel, Irish terrier, Irish water spaniel, Irish wheaten terrier, Irish wolfhound*. Note that the *Irish greyhound* is not only a dog.

Irish blunder 'To take the noise of brass for thunder' (Jonathan Swift, *Wood the Ironmonger*, 1725). An allusion perhaps, to the Irishman's supposed gullibility.

Irish boat This is probably another name for what is more commonly called a *Paddy boat*, a 'fishing cutter' built in America from the 1850s by Irish immigrants (Rawson, 1991), especially off the coast of Boston 'derived from an Irish model and having a cutter rig' (for one of the rare sources where it is called an 'Irish' rather than a 'Paddy' boat, see www.infoplease.com). See also *Irish battleship, Irish man-of-war, Irish two-boater*.

Irish bog butter Substance found in Irish bogs. 'Irish bog butter ... consists chiefly of free fatty acids' (Encycl. Brit., Vol. 16) and is used for making soap or candles.

Irish bog-trotters The prefix 'Irish' is used with *bog-trotter* in *Chambers Twentieth-Century Dictionary* (under the entry 'Tory' – for which see *Irish tories*) and refers particularly to a rebel Irishman or *Irish rapparee*. Almost everywhere a source of racial (and often racist) nicknames derive from geographical phenomena. Thus the word 'bog' (a feature of the Irish landscape) exists in many phrases related to the Irish: 'Bogland' was Ireland and a 'Boglander' in the late seventeenth century was an Irishman (Partridge, 1937). There was an Irish craftsmen's jargon called 'Bog Latin' and in the late nineteenth and early twentieth centuries an

Irish immigrant was referred to as coming 'straight from the bog' (Partridge, 1937). Another pejorative synonym is 'Irish bog dweller' (www.cycad.com). Irishmen are themselves guilty of using such insults about their fellow countrymen. For instance, the Dub or Jackeen, i.e. Dubliner, sometimes refers to the 'culchie', i.e. non-Dubliner, especially one from a rural area, as a 'bogger', 'bog-trotter' or 'bogman'. Moreover, Dubliners sometimes refer to *Irish football* as 'bog-ball'. Green (1996) provides other derogatory synonyms: 'bogger', 'bog-hopper' and 'bog-rat' (no relation to the *Irish rat*). Share (1997) also gives the terms 'bog man' and *Bog Irish* (see Appendix 4), referring specifically to Irishmen who are working or living in bogland areas rather than to all Irishmen. Bog oranges are potatoes (Partridge, 1937; see also *Irish apricot* and *Irishman's harvest* in Appendix 3, as well as *Irish potato*). There is also 'the Bogside' – the working-class Catholic area of Derry. For more positive nicknames derived from Ireland's unsurpassably beautiful landscape see, for example, *Irish favourite*.

Irish bogwood Type of wood found in Irish bogs and one of the best types for skilled wood-carving (*Antique Collecting* magazine, No. 21).

Irish Bohemian Sobriquet of journalist and novelist John Augustus O'Shea (1839–1905) (Welch, 1996).

Irish boiled dinner Potatoes, corned beef, sliced head of cabbage, carrots, onions and turnip (Donnelly, 1987). No relation to an *Irishman's dinner* or *Irish seven-course meal*. Yet the term *Irishman* (see Appendix 2) on its own can connote a 'boiled dinner' (Green, 1996). See also *Irish breakfast*.

Irish boiled fruit cake A Christmas cake containing plenty of Guinness. Voth (1981) tells us that because of this cake, 'in one part of Ireland Christmas Eve was called "the night of the cakes".' See also *Irish Christmas pudding*.

Irish boiled ham Ham boiled with Guinness and then covered in breadcrumbs (Sheridan, 1996). See also *Irish bacon*.

'Irish' Bond Street With reference to the London Street famous for its expensive stores, Morton (1930) writes that 'Grafton Street, Dublin, is the Bond Street of Ireland; St Patrick's Street, Cork, is the Regent Street.' St Patrick's Street was destroyed in the Troubles of 1920; was subsequently rebuilt and is now a thriving shopping street.

'Irish' Bonnie Prince Charlie Or rather 'the Bonnie Prince
Charlie of Ireland', as Michael Collins (1890–1922) has been
dubbed (see Morton, 1930) with reference to Bonnie Prince
Charlie, or Charles Edward Stuart (alias the young Pre-
tender, 1720–88), who led the Scots in the 1745 Jacobite Re-
bellion. Morton writes of Collins: 'Like Prince Charles Ed-
wards, he was young, handsome, fearless and a fugitive ...
But died, as Charles should have died on Culloden Moor.'
After the Battle of Culloden Moor (16 April 1746), Bonnie
Prince Charlie escaped to France. See also the *Irish Lenin*.

Irish booby The fortune-hunting Macahone, an anti-Catholic
stage Irish (see Appendix 4) character in George Farruhar's
The Stage Coach (1704) (Welch, 1996).

Irish boomerang 'It doesn't come back, it just sings songs about
how much it wants to' (see the website *Best of the Emerald
Isle Irish Jokes from the Gazette*), in reference to the Irish immigrant. This is an adaptation of the Welsh-boomerang joke
told by the Two Ronnies (quoted by McArthur, 1992). See
also *Paddymelon stick* (Appendix 5) and, for another meaning of 'boomerang', *Irish draught mare*.

Irish bordello A kip house. Benedict Kiely in *Honey Seems Sweeter*
(1954) describes the kip (also 'kip house') as 'the true native
Irish bordello. Fleas, disease and fights in the backyard'
(quoted by Share, 1997). The 'madame' in charge of the kip
was called a kip-keeper. (Dan. *kippe* = hut or alehouse). In
Wexford town, the word for such an establishment was
watlin' shop (Ó Muirithe, 1999). Now the word 'kip' has almost lost its former meaning and refers to 'dilapidated ac-
commodation', and to 'kip down' means to rest or sleep.
'The Murphy trick', an Irish-sounding crime term from
African-American slang (Major, 1971) also had a connection with a brothel: the term relates to a white person who
is told to wait for a (black) prostitute but is robbed (for the
confusion in black slang of equating Irish people with all
whites see *Paddy* and *Paddy Roll* in Appendix 5) See also
Irish clubhouse.

Irish Bostonian A Bostonian of Irish extraction (Arrowsmith,
2000). Boston has a particular significance for the Irish: it
was the home of the Kennedys and was even dubbed 'the

Dublin of America' (see online article *Anti-Irish Racism in the United States* and see also *Irishtown* where Dublin is a nickname for part of New York). North Carolina is called 'the Ireland of America' (Kane and Alexander, 1899). See also *Irish capital, Irish Riviera*.

Irish bouquet (US 1960s and 1970s) 'Any form of projectile, usually a stone or brick' (Green, 1998). See also *Irish confetti, Irish rose*.

Irish bouzouki Irish version of the Greek instrument. Vallely (1999) says of bouzouki exponent Donal Lunny: 'To compensate for what he considered the awkwardness of the Greek bouzouki ... he had a version made with a flat back and a shorter neck, this having now become known as the Irish bouzouki.' See also *Irish bagpipes*.

Irish Box 'An EU-designated fishing ground located largely in Irish territorial waters' (Knowles, 2000). See also *Irish Channel, Irish Sea, the*.

Irish box bed A type of bed. 'The Irish box bed was totally enclosed on all sides except the front, which usually had a door or pair of doors' (Kinmouth, 1993). See also *Irish camp bed, Irish dresser, Irish open frame settle, Irish press bed, Irish settle-bed, Irish Windsor chair*.

Irish boxty pancakes Pancakes that contain potatoes (Smith, 1995).

Irish brace A leash of Irish wolfhounds, usually a couple – on a lead – however, *Chambers* says a leash is three.

Irish brack A spicy fruit loaf (Jones, 1993).

Irish Braveheart As BrianBorú (Boruma), d. 1014, the king of Munster and great military leader has been called (www.brown.edu). The 'Welsh Braveheart' is Owain Glyndwr, fl. 1400s, under whose leadership English rule was temporarily ended in Wales (Edwards, 1998). No one has recorded his death and he simply 'disappeared' (later to return in the future like King Arthur) (Dewi Roberts, *BWA* 48, July 1997). The 'Cornish Braveheart' was 'An Gof', 'the Smith', the name of whom is a cognate of the Irish smith-god Goibniu. An Gof was executed after the Cornish Rebellion of 1497 (Payton, 1996). The original Braveheart was William Wallace (1270–1305) who lead the Scottish to victory over the English at the battle of Stirling Bridge (1297). After his defeat at the first Battle of Falkirk (1298) he vanished and was found in 1305 by the evil Edward I 'The Hammer of the Scots' who had Braveheart tortured to death.

'Irish bread' 1 (W. *bara Gwyddel*) The Welsh name for bread with potatoes. 2 'Irish bread' is milk bread with raisins and caraway seeds (see website *Irish Recipes from the Irish Kitchen Abroad*).

Irish breakfast Fried eggs, bacon, sausages, toast, *Irish soda bread*, juice, cereal, marmalade, tea or coffee (Bernstein, 1980; Mahon, 1991). In America on St Patrick's Day 'one can also find green eggs and ham for breakfast' (Tucker, 1996). See also *Irish boiled dinner, Irish fry*.

Irish breakfast tea A unique blend of tea that includes Ceylon tea (although Twinings Irish Breakfast uses Assam), coined perhaps by analogy to English breakfast tea. (The Irish drink even more tea than the English!) In Cockney rhyming slang, 'tea caddy' (= Paddy) means an Irishman (see also Appendix 5) (www.cockneycowboy.ic24.net). So closely is tea-drinking associated with the Irish that even in Australian slang the word 'mike' (an Irish labourer) means 'a cup of tea'. In Australian slang, another name for tea was the Irish-sounding 'Mother Machree' (Green, 1998 – from Ir. *mo chroí* = my heart).

Irish brehons Some writers (Mahon, 1991) use the prefix 'Irish' for brehons (Ir. *breitheamh* = judge). The brehons (judges) imposed law in old Gaelic Ireland. Their legal system, known as Brehon Law, was first codified in the fifth century; a specific ancient legal form of Old Irish (see Appendix 4), called *béarla féine*, was used. Despite being supplanted by the laws of the English colonists, the Brehon laws were still in use as late as the seventeenth century. See also *'Irish' Dublin Lawyer* and *Lawyer's Irish* (Appendix 4).

Irish bridge 'A type of bridge used in ... mountain districts. One or more pipes surrounded with concrete form a culvert which may submerge in a flood yet remain fordable' (Scott, 1958). See also *Irish land bridge*.

Irish Brigade A general term for several regiments in history. 1 The original Irish Brigade in French service after 1691 (Connolly, 1998). 2 Those who fought for the pope during the Italian *risorgimento* ('resurrection' or 'revival' of nine-

teenth century Italian Unification). See also *Irish Battalion of
St Patrick, 'Irish' greenfinch.* **3** Irish brigades fought on both
sides in the American Civil War (1861–5). **4** Those who
fought for the Boers (Dutch colonialists) against the English
colonialists in the Boer War (1899–1902). See also *Irish Transvaal Committee.* **5** Those led by Eoin O'Duffy who fought
for the *falangistas* (Franco's fascists) in the Spanish Civil
War (1936 –39). See also *Irish Blueshirts.* **6** Irish soldiers who
fought in North Africa and Italy in the Second World War
(Connolly, 1998). **7** The twenty-four Liberal MPs who opposed the Ecclesiastical Tithe Bill in 1851. They founded
the Catholic Defence Association and so were also derided
as 'the Pope's Brass Band'. With the Tenant League, the Catholic Defence Association formed the Independent Irish
Party. Despite achieving electoral success in 1852, it soon
disbanded (Hickey and Doherty, 1980).

Irish brigadiers 1 Soldiers in the *Irish Brigade.* **2** The twenty-
four Liberal MPs who opposed the Ecclesiastical Tithe Bill
in 1851.

Irish broadsides Sing-song ballad-sheets or broadsheets printed in Ireland since the 1570s and sold by 'patterers' (street
vendors). See also *Irish lays.*

Irish brogue 1 An old leather shoe (from Ir. *bróg*). One of the
possible etymologies suggested for the *Irish leprechaun* is
leath bhrógán = shoemaker (i.e. a synonym of *greasaí*); in
America, one word for shoe, used even by the non-Irish,
was *brógan* (Green, 1998). **2** A strong Irish pronunciation
(the prefix 'Irish' is sometimes used) (Macalister, 1937). This
is also called 'broguen' speech, a name which 'mixes the
brogue and a pun on "broken speech"' (Green, 1996). One
who speaks thus is called a 'broganeer' or 'broganier' (Share,
1997). A brogue is not to be confused with the more subtle
pronunciations of *Irish English.* It is interesting that another
term for the Irish brogue was a Grecian accent (Partridge,
1937). By coincidence, Oscar Wilde once called the Irish
'The greatest talkers since the ancient Greeks' (quoted by
Eagleton, 1999). Similarly, in the mid-nineteenth century,
an Irishman was called a Grecian or Greek (See also *'Irish'
Turks)*; Greek fire (an incendiary weapon of the Byzan-
tines) refers to bad whiskey (both Partridge, 1937). See also

Irish bouzouki, Irish by birth but Greek by injection, Irish pronunciation, received and *Irish twist*.

Irish bronze A plant with white flowers, whose young foliage has bronze tints.

Irish broth (Ir. *anraith Gaelach*) Made with stock, nettle tops, oatmeal, butter, onions, leek, egg yolk, cream, nutmeg, salt and pepper (Thomson, 1982).

Irish brown-red A breed of poultry, much favoured for cock-fighting (Encycl. Brit., Vol. 5). On the subject of cockfighting and the Irish, Green (1998) tells us that the phrase 'All on one side like Lord Thomond's cocks' derives from the nobleman's 'Irish cock feeder', who, presuming the cocks were all friendly, as they were on the same side, caged them all up together before the fight – with obvious consequences! See also *Irish gilder, Irish gray*.

Irish brown soda bread A recipe for a type of *Irish soda bread* made with baking soda, wheat flour, rolled oats and buttermilk (see webpage allrecipes.com /directory). See also *Irish American soda bread, 'Irish bread'*.

Irish buffoon A term that Ó Ciosáin (1998) uses as a synonym for *Irish rogues*, especially for the two characters mentioned in his book *Smith's Complete History*: Patrick Fleming and William Maguire, alias *Irish Teague*. The term is derived from a form of buffoonery in their robbery: for example, Maguire declared that he was only 'borrowing' the money he was taking by force. See also *Irish rapparee*.

Irish buggy A wheelbarrow (Partridge, 1950; Share, 1997). For synonyms see *Irish baby buggy*.

Irish bull A contradictory, illogical statement seen in many an *Irish joke*. According to Ó Muirithe (1999), the word 'bull' in Middle English meant a falsehood and is a cognate of the Icelandic word for 'nonsense'. Similarly in Old French, *boule* meant trickery. Yet Grose traced the expression 'Irish bull' from a 'blundering lawyer' of the fifteenth century called *Obadiah Bull* (cited by Green, 1998). See also *Irish answer, Irish logic*.

Irish 'bullie' Or rather *la bullie Hibernian*, which is 'fake restaurant French for a distinctly plebeian dish that is also known as an Irishman or a boiled dinner' (Green, 1996).

Irish burgoo A synonym of *Irish stew* (www.realdictionary.com).

'Burgoo' is a sailor's dish of boiled oatmeal, salt, butter and sugar; it is also a thick soup for American picnics (*Chambers*). See also '*Irish caviar*'.

'Irish' Bury pudding The English traveller Morton (1930) wrote 'if you see a man ... devouring what appears to be a chocolate-coloured python, you can be certain that he comes from Cork ... Now drisheen is a kind of sausage, made ... mainly from sheep's blood and milk. It is the Irish cousin of the Bury pudding ... one might call it the caviare of Cork.' See also *Irish caviar*.

Irish button 'A syphilitic bubo that develops in the groin' (Green, 1996). The Irish 'connection' is very rare; usually the poor French are the supposed victims of this disease, which is variously described as French crown, French disease, Frenchman, French marbles, French pig and French pox (Green, 1998). See also *Irish mutton*.

'Irish by birth but Greek by injection' Gay (Green, 1996; Share, 1997). Here Irish and Greek stereotypes are combined. Yet Seán Ó Faoláin is probably more correct when he says: 'An Irish queer is a fellow who prefers women to drink' (MacHale [nd]). As regards the 'Greek by injection' part of the phrase, similarities can be found in the phrases 'Dutch by injection' (referring to a woman living with a foreigner) and 'French by injection', which refers to a gay sexual act (both Green, 1998). Apparently, American homosexuals have invented slang words for almost every racial combination, including the newly coined 'Gaelick' (a pun on 'gay' and 'Gaelic') to denote a gay Irishman (Green, 1998).

C

Irish cabbage In American slang the 'St Patrick's Day meal of corned (salt) beef, cabbage and Irish potatoes' (Green, 1998). See also *Irish potato, Irish turkey*.

Irish cabin The word 'Irish' is often prefixed to the modest Irish home (Kinmouth, 1993). This dwelling, according to the 1841 Census, was the poorest of the four grades of houses recorded: it 'comprised all mud cabins having only one room' and by the end of the nineteenth century was a rarity. See also *Irishmen's cottages*.

Irish Cajun A blend of traditional *Irish music* and music in the

Louisiana Cajun country style, with prominent fiddle playing. At Jethro's club in Cornwall there is even an Irish Cajun Day (*Cornwall Today*, Vol. 2, No. 12, Sept 1996). See also
Irish Athabaskan, Irish fiddling.

Irish cake dance Not an actual dance but a dance competition.
Competitors would dance around a tall maypole-like pike
decorated with flowers and on top of which was a cake.
The winner of the cake was the one who had the stamina
to dance the longest.

Irish calendar A unique numerical solar calendar with sixteen
months of twenty-four or twenty-one days each (as opposed
to the ancient British calendar of sixteen months of twenty-
two or twenty-three days) (Thomas, 1988). See also *Irish
Easter.*

Irish cambric handkerchief An Irish embroidered handerchief;
often given as a present to a bride. Queen Victoria bought
Irish cambric handkerchiefs and other embroidery from
Robinson and Cleaver in Belfast. Connolly (1998) refers to
the Protestant Holland weavers round Lurgan, Co. Armagh,
on May Day 1737 as 'each attired in uniform of shirt and
black trousers, cockades in their hats, and basket-hilt swords
drawn in one hand and Irish cambric handkerchiefs in the
other.'

'Irish' Camelot With reference to the ancient seat of the legendary King Arthur of Britain, Bremner (1998) describes *Tír
na nÓg* as 'Ireland's Camelot'. This was the land of eternal
youth where nobody would grow old. Ellis (1987) also suggests that the name of the Fianna leader Cumal is related
to the British fort of Camulos and 'seems cognate with
King Arthur's famous court at Camelot'. Similarly, Navan
Fort in Armagh has been dubbed 'Ulster's Camelot', as it
was the seat of the Ulster high kings (Law, 1998). See also
'Irish' Atlantis, Irish Elysium.

Irish camp bed Also called *Irish canopy bed,* as it has a wooden
canopy over it. See also *Irish box bed.*

Irish campaign, the So the evil incursions of Cromwell into Ireland are sometimes called. See also *Irish stroker, the; Irish
wrenboys.*

Irish canary Not a bird but a rare medium-sized, yellow variety
of apple from Northern Ireland (see *NAR*).

Irish canopy bed See *Irish camp bed*.

'Irish' Canterbury Or rather 'Ireland's Canterbury' – as Morton (1930) referred to Armagh. Canterbury has always been the most important religious centre in England and since the Reformation, the Archbishop of Canterbury is, after the monarch, the most senior figure in the Anglican church. Armagh has two cathedrals (one Catholic, the other Protestant) on the hills and the archbishop of Armagh is perhaps the equivalent of the Archbishop of Canterbury. See also *Irish capital, Irish Lourdes, Irish Thebaid*.

Irish capital Dublin (Ir. *Baile Átha Cliath*). The name 'Dublin' is itself derived from Irish (*Dubh linn*), meaning 'black pool'. In rhyming slang, Dublin is *Alpolnoghaire*, from 'alp' = 'town' in Irish mason jargon and O'Laoighire, the surname (Macalister, 1937). Yet Tara Hill, Co. Meath, where many kings were crowned, was, according to the seventh-century *Life of St Patrick* 'the capital of the Irish' (Brady, 2000). Galway has been called 'the capital of the west' (Shaffrey, 1979); it has also been called 'the Gaelic capital' (Floyd, 1937) – a title shared by *Belfast*, which, as Napier (1989) notes, was in the early nineteenth century 'the Irish-language capital of Ireland'. Armagh has been described as 'the ecclesiastical capital of Ireland' (Killanin, 1962; Connolly, 1998) (see the '*Irish' Canterbury*); and the Curragh is 'the capital of Irish horse-racing' (Bernstein, 1980). Moreover, according to Hughes (2000), Kinsale is 'the gourmet capital of Ireland'. Morton (1930), with reference to the fact that 'these young people have their minds on America', states that 'the real capital of Connemara is New York': there are indeed many more Irish people in New York than even in Dublin. Morton adds about Connemara that 'its nominal capital is Clifden, but its real capital is Boston' (see also *Irish Bostonian*). See also '*Irish' Athens, 'Irish' Glasgow, 'Irish' Sodom, Irishtown*.

Irish car 'The common Irish car was better adapted to the needs and skills of the people as well as to the condition of the roads' (Evans, 1957). As Jenkins (1962) observes, the vehicle existed in Wales by the name *car Gwyddelig* (i.e. 'Irish car'). See also *Irish cart, Irish covered car, Irish jaunting car, Irish outside car, 'Irish' sidecar, Irish slide car*.

Irish caravan In contrast to the heavier, square, timber caravan

of English gypsies, 'the Irish caravan is really a development of the round-topped, barrel-shaped tent built on the
flat cart instead of on the ground' (Logan, 1986). See also
Irish bender tent, Irish Travellers.

Irish cart A unique type of farm vehicle very similar to the
Cornish 'wain' and Welsh *gambo* (Evans, 1959).

Irish carthorse Listed as a unique breed of horse synonymous
with the *Irish draught* (Mason, 1951). See also *Irish Clydesdale, Irish cob, Irish draught, Irish hobby, Irish hunter, Irish
thoroughbred*.

Irish Caruso John McCormack (1884–1945), who sang ballads
rather than heavier opera material, was one of the greatest
tenors of all time. In fact during the First World War, sales
of his records in America at one point surpassed those of
the great Caruso himself. See also *Irish nightingale, 'Irish'
Prima Donna*.

'Irish' catacombs The basements of Georgian houses, especially in Dublin. See also *Irish Georgian*.

Irish Catholic, White (WIC) Americans of Irish extraction or
Irish people generally, in the same way as 'WASPs' are
White Anglo-Saxon Protestants (see the website *The Racial
Slur Database*, www.rsdb.org).

Irish cattle Pigs, in Liverpudlian dialect (see webpage *Mersey-
talk9*). See *Irish pig*.

Irish Cattle Acts English Acts of Parliament (passed in 1663,
1671, 1681 and 1758–9) preventing Irish livestock from being
imported into Britain. The Acts were repealed in 1759. See
also *Irish Dun, Irish moiled*.

'Irish caviar' In 1930s American slang, *Irish stew* (Green, 1998).
Note that 'Welsh caviar' is laverbread (W. *bara lawr*), or
edible seaweed. The Irish too eat some types of seaweed
(such as dulse) and use *Irish moss* for cooking. Newby (1987)
said of *Irish bacon* that 'bacon is to Limerick what caviar is
to Astrakhan'. See also *'Irish' Bury pudding*.

Irish *céilí* band A small band of musicians playing *Irish music*
for a *céilí* (Vallely, 1999). The band would comprise four or
five members whose instruments would include guitar,
fiddle, drums and possibly the *Irish traditional button accordion*. With fewer musicians and amplification, in the 1970s
and 1980s the Irish céilí band evolved into the set-dance

band (see *Irish set-dance*). See *Irish fiddling, Irish Guards Band*.

Irish Cessation Term (used by Encycl. Brit., Vol. 10) to refer to the truce made between the English King Charles I (through his lieutenant) and the *Irish rebels* in 1643. Charles had a two-fold aim in reaching the agreement: to allow him to deploy troops against the Cromwellian Parliamentary forces and to secure possible Irish support against Parliament.

Irish chain The border for *Irish patchwork* is completed 'on a mosaic patchwork block pattern known as Irish chain' (Shaw-Smith, 1984). See also *Irish crochet, Irish flax, Irish flowerer, Irish lace, Irish linen, Irish poplin, Irish quilt*.

Irish chain, double A pattern of mosaic patchwork (Ballard, b). See also *Irish chain*.

Irish chair An ancient triangular-shaped chair with three legs. Also called a Sligo chair or board chair (see Kinmouth, 1993). See also *Irish comb-back chair, Irish form, Irish Windsor chair*.

Irish champ The word 'champ' alone is usually sufficient for the traditional Irish dish of mashed potatoes, milk and scallions. However, the word Irish is sometimes prefixed, as for instance on the website of *The Galway Bay Irish Restaurant and Pub* (www.thefoody.com).

Irish Champion Stakes An important horse-racing event. which takes place at the Leopardstown Racecourse, Co. Dublin in September. See also *Irish Classics, Irish Derby, Irish Grand National, Irish Oaks, Irish 1000 Guineas, Irish 2000 Guineas*.

Irish Channel 1 The *Irish Sea* itself or an outlet to it (Floyd, 1937). **2** A rough neighbourhood in mid-nineteenth century New Orleans, so called as it was populated mainly by Irish immigrants (Urdang, 1991).

Irish chariot A wheelbarrow (Rawson, 1991; Green, 1996). For synonyms, see *Irish baby buggy*.

Irish Charivari *Zoz*, or the *Irish Charivari* was a comic magazine published by Zozimus (Michael Maron) from 1876 to 1879. The word 'charivari' also means 'rough music' or the serenading, usually with a cacophonous din, of an unpopular couple (for instance, a widower with a new wife) on their wedding night. The Irish equivalent of this custom was called 'blowing' or 'horning', from the sound made.

Irish Charles Bukowski Shane MacGowan, founder of the rock group the Pogues (for more on the word 'pogue', see *Irish arse, kiss my royal*). He is also a writer (and is so described by Stephen Lemons on the *Salon.com* website). Bukowski (1920–94) was a poet, short-story writer and novelist. See also *Irish Dickens, 'Irish' Homer, Irish Keats*.

Irish charm An old rose variety (Brett, nd).

Irish chateaux Castles in France occupied by exiled *'Irish' Wild Geese*.

'Irish' chaw The prefix Irish is not normally used. In American slang, 'chaw' or 'chawbacon' meant 'variously a yokel, a peasant and an Irish immigrant' (Green, 1996). In *Irish English* (1997), Bernard Share records the term 'hard chaw' to refer to a 'tough individual'. This phrase may or may not be related to the term chaw-mouth (a synonym of *Irish flannel-mouth*).

Irish checkers A variation of checkers. 'Irish checkers ... uses a die to determine movement' (see www.greathallgames.com). See also *'Irish' backgammon*.

Irish cherry A carrot (Rawson, 1991; Green, 1996). See also *Irish apple, Irish vegetables*.

'Irish' chess The ancient Irish board game *fidchell* or 'wooden wisdom' (which has the same etymology as the Welsh game *gwyddbwyll*). The exact rules have been lost but historians believe it was similar to the game Fox and Geese. A similar Irish game was *brandubh* ('black raven'). See also *'Irish' backgammon, Irish gambit, Irish loo, Irish whist, Two-hand Irish* (Appendix 4).

Irish chicken Pork, in American slang of the 1920s and 1930s (Green, 1998). See also *Irish goose, Irish turkey*.

Irish chief secretary The chief administrator appointed during British rule in Ireland. In the seventeenth century, he was the lord lieutenant's personal assistant; yet by the nineteenth century, the chief secretary had a more important role. Some famous chief secretaries were Robert Peel (1812–18) and Arthur 'Bloody' Balfour (1887–91) See also *Irish Invincibles*.

Irish chimney cupboard A tall, very thin cupboard made of pine c.1900. Certainly narrow enough to fit at the side of a chimney but probably so called from its resemblance to one.

The door is simple yet beautifully panelled (see www.irish countryantiques.com). See also *Irish dresser*.

Irish Chippendale Term for *Irish rococo* furniture modelled on designs by Thomas Chippendale. 'Usually made of mahogany, Irish Chippendale furniture is characterised by very broad aprons on tables, the use of a lion's-paw foot and a lion's-mask motif, and carving' (Boyce, 1985). See also *Irish mahogany*.

'Irish' chloroform In allusion to Marx's famous quote that religion is the opium of the masses, Oliver St John Gogarty wrote that 'Politics is the chloroform of the Irish people' (in *As I Was Going Down Sackville Street*, 1937, quoted by Brady, 2000). See also *Irish people, the aardvark of the*.

Irish Christian Brothers 'Brother of the Christian Schools' (*Webster's*). A lay teaching order founded by Edmund Rice, who opened the first such school in 1802 in Waterford. The curriculum placed emphasis on the Catholic faith. See also *Irish Education Act, 1892; Irish hedge school; Irish Not*.

Irish Christian Front Extreme right-wing movement founded in 1935 by former Fianna Fáil member Patrick Belton. It had a close connection with the *Irish Blueshirts* and sympathised with Franco's regime in Spain.

Irish Christmas pudding The distinct Irishness of this Christmas pudding derives from its generous quantities of both *Irish whiskey* and Guinness (Cole, 1973). See also *Irish boiled fruit cake*.

Irish Church Although Ireland has always retained one of the most faithful Catholic traditions, the early Christian Church had some unique Irish characteristics, such as a priest abbot (a monastic overseer, not a bishop) instead of an episcopal see; an outmoded form of tonsure (see also *Irish tonsure*); and a distinct way of computing the date of Easter (see also *Irish Easter*).

Irish Church Act, 1869 The disestablishment of the Protestant Episcopal Church of Ireland, which had levied heavy tithes on both Protestants and Catholics. See also *Irish Tithe Act*.

Irish Church Temporalities Act, 1833 Act suppressing ten sees (bishoprics) of the Church of Ireland and reducing the revenues of the remaining twelve.

Irish Cinderella 1 As the Irish fairy tale 'Fair, Brown and Trembling' has been dubbed (see a host of websites, including *Irish Folk and Fairy Tales*). **2** Hollywood's Attic's silent film *The Irish Cinderella* (1922), starring Pattie MacNamara, set against a background of Irish politics (see www.hollywoods attic.com). Cinderella is also an Irish crochet pattern (Weiss, 1985).

Irish Circe Circe was the sorceress who turned the men of Odysseus (i.e. Ulysses) into pigs; Odysseus escaped Circe's spell with the plant moly given to him by Hermes. In relation to James Joyce's novel *A Portrait of the Artist as a Young Man* (1916), Henke writes about the beautiful young woman on the seashore on whom Stephen Dedalus is fixated: 'Like an Irish Circe the nymph in *Portrait* has the potential to drag Stephen down into the emerald-green nets of Dublin paralysis' (cited on website www.pwli.com). In Joyce's *Ulysses* (1922) 'Circe' is one of the chapter titles (but is not mentioned in the text itself). See also *Irish Odyssey*.

Irish Citizen Army Founded by James Larkin and James Connolly during the 1913 Dublin Lockout, when employers, headed by William Martin Murphy, began to fear industrial militancy and so told workers to withdraw from the ITGWU (Irish Transport and General Workers' Union). The Irish Citizen Army's role was to protect workers from the employers' hired thugs as well as from the Dublin Metropolitan Police. When the Lockout ended in 1914, the army's numbers dwindled, yet in 1916 it took part in the '*Irish' Easter Rising*. By the end of the *Irish Civil War* it had practically disintegrated.

Irish Civil War 1 This term is occasionally applied (e.g. by Connolly, 1998) to the Confederate War (1641–53), also known as the Eleven Years War. **2** Despite Dáil Éireann's 64–57 vote in favour of the *Anglo-Irish Treaty*, the republicans were split between those, such as Éamon de Valera, who still opposed the Treaty and those who supported it (the Free Staters). The disagreement between the two sides led to bitter civil war (1922–3). The sad legacy of division remained for some time between Irishmen and women who had previously fought bravely side by side in the *Irish War of Independence*. The Irish also fought in other civil wars: the English Civil War (see for instance *Irish kerne*), the American Civil War (see *Irish national anthem*) and the Spanish Civil War (see *Irish Brigade*).

Irish Classics This term refers to five major horse races in Ireland; all of them are run on the Curragh: the *Irish Derby, Irish Oaks, Irish 1,000 Guineas, Irish St Leger* and *Irish 2,000 Guineas*. See also *Irish Grand National, Irish National Hunt Steeplechase*.

Irish Classics, Home of the The Curragh Racecourse, Co. Kildare. One Arabic-racehorse website declares: 'The Curragh Racecourse is the headquarters of Irish racing and the home of the Irish Classics' (www.emirates.com). See also *Irish capital*.

Irish clay pipe As many refer to the distinct Irish pipe, the 'dudeen' or 'didgeen' (from Ir. *dúidín*) with its long thin stem and clay bowl; the bowl and mouthpiece are not separate but made from a single piece of clay. Another name for it was a 'Lord ha' mercy', since this was customarily said by one who was given the pipe to smoke (along with *Irish whiskey* to drink) by the bereaved family at an *Irish wake*. Sometimes even 'a gross of pipes' (i.e. 144) could be bought. The *Irish leprechaun* is also portrayed as smoking a clay pipe.

Irish cloak A garment that 'reached down to the feet' (Lysaght, 1986) and was also called the Kinsdale cloak (Connolly, 1998). Welch (1996) says that, since it was often worn by the *Irish kerne*, 'the Irish cloak ... became synonymous with Irish treachery.' See also *Irish coat, Irish fashion, Irish mantle, Irish rug, Irish sleeve*.

Irish clubhouse 1 A police station. Partridge (1950) observes that many police in America are of Irish extraction. Similarly, the police van or Black Maria has been called a *Paddy wagon*, and the American gangster would call a police officer an 'O'Malley' (Green, 1996, and see also Appendix 5). The hoodlum would call the police officer 'Johnny Gallagher' or another slang name was 'Shaun', i.e. Seán. The Flying Squad was called 'the Sweeney', as many officers were Irish. In early nineteenth century America, the police were referred to collectively as 'Gallagher and Sheehan', and a 'muldoon' or a 'shamrock' was a policeman. In Australian slang, a 'doolan' is a policeman, whereas in New Zealand a doolan is any Irish Catholic (Green, 1998). Liverpudlians would refer to a police officer in the docks as *Paddy Kelly* (see also Appendix 5). Likewise, in the 1930s a policeman's truncheon was called a 'Callahan', and fingerprints taken by the police were called 'Paddy prints' (Partridge, 1950). See also *Irish dividend, Irish theatre*. **2** A brothel (Green, 1996; Share, 1997). See also *Irish bordello*.

Irish cluster A variety of small apple with a red flush originally from Scotland.

Irish Clydesdale Large working horse that was introduced from Scotland in the early nineteenth century and remained in use until the 1950s (Connolly, 1998). See also *Irish carthorse*.

Irish coal tit *(Parus ater hibernicus)* A different bird from the British and continental species. It has a larger beak and sulphur-yellow tones on cheeks, breast and belly, as well as 'a buffish tinge on the grayish-green underparts' and a paler rump (www.birdsireland.com). See *Irish dipper, Irish jay*. See also *Irish grey partridge, Irish red grouse*.

Irish coat A unique Irish garment: 'The real origins of the Irish coat ... probably lay in the medieval gown. The fabric was measured through wrapping around the wearer's body and then cut to size ... and edges joined with cloth button rather than a seam. The coat was of unlined frieze, about knee-length, unhemmed and with unisex stand collars.' (Connolly, 1998). See also *Irish cloak*.

Irish coat of arms 1 A black eye (Rawson, 1989). **2** In a later work, Green (1998) gives the extended meaning of 'two black eyes and a bleeding nose'. No relation to *Irish arms*. However, the etymology of this word might be related to that of 'Lord Northumberland's arms', which also means a black eye. Green (1998), derives this from Northumberland's 'red and black spectacle-like badge' which resembled a black eye. See also *Irish beauty* and *Irish wedding, to have danced at an*.

Irish cob Unique Irish horse, usually an *Irish thoroughbred* or Connemara crossed with an *Irish draught* (Mason, 1951). See also *Irish carthorse*.

Irish cobbler An early variety of potato, popular also in America (Encycl. Brit., Vol. 18). See also *Irish daisy, Irish queen, Irish red*.

Irish cob loaf A large, square loaf (Bonthrone, 1960). See also 'Irish bread'.

Irish cocktail In American slang of the 1980s, 'a drink containing a substance that causes unconsciousness' (Green, 1998). Similarly, in Australian slang a 'Fitzroy cocktail' is a drink containing methylated spirits (the term is derived not from an Irish person but from a suburb of Melbourne; see Green, 1998). A 'Kerry cocktail' is half a glass of whiskey with another half (MacHale, 1979).

Irish codlin A variety of apple, also called Manks (i.e. Manx) codlin. See also *Irish canary*.

'Irish' Coercion Acts No fewer than 105 such Acts were passed between 1800 and 1921. Under these Acts, Britain gave the Irish administration special authority and power during times of extreme unrest (some writers, such as Pascoe [1968], use the prefix 'Irish').

Irish coffee 1 *Caife Gaelach*: Hot black (filtered) coffee with brown sugar and *Irish whiskey* which is then topped with thick double cream. It should be served in a (heated) stemmed *Irish whiskey* cup, glass or mug. When made with Scotch whisky, it is known as *Gaelic coffee* (see *Irish Gaelic*), but this is not to be confused with 'Scotch coffee', which is 'hot water flavoured with burnt biscuit' (Partridge, 1937). Another association between *Irish whiskey* and coffee can be seen in the term 'coffee still': a patent still that allows continuous distillation of 'wash' (i.e. fermented liquid that is present before the first distillation). It was named after Irishman Aeneas Coffee (see webpage *Glossary of Whiskey Terms*). **2** Irish coffee is also a hybrid narcissus (see www.hortpurdue. edu).

Irish coffee, Godiva Coffee containing *Irish cream* and Godiva liqueur; the liqueur is named after the eleventh-century lady who rode naked on horseback through Coventry to protest against her husband's taxes on the poor (see webpage for *Irish Beverage Recipes*).

Irish coffee glass A special tall glass through which the layers of the hot *Irish coffee* can be seen, and with a handle to prevent burning the fingers.

Irish cole titmouse An old name for the *Irish coal tit*. Swainson (1886) recorded the form 'cole titmouse', which corresponds with the Latin; he wrote that 'in Ireland it is called tomtit.'

Irish collar and elbow method A synonym for the distinct form of *Irish wrestling* in which wrestlers take hold of each other's collar with one arm and their elbow with the other. It is somewhat similar to Cornish wrestling and very similar to Cumberland wrestling from the old Celtic stronghold of Cumbria in north-west England (ESGP).

Irish colleen 1 A traditional Irish girl (from Ir: *cailín*). **2** 'The Irish Colleen' was the nickname of fiddler and accordion player Rose (née Conlon) Murphy, who was born in 1900 (Vallely, 1999).

Irish College Term used for several Irish seminaries founded on the continent, the first of which was at Salamanca (f. 1592), although unofficially a college was started in Paris in 1578 (Connolly, 1998). The year after Salamanca, an Irish college was founded in Lisbon. By the end of the seventeenth century, Catholic religious orders had already established some thirty colleges in Spain, France and Holland (then the Low Countries). In the late seventeenth century, the expulsion of the Jesuits from Spain and France reduced the number of such colleges. A few of the colleges, for instance the one in Paris, still exist today. See *Irish University Act*.

Irish comb-back chair A chair in which the back has a second smaller, narrower tier on top. See also *Irish chair*.

Irish combine (NZ) A flail (Orsman, 1997). See also *Irish banjo, Irish screwdriver, Irish toothpick*.

Irish come-all-ye Often simply called a 'come-all-ye'. A narrative song from Ireland in English, so called because the opening line of such songs was invariably 'Come all ye ... ' See also *Irish lays*.

Irish comics Obituary columns in a newspaper (Green, 1996). Also recorded by Green in a later work (1998) as 'Irish funnies'.

Irish compliment A backhanded one (Rawson, 1991; Green, 1996). Similarly, a 'north country compliment' or 'Yorkshire compliment' is a gift that is useless to both the donor and the recipient, while a 'Chinese compliment' is pretended interest in another's opinion while having already formed one's own opinion (Partridge, 1937). For other tenuous Chinese-Irish connections see *Irish screwdriver* and *Paddy* (Appendix 5). The phrase 'Jewish compliment' refers to telling someone that they don't look well (Green, 1996; the same phrase later acquired a vulgar connotation in relation to male genitalia).

Irish Confederation A union founded in 1847 by Young Irelanders who had seceded from the Repeal Association of Daniel O'Connell (who died that year). The Confederation sought self-government for Ireland from the British; its leaders were arrested in 1848 as the English had fears of an Irish uprising similar to the French revolution of that year. Although the Confederation disintegrated, two of its leaders, John O'Mahony and James Stephens, later founded the *Irish Republican Brotherhood*.

Irish Confederate Wars Term used by some (e.g. Lenihan, 1995) to refer to Irish participation in the English Civil War of 1641–9.

Irish confetti 1 Stone and bricks (particularly thrown as weapons) (*Webster's* and Rawson, 1991). See also the nickname 'stone-thrower' for a Tipperary man (RDGED, Vol. 3) and the mid-nineteenth century rhyming-slang phrase 'Dublin tricks' (i.e. 'bricks', see Partridge, 1937). In NZ usage, 'Irish confetti' means 'gravel' (Orsman, 1997). Other non-paper forms of 'confetti' include 'cowyard confetti' and 'Flemington confetti' – both meaning, in Australian slang, rubbish and nonsense (Green, 1998). See also *Irish bouquet, Irish rose.* **2** Semen (Green, 1996; Share, 1997). A semen stain on a sheet is supposedly called a 'map of Ireland', according to Green (1998). Yet Green also records that such a stain is more popularly known as a 'map of England' while the phrase 'to have the map of Ireland written all over one's face' merely means 'to be unmistakenly Irish'.

Irish Constabulary, Royal (RIC) Formed in 1836 as the Irish Constabulary as a 'reward' for the fact that its members had helped suppress the *Irish Republican Brotherhood;* the word 'Royal' was added in 1867. The force was not modelled on the British 'bobbies' but was a heavily armed military police force with dark green uniforms like soldiers. Mostly, this constabulary was used to enforce evictions (see also '*Irish' latch-key*) and stop *Irish faction fights*. In 1922 it was disbanded and replaced by the Garda Síochána in the Republic and the Royal Ulster Constabularly (RUC) (now the Police Service of Northern Ireland) in the north. See also *Irish clubhouse* for phrases connecting the Irish with the police, and '*Irish' Yeomanry*.

Irish contagion The *Irishisation* of foreigners, especially the English. Smith (1991) refers to the way in which, from the fourteenth century, the English in Ireland 'adopted the *Irish language* and customs, illustrating ... how the English government's fears about its subjects succumbing to what it saw as the Irish contagion were justified.' This *Irishisation* was perhaps first seen with the Normans who, it is said, became more Irish than the Irish themselves; see *Irish than the Irish, more*.

Irish Convention David Lloyd George's attempt to reach a settlement of the 'Irish Question' in July 1917–18. The meeting was chaired by Sir Horace Plunkett (more well known for his agrarian reforms) with over one hundred delegates in attendance. Nationalists and southern Unionists assented to self-government offered by the British but Sinn Féin boycotted the convention. Ulster Unionists demanded the exclusion of the six counties from an independent Irish state. See also *Irish Treaty, Anglo-*.

Irish cookery, the doyenne of The late Theodora Fitzgibbon (d. 1991), a 'famous Irish cook', according to the blurb of the 1991 edition of her book *Irish Traditional Food* (originally published in 1983) and the author of twenty-five books.

'Irish coon' Extremely derogatory phrase analogous to *Irish wog* and 'green nigger' (for which see the same entry and the analogous *sunburnt Irishman* in Appendix 3); this term was an insult both to the Irish and to black people, reflecting the discrimination suffered by both races. The phrase is actually derived from the song 'Bedelia', subtitled 'The Irish Coon Song Serenade', the music for which was written in 1903 by Jean Schwartz; William Jerome is to be blamed for the lyrics. By coincidence, illicitly distilled *Irish whiskey* (i.e. *Irish poteen*) in the American slang of 1920s and 1930s was 'coon dick' or 'coon juice' (Green, 1998). See also *Paddy Roll* and *White Paddy* (Appendix 5).

Irish coop dresser Also called *Irish hen dresser*. An *Irish dresser* with space at the bottom for hens.

Irish coracle A small wickerwork boat covered in watertight material, originally leather. A misnomer for the *Irish curragh* (Ir. *naomhóg, currach*) but used for example by MacCullagh (1992), who normally prefers the term *Irish curragh* – for the vessel that exists in various forms in Ireland. Only the River Boyne version closely resembles the Welsh coracle (W. *cwrwgl)*, the others being much longer and narrower. The Welsh word *cwrwgl*, like the Irish cognate, *currach,* may be derived from the Latin *corium*, i.e. leather, skin, referring to the hide covering the vessel. See also *Irish curragh raids*.

Irish Council Founded 1847; members included John O'Connell and John Mitchel. The organisation's aim was to alleviate Famine distress (see also *Irish Famine*). Before disbanding, it succeeded in having investigations conducted into social problems. Not to be confused with the Council of Ireland (1920–5), which aimed to hold meetings between representatives from both Northern Ireland and the Republic on issues such as commerce and transport.

Irish Council Bill, 1907 Also known as the Devolution Bill. The abortive attempt of Chief Secretary Birrell to give Ireland devolved powers.

Irish Counter-Reformation The revival of Irish Catholicism in the face of attempts to enforce the Reformation in Ireland after the Act of Supremacy of 1537. (The word 'Irish' is occasionally prefixed, e.g. by Brady, 2000). See also *Irish Act of Uniformity*.

Irish Country See *Irish and Country*.

Irish county tartans There are thirty-two distinct patterns (or as the Scots say, 'setts') which denote not clans but the Irish counties. Manufactured by the House of Edgar in Scotland (see webpage www.donaldsons-of-crieff.com). See also *Irish kilt, Irish national tartan, Irish tartan*.

Irish courage A variety of pink rose (Brett, nd).

Irish covered car Horse-drawn vehicle used in the southern counties from the early nineteenth to the early twentieth century. The car was covered by a valance and curtain (the covered 'car bed' was a bed used in Ireland that resembled this and also had curtains). See also *Irish car*.

Irish cow, old An old breed of Irish cow which Sir William Wilde described as being usually black or red, with medium-sized short legs and a big belly, difficult to fatten but good for milk (cited by Logan, 1986; the breed is also listed by Mason, 1951). See also *Irish Dun, Irish moiled* and *polled Irish* (Appendix 4).

Irish craft gods As Green (1992) calls the Triad of Goibniu the Smith, Luchta the Wright and Credne the Metalworker. They forged weapons for Lugh and the Tuatha against the Fomorians.

Irish cream A popular drink, the base of which is *Irish whiskey* and cream. The first Irish cream, Bailey's Original, was launched in 1974. Carolan's takes its name from the seventeenth-century blind Irish harpist, Turlough O'Carolan, while Emmet's is named after the great Irish patriot and *United Irishman* Robert Emmet (1778–1803). See also *Irish mist, Irish velvet*.

Irish crochet Sometimes also called Clones lace (from the town in Co. Monaghan). 'Irish crochet is related to plain crochet but it is worked on the finest of hooks, using very fine threads' (Ballard, a). Moreover, 'Irish crochet became known for its particular designs ... roses, trefoils, ferns and grapes, and a northern Irish form developed ... less open than the southern' (Boyle, 1964). See also *Irish lace*.

Irish crochet jewelry The term refers to exquisite patterns such as *Irish filigree* (see website of *Crochet Pattern Library Jewelry and Their Stuff*).

Irish crochet lace Term used in, for instance, Eithne D'Arcy's book *Irish Crochet Lace* (1984). This beautiful technique is used especially for the collar of *Irish dancing costumes*. See also *Irish crochet*.

Irish Croesus Croesus was the last king of Lydia in the sixth century BC and his wealth was proverbial. P. W. Joyce wrote, 'Damer of Shronell, who lived in the eighteenth century, was reputed to be the richest man in Ireland – a sort of Irish Croesus' (1910). Legend says that Damer made a pact with the devil, selling his soul for 'as much gold as would fill his boot'; the Irishman then cut a hole in his heel. No one knows what happened to his soul but perhaps an Irishman tricked the devil again?

Irish croppie The prefix 'Irish' is used by, for instance, Ó hAllmhuráin (1998). The croppies, so called because of their cropped hair, took part in the Rebellion of 1798. See also *Irish glib, Irishmen, United*.

Irish Cross Often used synonymously with Celtic Cross. Refers to a short cross, with four arms. The top, left and right arms are the same length, whereas the bottom is longer and forms the base. There is also a circle connecting the four arms and hence the name 'ringed cross'. It is often thought that it may be a combination of two symbols, the Christian cross and the Celtic sun. Apart from this beautiful, often stone, cross, other unique crosses appear in Irish folklore. For instance on St Brigid's Day (February 1) (see *'Irish' Mary*), a *cros Bríde* or *bogha Bríde* (i.e. St Brigid's cross) was made out of straw, to be hung in the home or byre. This cross usually had a lozenge shape but in Co. Cork often resembled the Irish Cross (Danaher, 1972). Similarly, on St Patrick's Day (see *Irish patron saint*), a St Patrick's cross is made with paper and ribbons; one form of this cross also resembles the Irish Cross with the circular frame (Danaher, 1972).

Irish Crossroads 1 An American charitable organisation whose goal is to 'foster peace and unity among Protestant and Catholic youngsters in troubled areas of Belfast.' **2** The epithet 'the Crossroads of Ireland' is used for Co. Laois.

'Irish crow' (W. *brân Iwerddon*). The Welsh name for the hooded or Royston crow.

Irish crowned harp Emblem that combined the *Irish harp* with the English crown. The arms of Norman Ireland had used three crowns on a blue shield, without a harp. Hence the inclusion of a crown on any flag or emblem implied that Ireland was not independent. This is why James Connolly (see *Irish Citizen Army*) at the 'Solemn Ceremony of Hoisting the Irish Flag' in his oath referred to 'the Green Flag of Ireland, emblazoned with the harp without the crown' (see also *Irish Green Flag*). The Irish crowned harp also featured on some *Irish punchmarks*.

Irish Crown Jewels, theft of the The disappearance of the Irish Crown jewels from Dublin Castle's Bedford Tower in 1907. King Edward VII dismissed four employees responsible for the jewels' safekeeping. Neither the jewels nor the culprits were ever found (Pickering, 1991). Not to be confused with *Irish diamond, Irish gold* or *Irish silver*.

Irish cry 'Keening, from Irish *caoineadh,* also referred to as the Irish cry, the custom of delivering a lament, accompanied by wailing and cries of grief over the body of a dead person' (Connolly, 1998; Vallely also refers to the Irish cry, 1999). See also *Irish wake*.

Irish crystal Made with potash, litharge and sand. According to some (e.g. Booth, 1995), it enhances the taste of *Irish whiskey*. It has deep-cut patterns, with motifs of flowers and trees decorating the original blank. Co. Waterford has been nicknamed the Crystal County (see website *Yahoo: Nicknames of the Counties of Ireland*). See also *Irish blowers, Irish glass*.

'Irish' Cupid Mc Guire (2000) describes Aonghus Óg as a Celtic Cupid (Cupid was the Roman god of love). Aonghus had four birds symbolising kisses that flew above his head. See *Irish god of love*.

Irish curragh Term used in J. Hornell's book *British Coracles and Irish Curraghs* (1938). For which, see *Irish coracle*. See also *Irish curragh raids*.

Irish curragh raids Ancient plundering raids on Welsh and west British coasts carried out from *Irish curraghs* (Mac Cullagh, 1992).

Irish curtain Mainly NZ usage, for cobwebs (Orsman, 1997). A synonym of *Irish draperies,* yet the phrase 'Irish curtain' does not have the same secondary connotations that *Irish draperies* has acquired. Bernstein uses the phrase 'shamrock curtain' to refer to the invisible line between the English-speaking areas of Ireland and the Gaeltachtaí of the west of Ireland (1980) (see *Irish-speaking area)*. See also *Irish lace*. Not to be confused with *lace-curtain Irish* (see Appendix 4).

D

Irish daisy 1 A dandelion (Rawson, 1991). **2** According to a Japanese botanical website (www.jekai.org), Irish daisy is listed together with *Irish cobbler* with reference to the Irish potato, i.e. *solanum tuberosum*. In Irish slang, a 'daisy picker' is a chaperone for two young lovers (Share, 1997). Another name for dandelions is 'piss in the beds' (www.thepale boys.com).

'Irish Dames of Ypres' As the Benedictine nuns who settled in Kylemore, Co. Galway, after the First World War were called. The nuns have a convent (with school) there (Killanin, 1962). See also *Irish Sisters of Charity*.

Irish Dan Daniel O'Connell (1775–1847). A ballad from Co. Cavan around the time of the Reform Bill (1832) includes the lines (quoted by Logan, 1986): 'And on the first banner was brave Irish Dan, The man for the people the great Liberator.' See also *Irish Agitator, the; Irish king, uncrowned*.

Irish Dance, Lord of *Daily Mail* journalist Jack Tinker described Michael Flatley as 'the fantastic Lord of Irish Dance'. See also *Irish step-dance stage show*.

Irish dancing costume The costume worn by Irish dancers and the title of a book by Robb (1998); for which see *Irish national dancing costume*. See also *Irish Washerwoman outfit*.

'Irish' dark rosary (Ir. *paidrín gorm*) A unique Irish form of rosary, the beads of which are made of silver with 'blue Iris bead' (supplied by the Silver Grove Studio, in Wrentham, Massachusetts, USA). In some traditional Irish houses, the rosary was kept in a special fireplace recess in the kitchen called a 'keeping hole' or *poll an phaidrín* (i.e. *'hole for the rosary'*: Kinmouth, 1993). See also *Irish penal rosary*.

Irish dawn goddess The epithet of Tuag (CGG). Tuag, or Inbir, was a beautiful maiden who was kept away from the eyes of men. Manannan Mac Lir (see also *Irish sea god*) wanted her, and so sent the druid Fer Fidail to fetch her. The druid wanted Tuag for himself however, so Lir drowned the maiden with a wave and killed Fer Fidail.

Irish death coach Also called a 'headless coach' and 'coach a bower' (Lover and Croker, 1995). This term is derived from the Ir. *cóiste bodhar* = silent coach. It is a death omen or harbinger of misfortune. In Co. Tyrone, the black coach is driven by the *dullahan* (or headless rider, who normally rides alone). The coach is pulled by six black horses; it burns bushes in its trail and all gates open for it.

Irish death god The epithet of Balor of the Evil Eye (CGG). His eye was so evil that it could destroy whatever he looked at. In fulfilment of prophecy, he was slain by his grandson Lugh (see *Irish god of light*), who set a *tathlum* (magic stone ball) in his eye.

Irish death messenger As Lysaght (1986) calls the banshee (literally 'the fairy woman', from Ir. *bean sidhe*), whose wailing outside a house – usually on three consecutive nights – is a warning of the impending death of someone in the household. See also *Irish Lady, Irish phantom funeral, Irish vampire.*

Irish Debtors Act, 1872 Act that abolished the imprisonment of debtors (Encycl. Brit., Vol 3). Hitherto, debtors (sometimes along with their families) were incarcerated in special 'debtors' prisons', for instance on Merchant's Quay and Four Courts Marshalsea, both in Dublin. (The latter was converted into a barracks after this Act.). See also *Irish Siberia.*

Irish declaimer As Rimmer (1969) calls the *recaire* or reciter of poetry/song who once accompanied the *Irish harper.*

Irish deer, great (Ir. *fia mor na mbeann*; Lat. *Megaloceras giganteus* – '*megaloceras*' is Greek for 'large-horned'). A unique species of deer, now extinct, the remains of which have been found in caves above Lough Gur, Co. Limerick, and in a number of bogs. The beast's skull and giant antlers can be seen in the Cork Geology Museum. It is also called the great *Irish elk* and Irish great deer, but some writers (e.g. Evans, 1942) refer to it as 'great Irish deer'. The OED uses both 'Irish deer' and 'Irish elk'. The first scientific study of this species was carried out by Sir Thomas Molyneux (1661–1733). See also *Irish hare, Irish stoat, Irish weasel*

Irish delftware Irish imitations with different designs of a type of pottery the name of which derives from Delft, the Netherlands, where this type of earthenware was originally made. Irish delftware is usually displayed on an *Irish dresser.*

Irish Deluge As Ellis (1987) describes the equivalent of the Biblical flood in Irish mythology. There were only four survivors outside the Ark, including Fintan, who escaped by becoming a salmon. See also *Irish fish, the; Irish trout.*

'Irish' Demosthenes Joseph Devlin (1871–1934), a nationalist who organised the National Volunteers to balance Edward Henry Carson's Ulster Volunteers. T. M. Healy called him 'the duodecimo Demosthenes' (Boylan, 1998).

Irish deputy The *tánaiste* or deputy prime minister, second only to the *taoiseach* or prime minister. In history, the terms referred to the heir presumptive and chief of the clan/tribe respectively. See also *Irish parliament.*

Irish Derby An important horse race for three-year-olds held since 1886 at the Curragh, in June, over a mile and four furlongs. Apart from the Epsom Derby in England, there was also the Manx Derby, instituted in 1628 and run at Langness, as well as the Welsh Derby, which is held at Chepstow in July. See also *Irish Classics*.

Irish dexter A small breed of cattle producing high-quality meat and milk. They are either dun or black. The breed originated in Kerry in the mid-eighteenth century and in Ireland is referred to simply as the Dexter. In America, where it is the smallest cattle breed, the prefix 'Irish' is invariably used. Irish dexters 'are one of the ten rarest breeds of cattle in the world', according to the American website www.iland.net. See also *Irish cow, old*.

Irish diamond Like a Welsh diamond (Edwards, 1998) a worthless rock crystal (Rawson, 1991; and OED). According to the *Illustrated Dictionary of Jewelry* (www.allaboutjewels. com) an Irish diamond is not just any crystal but 'rock crystal from Ireland'. In Northern Ireland, the 'diamond' is the town square (Christensen, 1996). See also *Irish favourite, Irish touchstone*.

Irish diamond dresser A traditional pine *Irish dresser* with a glass case, perhaps so called due to the lozenge patterns on the glass casing (see www.glenmoreantiques.com). See also *Irish spice dresser*.

Irish diaspora The term refers to all those Irish people who live outside Ireland. Many are descendants of those who escaped the *Irish Famine* and went to America or whose ancestors were forced to go as convicts to Australia and elsewhere. Law (1998) estimates that 'some 70 million people worldwide now claim Irish descent': there are many more Irish people in America than in Ireland! Talking of Irish-Americans, it is possible that the expression 'Uncle Sam' is Irish in origin. Perhaps an Irishman back home may have written on the thank-you letter to his generous uncle abroad: 'S.A.M.' (i.e. *Stáit Aontaithe Mheiriceá* = USA). On the other hand, many Americans derive it from the initials of the patriot U. S. Wilson [U. S. = Uncle Sam] (see Alicia Duchak's *An A-Z of Modern America*, 1999). The existence of an Irish diaspora in America also gave Irish-English some interesting expressions, like the 'American wake' held on the eve of the departure of someone Irish (see also *Irish wake*). Aran was referred to as 'the next parish to America' and fatty bacon was known as 'American lad' (for which see *Irish bacon*). The Irish also went to the West Indies (see *Black Irish* in Appendix 4), as well as on the continent (see *'Irish' Wild Geese*).

Irish Dickens 1 Frank McCourt, writer of the 1997 Pulitzer Prize-winning memoir *Angela's Ashes,* set in Limerick. The *Irish Times* has dubbed him 'our first Irish Dickens'. **2** Similarly, James Joyce has been described as 'an Irish Dickens or a Myles na gCopaleen without the jokes' (*New York Times,* 16 June 1996). Myles na gCopaleen was the pseudonym used by Irish novelist Flann O'Brien. See also *Irish Charles Bukowski, 'Irish' Homer, Irish Keats, 'Irish' Shakespeare.*

Irish dinner The term 'Irish dinner' is used by some (e.g. Green, 1996) for *Irishman's dinner* (see Appendix 3).

Irish dip 1 Sexual relations (Green, 1996). **2** Gay sexual relations (Share, 1997).

Irish dipper *(Cinclus cinclus hibernicus)* Unique Irish bird which has a darker head than both the British and continental species. The chestnut band on the breast is narrower and duller and the upper parts are darker. The Irish dipper can also be found in the west of Scotland. According to Swainson (1886), a popular Irish name for it is 'river pie'.

'Irish' Disneyland 1 In relation to Ireland's beauty and tourist potential, Eagleton (1999) writes: 'The country is well on the way to becoming one enormous theme park, a kind of Celtic Disneyland with Queen Maeve standing in for Mickey Mouse.' Eagleton also calls Ireland 'a spiritual Disneyland'. Walt Disney in fact did make a film about Ireland, namely *Darby O'Gill and the Little People.* **2** Ballymena, Co. Antrim, is, according to Pepper (1983), 'sometimes called Disneyland because of the constant references to it heard there, as in, "The child disney like her breakfast" and "My man disney like Tap aff th' Paps".' See also *Irish Cinderella.*

Irish distillers Term often used (e.g. by Magee, 1980) to refer to the distillers of *Irish whiskey:* they distill the drink three times, as opposed to the distillers of Scotch whisky, who do only a double distillation.

Irish dividend 1 Police extortion (Partridge, 1950) or, as Green (1998) says, 'a shakedown by the police'. Again, the Irish seem to be targeted in this phrase because many American police officers are Irish, irrespective of whether Irish police-men took part in any extortion or not. See also Iris*h club-house*. **2** A tax assessment which takes rather than gives money (Green, 1996) or generally 'an assessment on stock' (*Webster's*). See also *'Irish' Maffia*.

Irish Division, Sixteenth Together with the Thirty-sixth (Ulster) Division, they fought in the Battle of the Somme (began September 1916).

Irish Division, Tenth The first Irish division put together by the British army. Many were sacrificed needlessly at the stupid assault on Gallipoli (1915).

Irish dodo The actual dodo was a large Mauritian bird that was first discovered in 1598 but had become extinct by 1681. As it did not fear predators, it was called by Portuguese sailors *doudo*, i.e. 'stupid'. Similarly, because of humans – who fish and cause pollution – the salmon is also endangered in Irish waters. One website asks: 'Will salmon become merely a memory, like the bittern of Ireland and the dodo of Mauri-tius? Some people already refer to it as the Irish dodo' (www.iol.ie/~mfogarty/salmon.htm).

'Irish dogs' An insult once directed at the Anglo-Irish (and English settlers) rather than the native Irish. In the time of King Edward II, 'Englishmen from England were forbid-den to abuse the colonists, faithful lieges to the lord king, by calling them Irish dogs or the like' (cited by Simms, 1989). Similarly (perhaps due to the Irishman's naturally fierce hostility to invaders), the word 'bark' was once used for an Irish person (Partridge, 1937 – who also notes that 'Bark-shire' existed until the nineteenth century as a name for Ireland). This may be related to the fact that, due to the Eng-lishman's inability to produce Irish rhotic sounds, the 'R' sounded like a snarl and was called the 'dog's letter' (Ó Muirithe, 1999). In retaliation, Irish Catholics (especially in the north – see Share, 1997 – and Liverpool) have used the term 'Proddy dog' for a Protestant. See also *Irish wolf*.

Irish doll A variety of Iris.

Irishdom Should be 'Gaeldom'. See *Irishry*.

Irish Dominion League Founded in June 1919 by Sir Horace Plunkett with the aim of founding a self-governing Ireland within the British empire. Apart from displeasing Unionists, the short-lived League was too late, since in January of the same year an *Irish Republic* had already been proclaimed at the first Dáil Éireann.

Irish double-headed stone Ancient stone monument with two heads; see, for example, on Boa Island, Co. Fermanagh.

Irish double jig (Ir. *port dúbailte*). An *Irish jig* in six-eight time.

Irish Downhill harp Phillips uses the prefix 'Irish' for this beautiful, lightly strung *Irish harp,* made c.1702 for Arthur Guinness and Co. in Dublin *(Cambria,* March/April 1999).

Irish Dragon An old vignette (c.1649) depicts one of Cromwell's troops standing on a small lizard holding a sword in one hand and a decapitated, bearded head in the other. The caption reads: 'St George trampling upon the Irish Dragon' (Foster, 1989). See also *Irish Nessie.*

Irish Dragoons As the heroic Irishmen who fought with Sarsfield have been called because of their dashing bravery, which would match that of any dragoon (Morton, 1930); the Irish Dragoons were Jacobites.

Irish draperies 1 Cobwebs (Partridge, 1937; Dickson, 1997). See also *Irish curtain, Irish lace.* **2** Drooping breasts (Green, 1996; Share, 1997).

Irish draught 'The Irish draught was big and powerful, with a thick-set, short-legged build, and unlike other carthorse breeds had no "beard" on its legs' (Sharkey, 1985). Today the offspring are appreciated as excellent jumping horses, and are often cross-bred with the *Irish thoroughbred* to produce the *Irish hunter.* See also *Irish carthorse* for other Irish breeds of horses.

Irish draught mare Used for cross-breeding. Logan (1986) refers to 'half-breds, sired by blood stallion out of an *Irish draught mare.* A foal resulting from such a cross might be anything – an Arkle or a Boomerang [no relation to the *Irish boomerang*], a Dundrum or a Limerick Lace'. See *Irish draught.*

Irish dresser 'The Irish dresser is ... easily distinguished from its Welsh and English counterparts because it was traditionally made in one piece rather than two' (Kinmouth, 1993). It is also usually thinner (see Shaw-Smith, 1984). In Irish it is called *drisiúr* and in Shelta (*Irish Travellers' Cant*) *misur* (Macalister, 1937). See also *Irish diamond dresser, Irish hen dresser, Irish spice dresser*.

'Irish' drugget skirt Large wraparound apron. Sharkey (1985) says that, because of their size and shape, 'black druggets often doubled as shawls'.

'Irish' Dublin Lawyer The prefix 'Irish' is sometimes used for this recipe of fresh lobster prepared with *Irish whiskey* and cream. No relation to a 'Tipperary lawyer', which is a cudgel (Partridge, 1937). See also *Irish brehons*.

Irish Dun An old breed of cow which Mason (1951) says was most similar to the Suffolk Dun; the Irish Dun survived until 1974. A synonym for 'Irish Dun' is the *polled Irish* (see Appendix 4). Logan (1986) writes that extinct cattle breeds 'included the Donegal Red and Irish Dun, and ... a breed which they called Yellow Polly'. See also *Irish moiled*.

Irish dwarf pine (*Pinus sylvestris hibernica*) A miniature garden variety of pine tree (see webpage for *Altamont, Co. Carlow*). This tree is not used for Irish pine furniture! See also *Irish juniper, Irish mahogany, Irish whitebeam, Irish willow, Irish yew*.

E

Irish earth goddess The epithet of Tailtu (CGG) who was the foster mother of Lugh. The Lughnasa feast of games was held in her honour. See also *Irish Olympics*.

Irish Easter The early *Irish Church*'s distinct way of computing the date for Easter adhered to an eighty-four-year cycle, as opposed to the Roman nineteen-year cycle, i.e. the Irish celebrated on the day of the Paschal moon rather than the following Sunday. Even after the Synod of Whitby (664), a few Irish ecclesiastical communities retained this system until 716. See also *Irish calendar*.

'Irish' Easter Rising Or more commonly simply 'the Easter Rising' (1916). A revolution so named as it commenced on Easter Monday (April 24). The *Irish Republican Brotherhood* had planned the rising a day earlier but German arms carried on the boat *The Aud*, intended for the *Irish Volunteers*, were intercepted by the British. The *Irish Volunteers*, with the smaller *Irish Citizen Army*, took over the General Post Office in O'Connell Street (then Sackville Street), making it their headquarters, and proclaimed the *Irish Republic*. Other important buildings were taken afterwards. Heavily outnumbered, and with communications cut between the rebel outposts, the Irish leaders surrendered at the end of the week after a heroic struggle. The British lost 103 soldiers, while 64 Irishmen were killed in the fighting and another fifteen executed. See also *Irish Revolution; Irishmen, United*.

Irish ecclesiastical capital For this and other capitals see *Irish capital*.

'Irish' Edinburgh See *'Irish' Glasgow*.

Irish Education Act, 1892 This Act aimed to make national schooling compulsory and abolished fees for children aged three to fifteen. See also *Irish Christian Brothers, Irish hedge school, Irish Not*.

'Irish' eel There may not be any snakes in Ireland because of St Patrick, but there is a unique subspecies of eel found in Irish waters: the *Anguilla hibernica Couch* (see the website *List of Nominal Species of Anguillidae*). See also *Irish Nessie*.

Irish eggs Like Scotch eggs (hard-boiled eggs covered with sausage meat and then breadcrumbs), Irish eggs are hard-boiled eggs covered with potato which has been mashed with garlic, rosemary and Dijon mustard, according to the recipes webpage at www.geocities.com. See also *Irish shortbread*.

'Irish' El Dorado The Wicklow Hills. 'The great wealth of Ireland in copper, tin and alluvial gold found ... made it a kind of El Dorado of the Ancient World' (Thomas, 1939). See also *Irish gold*.

Irish elbow pipes As some (Christensen, 1996) call the *uilleann pipes* (from Ir. *uillinn* = elbow), since the *Irish piper* must have used both elbows to play. David C. Daye, while agreeing with this etymology, adds that 'an archaic meaning may also be "elder tree" [see also *Irish mahogany*], whose bark was once used to make reeds for this instrument' (www.bprc.mps.ohio_state.edu). Also called *Irish pipes* or *Irish Union pipes*.

Irish elegance 1 A rare variety of red rose (Brett, nd). **2** A variety of columbine.

Irish elk Some writers (Christensen, 1996) have a preference for the name 'Irish elk' or 'great Irish elk' instead of *great Irish deer*.

Irish Elysium With reference to the *Irish Otherworlds*, Mahon (2000) writes: 'the dead went to Tír na nÓg, "the land of eternal youth", or to the old Irish Elysium, Magh Meall, "the Plain of Honey".' See also *'Irish' Atlantis*.

Irish Emergency Army Also called the Irish Defence Forces and 'Soldiers of the Rearguard'. Special force established for the duration of the (Irish) Emergency (1939–46), while Britain and Germany were at war. Those who enlisted were also called 'durationists' or 'E-men' (Share, 1997). This force served essentially to protect the Republic's policy of neutrality. Despite this neutrality, immediately after the Belfast Blitz (15 April 1941), the Irish Republic sent fire engines and other assistance. The *Irish Emergency Army* is not to be confused with the 'Emergency Men' (loyalists who worked for boycotted landlords during the *Irish Land War*).

'Irish emperor' Or *Imperator Scottorum*. The title used by Brian Ború, high king of Ireland, when he presented himself at Armagh in 1005. See also *Irish high king, Irish lord*.

'Irish' Encumbered Estates Act Act of 1849 which facilitated the sale of estates belonging to those made bankrupt by the *Irish Famine*. Owners were not compensated for improvements made on their land, and new owners, especially in the west of Ireland, evicted tenants. (Pascoe uses the prefix 'Irish', 1968).

Irish English As distinct from *English Irish* (see Appendix 4). Irish English (also called Hiberno-English) is the form of English spoken by the Irish. Due to the rich vocabulary (especially that derived from the *Irish language)*, many words are unintelligible to other English speakers. This prompted George Bernard Shaw to remark that 'the English and the Irish are divided by the same language' (quoted and adapted by Eagleton, 1999). See also *Irish brogue; Irish literary revival, language of the; Irish pronunciation, received; Irish vocabulary, stage*.

Irish ensign As opposed to the *Irish harp* flag of a harp on a blue background used by some continental Irish regiments led by descendants of 'Wild Geese' (see *'Irish' Wild Geese*), this one 'was a flag ... in which the harp on a green field was combined with a canton of St George's Cross (and later the Union Jack). This flag (sometimes called the Irish ensign and sometimes the Irish Jack) was regularly included in flag charts and seems to have had a limited use as a kind of "loyal" national flag' (Ó Brógáin, 1998). See also *Irish flag, Irish harp emblem, 'Irish' Starry Plough, Irish Tricolour*.

Irisher 1 A synonym of an Irish person (OED). **2** (US slang) 'An Irish settler in the United States' (*Webster's*). By extension, the word 'Mickser', with the same meaning (see also *'Irish' mick*) has also been coined (Green, 1998). **3** The comparative form of 'Irish', i.e. more Irish (see *Irishest)*.

Irishes 1 Plural of Irish (see Appendix 1), in the sense of 'Irishman' (OED). **2** In the eighteenth century, used to refer to Scots (McArthur, 1992).

Irishese Facetious internet neologism for some form of Irish jargon or even *Irish English,* coined by analogy to Americanese, Australianese and so on (McArthur, 1992).

Irishest The superlative form of 'Irish', i.e. the most Irish. On one internet site, the author writes: 'I quickly learned the realities of the conjugation Irish – Irisher – Irishest' (www.nhc.rtp.nc.us).

Irish Estates Act, 1460 (Encycl. Brit., Vol. 12) In the previous year (1459) Richard of York had already been deprived of his title, Lieutenant of Ireland, by the Lancastrian king Henry VI. Therefore this act at Drogheda was an attempt by Richard to reclaim his Irish estates and to receive support from the Irish (or rather a promise not to rebel) by reaffirming the *Irish parliament.* The act was short-lived however, as Richard was killed the same year in the War of the Roses.

Irishette Not a little *Irish colleen* but the Norwegian name for a variety of fungus (see website *Norske Soppnavn*).

Irish evidence False evidence or perjury (first recorded by Grose, 1785; quoted in Partridge, 1937). The origin of this phrase may reflect not so much the Irishman's supposed lying nature, but his refusal to betray fellow rebels to the English. Similarly, a 'Kerry witness' is one 'who will swear to anything' (Share, 1997) and 'Kerry security' is an oath pledged in return for money (Partridge, 1937).

Irish exactions The origin of 'coyne and livery' (Ir. *coinnmheadh* = guesting; Eng. *livery* = something, i.e. straw given to

horses), under which 'a lord was entitled to free entertainment from his tenants for himself and his retinue at a certain period of the year' (Smith, 1991).

Irish eye-water More commonly 'Paddy's eye-water', i.e. poteen (Share, 1997), as distinct from common (i.e. non-Irish)
eye-water, which is gin (Partridge, 1950). No connection
with 'Larry Duggan's eye-water', which meant blacking –
named after the eighteenth-century Dublin shoe-black (i.e.
shoe shiner) (Partridge, 1937). See also *Irish poteen*.

Irish eyes 1 A variety of orchid. **2** A variety of coneflower. **3** A
variety of sanritala (another flower). **4** Cocktail of *Irish
whiskey*, cream and crème de menthe (Sennet, 1977).

F

Irish faction fights Fights, mainly in the early nineteenth century, between rival gangs (e.g. the 'Caravats' and 'Shanavests' in Co. Kilkenny), who were usually armed with cud-
gels (see also *Irish shillelagh)*. The cudgel used – often loaded
with a stone or lead – was called a *cipín, maide* or *bata;* another word for one was a 'podger' (Share, 1997). The gangs
would decide on a place beforehand, which was often a
fair or *Irish pattern*. 'Sometimes the women joined in the
fighting using a *doirling* stone in a strong woollen stocking'
(Logan, 1986). Some of the gangs were members of secret
societies or sectarian groups. See also *Irish stick-fighting*.

Irish fada (Ir. *fada* = long) Accent (written the same as the French
acute accent) that lengthens the vowels in many words in
the *Irish language*.

Irish fairmaid Or rather what *Brewer's* called the 'fairmaid of
Ireland'. This is the will-o'-the-wisp or *ignis fatuus*, the Irish
name for which is *tine ghealain* (bright fire), a mysterious
light seen at night in the countryside. Ó hÓgáin (1995) says
that this strange light is 'the soul of a master gambler who
defeated the devil at cards but was refused entry into
heaven' and therefore roams. Another Irish word for this
'misguiding light' is *solas sí* (fairy light).

Irish fairy cattle Jessica Hemming's term for the supernatural
cows of Irish mythology (*Folklore* 113, 2002). Cattle have always had a special importance in Irish tradition. A druid
was imbued with the power to dream of the one who would

become *ard rí* (see also *Irish high king*) if he consumed the blood and meat of a white bull (Ellis, 1987). Like the supernatural *Ychen Bannog* (or long-horned oxen) of Welsh folk tales, these early cows belonged to the fairies. O'Sullivan (1991) says that 'the colour of all Irish cows was a mixture of red and white; only fairy cows were pure white.' Moreover, their milk could 'make silly people'. The milk could also be taken by a witch who had taken the form of a hare (see *Irish hare*). So rather than being magical, cows were often vulnerable to magic; for this reason, there would be a horseshoe in the cowshed (see *Irish luck*) and a St Brigid's cross (see *Irish Cross* and *'Irish' Mary*) or a *rath doire* or piece of oak.

Irish fairy king 1 Finvarra (Fin Bheara), according to Briggs (1976). Finvarra was king of the Connaght fairies in Cnoc Meadha, where he lured beautiful women. There are many legends about him, including one that he played a hurling match with his fairies each year (see also *Irish hurling*) against other provinces. **2** Dagda is so called by Jones (1995). For more on Dagda see *Irish father god*.

Irish fairy queen Boann, according to Jones (1995). Her name is usually rendered 'Boinn'. She was associated with the River Boyne, the source of which was a well called *Sídh* of Nechtan = fairy dwelling of Nechtan (Nechtan was her husband). The water of her river gave anyone who drank it the power to become a poet or seer (see Ó hÓgáin, 1990). See also *Irish queen of the fairies*.

Irish fairy spell As Briggs (1976) calls a *pishogue*. The Irish word *'piseog'* means a folk charm or spell to ward off witchcraft or disease (or even to harm someone, for instance by burying eggs in his haycock, according to Share, 1997, quoting Frank Kelly). Alternatively, a *pishogue* could be intended to help a farmer increase his milk yield (by 'placing a cow's afterbirth under the milk-keelers' (Hickey and Doherty, 1980). The same Irish term could also include love charms. By extension, the word *'piseog'* is so wide in meaning that, as Kavanagh (1959) says (using the form *'pistrog'*), it can refer to 'anything superstitious'. Joyce (1910) also gave the forms *pisheroge* and *pishthroge*; other forms, such as *'pishrob'* and *'pishlag'* exist in Ulster (Macafee, 1996).

Irish fairy tunes Jones (1995) writes that the 'coulin' are the 'Irish fairy tunes ... which are said to have been heard by musicians from the invisible harps of the *sídhe* [fairies].' See also *Irish harp*.

Irish fakirs Lady Wilde (nd) referred to a group of 'professional prayer-men' by allusion to the Arabic word *faqir* (poor men), i.e. a muslim ascetic/mendicant: 'the *Irish Fakirs*, or sacred fraternity of beggars, lead a pleasant, thoroughly idle life. they carry a wallet and staff and, being looked on as holy men endowed with strange spiritual gifts, they are entirely supported by the voluntary gifts of the people, who firmly believe in the efficacy of their prayers and blessings and prognostics of luck.' These 'professional prayer-men' may be the same as the so-called 'mock litany men' of nineteenth-century Ireland who begged 'in a sing-song or versifying manner' as if reciting a litany (Green, 1998). Similarly, in 1785, Grose mentioned another category of Irish 'beggar', the 'save-alls': 'boys running about gentlemen's houses in Ireland, who are fed on broken meats that would otherwise be wasted' (quoted by Partridge, 1937). See also *Irish toyle.*

Irish Famine (Ir. *An Drochshaol*) The Great Famine or Great Hunger (1845–9) caused by the *Irish potato famine fungus* and blight. As the *Irish potato* was so vital to the Irish diet, the successive failures of the crop caused the death of over a million people and prompted at least another million to emigrate. The Famine occurred despite the Indian corn brought by Sir Robert Peel as a substitute for potatoes, and unsuccessful relief schemes. There was also the 'aid' of Protestant proselytisers: for instance, 'souperism', whereby soup was offered to Catholics who renounced their faith (see also the 'rice Christians' in the East – Green, 1996). Such a 'convert' (who received a 'pot' of food) was called a 'pot convert' (Green, 1998). Apart from the great tragedy in losing half the Irish population, the Famine was undoubtedly the most severe blow to the *Irish language,* as the western parts of Ireland (the *Irish-speaking areas*) were the most badly affected by the disaster.

Irish famine dropsy Or simply 'famine dropsy', the common name for hunger oedema. This was one type of fever com-

mon in the *Irish Famine,* the others being black or spotted
fever (typhus), yellow fever (dysentery) and blackleg
(scurvy). See also *Irish ague; Irish Plague, the.*

Irish famine fever See *Irish fever.*

'Irish' famine road Or simply 'famine road', which was a 'road
(often leading nowhere) built under the relief scheme set
up by the government to provide employment for the poor
during periods of famine, especially in the 1840s' (Christensen, 1996). See also *Irish Road; Irish Way, the.*

Irish fan A spade or shovel (Green, 1996). For other jocular names
for tools, see *Irish banjo.*

Irish farmhouse As a prefix to various recipes, this term suggests plain, traditional, home Irish cooking, unaffected by
modern or foreign influences. It is thus the opposite of what
Hughes (2000) terms 'new Irish cuisine'.

Irish fart Also Irishman's fart. Legman describes someone's
family as 'like an Irishman's fart – always making a lot of
noise and raising stink and never wanting to go back where
they came from' (quoted by Rawson, 1991). On similar
lines, the pseudo-Irish name 'Doyle Carte' means the same
in rhyming slang (see website *Roger's Profanisaurus*). An
Anglo-Irish synonym of the *Irish jaunting car* was a 'farting
trap' (Green, 1998). Although Green does not acknowledge
this, the derivation may not be from the vulgar meaning
but could be a cognate of 'farthing' (a quarter of an *Irish
penny)* reflecting the fact that four passengers could sit in it.
In Irish slang, a 'Tinker's fart' (see *Irish Tinkers* or *Travellers*)
means a 'nugatory amount' (Share, 1997). Parallel ethnic
combinations include a 'Dutchman's fart' (a sea urchin –
Green, 1998).

Irish fashion Refers to couched embroidery, silk garnishing or
applied jewels on gowns. Like the *Irish mantle,* such decoration on clothes was prohibited in the time of King Henry
VIII (Connolly, 1998). See also *Irish cloak.*

Irish fashion', 'to take a reef in the Green's translation (1996)
of the French navy's phrase *'prendre des ris a l'irlandaise',*
which means 'to handle the sails recklessly, often slashing
them to ribbons.' This phrase may be related to the term
Paddy wester (see Appendix 5), an incompetent seamen or
one with a dead man's papers (so named after one Paddy

West, who sold fake seamen's papers in nineteenth-century Liverpool – Green, 1996). See also *Irish pennant*.

Irish fate goddess So Fedelm or Feithline, daughter of Conchobar, is dubbed (CGG). She was a woman of the Sídhe Cruachan, Hell's Gateway, and prophesied to Queen Medb that an invasion of Ulster to capture the Brown Bull would be unsuccessful. She also predicted Medb's death.

Irish father god As Dixon-Kennedy (1997) calls Daghdha or Dagda. Green (1992) calls him 'an Irish tribal father god'. His name means 'good god'. He is often portrayed dragging a huge club (see also *Irish shillelagh*) on wheels. No one could leave hungry from his cauldron, and his harp (see also *Irish harp)*, which had been stolen by the Fomorii, sang at the sound of his voice. See also *Irish craft gods*.

Irish favourite An emerald (Partridge, 1950). This term was used since the early 1920s by reference to Ireland as the Emerald Isle (for reference to other islands also dubbed the Emerald Isle, see *Black Irish* in Appendix 4). Ireland is also called the the Green Isle (*Brewer's*). By the same token, from the mid-nineteenth century an Irishman was also called an Emeralder (Green, 1996). One synonym of the phrase 'the Celtic Tiger' (which refers to Ireland's booming economy) is, according to Eagleton (1999), 'the Emerald Tiger' (see *Irish Tiger*). See also *Irish diamond, Irish national colour*.

'Irish' fern A prehistoric and unique variety of fern *(archaeopteris hibernica)*, the fossil of which can be seen in the Cork Geology Museum. See also *Irish tatting fern*.

Irish fertility and fate goddess So Eriu (an aspect of Morrigan) is called. She could change shape from a maiden to a hag or from a bird to an animal.

Irish fertility goddess of spring An epithet of Lasair (CGG). With her sisters Latiaran and Inghean Bhuidhe (symbolising growing, ripening and harvesting respectively), they are the Irish equivalent of the Three Fates.

Irish Fest The largest Irish festival in the world, held at Milwaukee, Wisconsin.

Irish Feud, Cornish- The prolonged tension in labour relations between Irish workers and the more privileged Cornish miners in Butte, America, in the early twentieth century (Rowe, 1965).

Irish fever 'Irish emigrants fleeing to England brought typhus, or Irish fever, with them' (Kohn, 1995). W. R. Wilde (1852) wrote: 'the spring of 1823 had passed by and with the early summer appeared a partial outbreak of the Irish fever, which annually bursts into flame about May or June.' See also *Irish ague, Irish pestilences, Irish Plague, the*.

Irish Fever Act, 1847 This Act gave relief committees responsibility for using government funds in time of famine to provide for the building of hospitals and the burial of those who died in the famine. This legislation was in force until 1850. See also *Irish Famine*.

Irish fiddling An Irish style of violin-playing in *Irish music* (Ó hAllmhuráin, 1998). This term is used to distinguish it from similar though distinct fiddling styles such as Scottish and Orcadian (from Orkney: a mixture of Irish, Scottish and Norse styles). When one Kerryman was asked if he could play the fiddle, he answered: 'I don't know, I've never tried' (MacHale, 1979).

Irish fifth (Ir. *cúige* = a fifth). One of the five ancient provinces of Ireland; since medieval times there have only been four. *Cúig cúigí na hÉireann* (five fifths of Ireland) was the collective name for the five provinces into which Ireland was divided by the *Fir Bholg*. See also *Irish septs*.

Irish figure dances Many Irish-music experts (Ó hAllmhuráin, 1998, and Vallely, 1999) use this term to describe pure Irish *céilí* dances, as opposed to the foreign, imported so-called *Irish set-dance*.

Irish filigree 1 As the beautiful pattern overlaid on the Tara brooch is described (www.ireland.org). **2** A type of *Irish crochet*.

Irish fine lady's delirium 'The Irish fine lady's delirium or the London vertigo', exhibited by the heroine of Charles Macklin's *The Irish Fine Lady* (1762) (or *The True Born Irishman*), refers to the pretensions of the Irish wife of O'Doherty, MP, to ape English ways (cited by Welch, 1996). In other words, the same as trying to be 'Englified' (Share, 1997). See also *Castle Irish* (Appendix 4).

Irish fire Also called Irishman's fire. 'A fire that burns only on top' (Rawson, 1991). In late nineteenth-century rhyming slang, the word for 'fire' was the Irish name Mick O'Dwyer

and in Australian rhyming slang the Irish-sounding Bar-
ney Maguire (Green, 1998). Many will be familiar with the
May Day bonfire festival, *Bealtaine*. The final element of
this word comes from the Irish word for fire: *tine* (see also
Shelta *tini* and Welsh *tân*). Green (1998) misspells the Irish
word as *teine* but nevertheless believes that it was from this
Irish root that 'tinny', the English slang word for fire, is
derived; it is thus an example of an *Irish loanword*. There
are also phrases like 'tinney-hunter' (a thief operating after
fires – see Partridge, 1937).

Irish fire pot The flat-bottomed utensil for baking in the fireplace (Cole, 1973).

Irish fireflame A bright orange variety of rose (Brett, nd).

Irish fish, the As Bluett (1994) calls the salmon. In Irish mythology, the salmon features prominently. It is the fish of
knowledge: Fionn derived wisdom from it (the salmon
had obtained this wisdom by eating nuts from nine hazel
trees at the bottom of the sea). Note that the so-called *Irish
salmon* is not a fish. The term 'mackerel snapper' has been
used in America as a nickname for a Catholic, and particularly an Irish Catholic (see *Irish Catholic, White*). This may
be because the fish is common in the North Atlantic or,
more likely, because Catholics often eat fish rather than
meat on Fridays. Fortunately, Irish waters have always been
blessed with an abundance of fresh fish: during the *Irish
Famine*, fish was known as 'famine food'. See also *Irish dodo,
Irish lord, Irish pollan, Irish trout*.

Irish flag 1 The Irish national flag, for which see *Irish Tricolour*.
See also *Irish ensign, Irish Green Flag, Irish harp emblem, 'Irish'
Starry Plough*. **2** In American slang, a diaper or nappy (Green,
1998). Green gives no explanation as to the origin of this
term; possibly coined by analogy to the *Irish baby buggy*.

Irish Flag, 'Eire' The *Irish Tricolour* with an *Irish harp* on the
central white stripe, above which is the name Eire (see
website *Island Ireland Marketplace Index*).

Irish flag', 'Solemn Ceremony of Hoisting the Historic ceremony (see Ó Brógáin, 1998) during the *'Irish' Easter Rising*.
On 16 April 1916 the *Irish Citizen Army*, with a special oath,
hoisted the flag at Liberty Hall in Dublin (for which see
Irish Green Flag).

Irish flag garden A garden where the floral arrangement is in the form of the *Irish Tricolour*. The term is used to describe a garden with green, white and gold flowers (see website *Album Dun Laoghaire Ecole Holy Family*).

Irish Flanders As Evans (1942) calls 'the isolated tract in Co. Wexford comprising the baronies of Bargy and Forth'. See also *'Irish' Athens* for toponyms.

Irish flannel-mouth Or just 'flannel-mouth' or 'chaw-mouth' (see also *'Irish' chaw*). An American term first used around 1670 for 'a smooth talker, a braggart, especially an Irishman' (Rawson, 1991). See also *Irish assurance, Irish blarney*.

Irish flax This material is plain-woven and full-bleached to make *Irish linen* (Wilcox, 1969). See also *Irish crochet, Irish lace, Irish poplin*.

Irish fling Type of dance which is very similar to the Highland fling.

Irish flowerer The title of E. Boyle's book, *The Irish Flowerers* refers to people who did 'flowering' (i.e. embroidery) or made *Irish lace*.

Irish flute 'The Irish flute, also called the session flute, is a crossworked wooden flute with six holes, in the key of D' (www.harpanddragon.com). It resembles the seventeenth- and eighteenth-century baroque flutes; the concert version has three pieces, compared to the cheaper, often two-piece plastic, Irish flute. See also *Irish tin whistle*.

Irish food, the high altar of Like 'the headquarters of modern Irish cuisine' (Hughes, 2000), this is an epithet of Ballymaloe House, which is noted for the finest traditional Irish cookery, as opposed to what Hughes calls 'new Irish cuisine'. Ballymaloe is associated with the famous cooks Myrtle Allen and her daughter-in-law Darina, whom Hughes dubs 'the saviours of traditional Irish food'.

Irish football 1 The term is used occasionally (Healy, 1998) as a synonym for the more usual term 'Gaelic football'. Healy writes: 'a form of Irish or Gaelic football was played in Ireland as far back as the fourteenth century.' Irish football players and fans call it simply 'football' (as opposed to soccer). A Gaelic football match features two teams of fifteen players who score by kicking the ball over the crossbar for a point or under it and between the posts for a goal (three

points). Since it is a pure Irish sport and therefore associated with Irishmen of the rural areas, some of the more
'sophisticated' soccer supporters of Dublin call it 'bogball'
(see *Irish bog-trotters*). **2** According to Green (1998), an Irish
football is another term for the potato. See also *Irish hurling*.

Irish footing Distinct steps in Scottish dancing based on Irish
folk dances (Thurston, 1954). There are different variations
as well as combinations with other dancing steps: Irish
footing and back step, double Irish footing, single Irish
footing, double Irish footing and double cut, and double
Irish footing and three shuffles. See also *Irish haye*.

Irish foot-plough The ploughman had to bend when using this
plough, so the Irish name for an early type of this tool was
cos-chrom or 'bent foot' (Sharkey, 1985). See also *Irish ard,
Irish plough*.

'Irish' Forgeries Correctly, the 'Ireland Forgeries' (*Brewer's*): the
bogus works of William Henry Ireland (1777–1835), in-
cluding two plays, *Vortigern* and *Henry II*, purporting to be
the work of Shakespeare. The only real Irish connection
with these works is that it was the Irish Shakespearean
scholar Edmund Malone (1741–1812) who exposed them
as frauds in 1796. (In 1782 he also exposed the 'Rowley
Forgeries' of Thomas Chatterton – again supposed to be by
Shakespeare.) See also *'Irish' Shakespeare*.

Irish fortune 1 Female genitalia (Partridge, 1937). The same as
meaning as Grose's 'Tipperary fortune' (quoted by Partridge, 1937). Likewise, in Australian slang a woman's private parts are labelled by the (common Irish) name of Mick
or Mickey (Hughes, 1989; Simes, 1993). Similarly, a woman's
posterior has been referred to as Ireland (Neaman and Silver, 1983). 'The Netherlands' has also been used in this sense
(Green, 1998). **2** Rawson (1991) provides the same definition but adds 'and a pair of clogs'. **3** A woman 'with no fortune other than her body' (Green, 1996). See also *Irish draperies*.

Irish foxhound Apparently, popular opinion 'points to the Irish
foxhound as one of the primary ancestors' of the unique
Catahoula leopard dog found in the southern states of the
USA (www.catahoulaleopard.com). See *Irish setter* for other
dog breeds.

Irish foxhunter's jig A variation of the *Irish jig*.

Irish frame drum As both Baines (1992) and Vallely (1999) refer to the bodhrán, which is like a tambourine without jingles and covered with skin. The base of the *bodhrán* may originally have been a winnowing tray (as its Irish synonym *dallan* and Scots Gaelic equivalent *dallach* suggest). Apart from its renewed popularity in *Irish music,* it has traditionally been used by the *Irish wrenboys.* See also *Irish bagpipes, Irish tambourine.*

Irish Franchise Act, 1850 This Act increased the size of the Irish electorate from 45,000 to 164,000. This was achieved by restructuring the registration system and reducing the price of the borough and county franchises (to £4 and £8 respectively) and linking the latter to occupation instead of ownership. It by no means meant universal suffrage though, it just gave the vote to the semi-wealthy.

Irish Frankenstein Unlike the *Irish vampire* (which is part of Ireland's rich folklore), the so-called Irish Frankenstein was nothing but a caricature by John Tenniel which appeared in *Punch* magazine in 1882. It is depicted like a monster wearing an *Irish cloak* and holding a dagger dripping with blood (www.people.virginia.edu). The figure's ape-like face indicates that it was not an original sketch on Tenniel's part but merely a variation of the *Simian Paddy* (see Appendix 5).

Irish freckle bread Type of bread so called because of the pieces of chopped dates in the dough (for recipe see www.recipe usa.org). The name may have been coined by analogy to the Welsh 'speckled bread' or *bara brith.*

Irish Freedom, Friends of US-based Republican organisation founded in 1916 at the *Irish Race Conventions.* It raised £35,000 for the Relief Fund for the families of those who were killed, injured or imprisoned after the '*Irish*' *Easter Rising*; a further £5 million was sent for the cause after an appeal by Éamon de Valera. In 1920 de Valera fell out with the leaders and in 1932 the organisation disbanded.

Irish Free State (Ir. *Saorstát Éireann*) The name suggested by Arthur Griffiths for the newly-created country which then had the same constitutional status as Canada, Australia, New Zealand and South Africa. This name was used between 1922 and 1937 and was then replaced under Article

4 of the Constitution by the name *Éire* or Ireland.

Irish Free Stater 1 A member of the *Irish Free State* forces in the *Irish Civil War*. **2** A supporter of the *Anglo-Irish Treaty*.

Irish Free Trade Agreement, Anglo- Agreement reached in 1965 that removed the tariff barriers of the 1930s between Ireland and England and aimed to achieve free trade by 1975. It is a paradox that the volume of Irish exports to Britain dwindled after this agreement (from 75 per cent of total exports in 1960 to 43 per cent in 1980), even though half of Irish imports were from Britain in the same period.

Irish friendship bracelet There seems to be a custom in Ireland and overseas of giving a special silver bracelet inscribed with a wish as a symbol of friendship (like the Claddagh ring).

Irish frieze (W. *deuliw Gwyddelig*) A Welsh name for a frieze (woollen cloth) with two colours (GPC).

'Irish fright' The mass panic in England in December 1688 caused by reports of pillage and massacre by Irish Catholic soldiers brought over to support King James II. The panic led to attacks on both Catholics and those suspected of being members of this faith (Connolly, 1998).

'Irish' Frizzler Or just 'frizzler'. In mid-nineteenth century slang, it meant 'an Irish hawker' (Partridge, 1950). The term is perhaps derived from the term 'driz fencer', i.e. a person who sells lace. See also *Irish lace*.

Irish fry The prefix 'Irish' is often used (for example by Hughes, 2000) for this breakfast meal (see also *Irish breakfast*) of *Irish bacon*, sausages, black pudding, white pudding, eggs and tomatoes. Similarly, there is also the Ulster fry (sausages, bacon, eggs, fried bread and slim, i.e. potato bread – see Law, 1998).

Irish funeral howl In 1824, T. C. Croker wrote (quoted by Lysaght, 1997): 'The Irish funeral howl is notorious, and althout [*sic*] this vociferous expression of grief is on the decline, there is still, in the less civilised parts of the country, a strong attachment to this custom, and many ... are keeners or mourners by profession.' See also *Irish cry, Irish keeners, Irish wake*.

'Irish' fungus There is an endemic variety of fungus called *phoma hibernica*. See also *Irishette, Paddy hat* (Appendix 5).

Irish funnies A synonym of Irish comics.

Irish furze *Ulex europaeus strictus*. As a cure for horse-worms, O'Sullivan (1991) recommends 'grounding the tops of Irish furze, *aitinn Gaelach*, and mixing it with chopped marigolds or turnips.' See *Webster's* and see also *Irish whin*.

G

Irish Gaelic Term sometimes used (for example in the OED) to refer to the *Irish language*. The word 'Gaelic' should logically be used in the sense of Irish, as it is in several instances, e.g. the Gaelic League (founded in 1893 to revive the Irish language – not to be confused with the *Irish League*). The historical term 'the Gaelic recovery' refers to the gradual process of emancipation of Irish chieftaincies from English control from the mid-thirteenth century (Connolly, 1998). There is also Gaelic football (or *Irish football*). Without a prefix (in non-Irish usage), however, 'Gaelic' generally refers to Scots Gaelic or means Scottish, e.g. Gaelic coffee (the Scottish version of *Irish coffee*, but with Scotch whisky instead of *Irish whiskey*) and 'Gaelically utter' refers to 'The Scottish accent' (Partridge, 1937). To add to the confusion, the word 'Scots' on its own means the Scottish language, i.e. the dialect of English analogous to Hiberno-English or *Irish English*. The word 'Irish' alone is sufficient to refer to the *Irish language* (*Gaeilge*) – yet 'Gaelic' can be added to distinguish it from Scots Gaelic (*Gaidhlig*) and Manx Gaelic (*Gaelck* [Kelly, 1866] or *Gaelgach* [Cregeen, 1835]). See also *Irishes, Irish Scot, Gaelic Irish* (Appendix 4), *Scotch Irish* (Appendix 4).

Irish gale-days With reference to the old Celtic festivals of Samhain and Bealtaine respectively, Evans (1957) writes that 'the first days of November and May are still the Irish gale-days, the times when rents fall due.'

Irish gambit A chess move technique synonymous with the Chicago gambit. There is also a Scotch gambit. See also *Irish attack, 'Irish' backgammon, 'Irish' chess*.

Irish game An old name for the dice game, dublets (Hazlitt, 1905)

Irish Gandhi With reference to Mahatma (i.e. 'great soul') Gandhi, known for his policy of *'ahimsa'* (non-violence), Naoise O'Boyle postulates that an 'Irish Gandhi' is the only type of person who could successfully bring about peace in Northern Ireland (www.geocities.com). See also *Irish babu, Irish hooley, Irish soma.*

Irish Gang, The As Joseph Geringer dubs the Irish-American followers of Bugs Moran (see his online article *George 'Bugs' Moran: His War with Al Capone*). Based in Chicago, they were occupied with bootlegging (selling spirits in speakeasies) during the Prohibition. Seven were murdered in cold blood by Al Capone's men in the St Valentine's Day Massacre of 1929. Despite Moran's criminal deeds, his humour, charm, *Irish blarney* and charisma endeared him to the public, who hated his Sicilian rival Capone and regarded Bugs as 'a good fella and even a Robin Hood'. See also *'Irish' Maffia, Irish Mob, 'Irish' Robin Hood.*

Irish gansey Knitted garment like a pullover worn especially by Irish seamen (from Ir. *geansaí* = jersey).

'Irish' Garden Or rather the Garden of Ireland or the Garden County, i.e. Co. Wicklow (Share, 1997).

'Irish' Garden of Eden Eagleton (1999) describes the popular image of the west of Ireland as a quiet, Celtic Garden of Eden as being in reality 'a bustling, fairly go-ahead sort of region'. He also refers to the Aran Islands as 'The End of the World and the Garden of Eden rolled into one'.

Irish Gascons Ó Faoláin (1941) said of Cork: 'It is a town with a sting, inhabited by the *Irish Gascons*, the most acidulous race we breed, the most alive, the keenest, the sharpest, the toughest.' A Gascon is a native of Gascony and has the reputation for being a natural boaster. According to *Chambers* he is also called a Gasconader – hence the words 'gasconade' and 'gasconism' as synonyms of 'boasting'. See also *Irish assurance.*

Irish Gate In Carrickfergus, Co. Antrim. The name of 'the Irish Gate or West Gate derives from the times when on Christmas Eve the Protestants would shut the gate on the Catholics as they went to mass' (St Clair, 1971).

Irish gem As the potato is sometimes called. 'Gem' is not to be confused with 'jem' (or 'jembo'), which is Irish slang for a Dubliner – though not as derogatory as 'jackeen' (Share, 1997). See *Irish apple* for other synonyms of 'potato'; see also *Irish diamond, 'Irish' jewel.*

Irish geology, father of Richard John Griffith (1784–1878), who produced the first complete geological map of Ireland in 1838 (Brady, 2000). See also *Irish green, Irish Valuation Act.*

Irish Georgian A unique Irish form of Georgian architecture. The term is often used, for instance in Herbert Ypman's work *Irish Georgian.* In 1958 the Irish Georgian Society was founded to conserve treasures of Irish architecture. See also *Irish Gothic, Irish Palladianism, Irish Romanesque.*

'Irish ghettoes' Phrase used by Eagleton (1999) to describe working-class areas of Irish immigrants in Britain. See also *Irishtown, shanty Irish* (Appendix 4).

Irish giant A large green, red-streaked, late variety of apple. See also *Irish canary.*

Irish Giant, the Charles Byrne (1761–83), who at nineteen was eight feet tall. A pantomime in London, *Harlequin Teague or the Giant's Causeway,* was named after him. His 'seven-foot-ten-inch' skeleton is in the museum of the College of Surgeons in Lincoln's Inn Fields, London; although *Brewer's* says that he was eight feet four inches tall. The following, unlike Byrne, were not known by the actual sobriquet 'the Irish Giant' but nevertheless were recorded by *Brewer's* as Irish giants: Patrick O'Brien, who died in 1804 aged thirty-nine, was eight feet seven inches tall; a man named Murphy, a contemporary of O'Brien, was eight feet ten inches tall and died in Marseilles; Patrick Cotter, who died in 1802, was eight feet seven inches tall; James McDonald, who died in 1760, was seven foot six inches tall; and Edmund Mellon, who was born in 1740, was seven feet six inches tall.

Irish Gilbert Stuart The great portrait painter Sir William Orpen (1878–1931) (Encycl. Brit., Vol. 15). The actual Gilbert Stuart (1755–1828) was an American artist who painted portraits and replicas of several American presidents, and of George III, George IV and Louis XVI. He also worked for five years in Ireland (Encycl. Brit., Vol. 21).

Irish gilder A once-popular breed of fighting cock (Encycl. Brit., Vol. 5). See also *Irish brown-red, Irish gray.*

Irish gingerbread sideboard Mid-nineteenth-century pine sideboard perhaps used for storing gingerbread or the utensils needed for making it. It consists of twin doors decorated in simple but beautiful relief, with a wide drawer above (for

picture see webpage of *Glenmore Antique Irish Pine)*. See
also *Irish dresser*.

'Irish' Glasgow Morton (1930) wrote: 'Belfast plays the Glasgow to Dublin's Edinburgh ... Dublin is feminine; Belfast is
masculine. Could they marry, the child of their union would
be a great and balanced nation.' (Morton was an Englishman!) He continued: 'Belfast is more like Glasgow than
any other city.' Another epithet for Belfast is 'Linenopolis',
due to the fact that it had a large Irish linen-manufacturing
industry (Green, 1998; similarly, Manchester was known as
'Cottonopolis'). *Polis* is, of course, the Greek word for city.

Irish glass Term for various forms of glasswork, the most
famous centres of manufacture for which are Cork, Waterford and Belfast. A characteristic of most Irish glass is the
unmistakeable deep-cut patterns. See also *Irish crystal*.

Irish Glen of Imaal terrier A unique Irish breed of terrier.
Sometimes it is called simply 'Glen of Imaal terrier' but
usually the 'Irish' prefix is used.

Irish glib In 1596 Edmund Spenser wrote of the thick, matted
hair over the forehead of Irishmen (quoted by Wall, 1995):
'Irish glibs are fit masks as a mantle is for a thief, for when
so ever he hath run himself into that peril of law that he
will not be known, he either cutteth off his glib ... or pull-
eth it so low down over his eyes that it is very hard to de-
scern his thievish countenance.' Similarly, the Manx (who
are usually pro-Irish) say: 'Ye might be Irish, the way yer
heer [hair] is all in thavvags [tufts]' (Moore, *et al*, 1924).
Perhaps such hair was greasy and so related to the word
'glib' in Co. Down which means 'slippery or smooth'? (Ó
Muirithe, 1997). An Australian rhyming-slang phrase for
'hair' is 'Dublin Fair' (Green, 1998); 'grogans' (mutton chop
whiskers) is an early-twentieth-century American term derived from the Irish surname Grogan, as many Irish-Americans had sideburns (Green, 1998). See also *Irish croppie, Irish
red, Irish shave, Irish stapple thatch*.

Irish goat A separate breed of goat that could be grey, white or
black with long hair (recorded by Mason as a distinct breed
in 1951). This breed is used for both meat and milk production. See also *Irish longwool, Irish shortwool*.

Irish goat-skin drum As the *bodhrán* is sometimes called. See also *Irish frame drum, Irish tambourine.*

Irish goddess of beauty So Cliodha is dubbed (CGG). She lived in *Tír Tairngire* (The Land of Promise), which she left to be with the mortal Ciabhan. Manannan Mac Lir, the *Irish sea god* sent a large wave to Cork to bring her back, however. She was accompanied by magical coloured birds that could soothe the sick with sleep.

Irish goddess of darkness and the underworld So Eo-Anu is called (CGG).

Irish goddess of destruction As Green (1992) calls Badbh. See *Irish war goddess.*

Irish goddess of healing and pleasure So Fand is dubbed. She was also a sea goddess living both in the Otherworld and on the Isle of Man (see *Irish Sea, Jewel in the*) and was the wife of Manannan Mac Lir (see *Irish sea god*). She could transform herself into a seabird to lure a mortal lover.

Irish goddess of hunting and wild animals Epithet of Flidais (or Flidhais) (CGG). The sacred deer were her 'cattle'; she is the equivalent of the Greek goddess Artemis or the Roman goddess Diana.

Irish goddess of poetry An epithet of Eadon. She was the nurse of the Tuatha Dé Danaan poets.

Irish goddess of the mist The epithet of Aobh/Aoife. She was the second wife of Manannan Mac Lir (see *Irish sea god*).

Irish goddess of the mist or dawn As Fionnuala (Fiongalla) is called (CGG). She was the daughter of Manannan Mac Lir (see *Irish sea god*). She and her brothers were changed into swans by their stepmother Aoife.

Irish goddess of wisdom The epithet of Nath (CGG). See also *Irish Solomon.*

'Irish' godfather Or rather 'the Godfather of the Irish'. Padre Varela (1788–1853), a priest from Cuba who was an abolitionist and helped the Irish immigrants in America to find jobs. He campaigned for their civil rights and petitioned for improved housing and educational opportunities for them (see the site by James Gilhooley at www.catholic.net).

Irish god of fertility As Bres (or Bress) is described. He was married to Brigid, goddess of fertility (see also *'Irish' Mary*).

Irish god of light As Dixon-Kennedy (1996) calls Lugh. His name means 'shining one'. As a baby he was in danger from his

grandfather Balor (see *Irish death god*), who, according to prophecy, he later slew. Lugh probably inherited his famous
sling from Balor. Lugh's son was the great warrior Cúchulainn (see *Irish Achilles, the*).

Irish god of love As Green (1992) refers to Oenghus (i.e. Aonghus)
of the Birds, who helped the lovers Midhir and Etain as
well as Diarmaid and Grainne. See also *Irish Cupid*.

Irish god of the dead The ancient Irish god, Donn (Green uses
the phrase, 1992). See also *Irish death god*.

'Irish Goebbels' Frank Gallagher (1898–1962), a journalist who
belonged to the *Irish Volunteers* and was on the publicity
staff of the Republican government 1919–1921, 1939–1948
and from 1951–1954 (on Éamon de Valera's return) was the
director of the Government Information Bureau. Some of
his publications were written under the pen-name David
Hogan. Graham Walker makes this exaggerated comparison
with Hitler's Nazi propaganda director in his article 'The
Irish Dr Goebbels: Frank Gallagher and Irish Republican
Propaganda' (*Journal of Contemporary History* 27, Jan 1992).
See also *Irish Mussolini*.

Irish gold Apparently there is really gold to be found in Ireland: the *Irish leprechaun* is right! According to the 1990 Wales
Tourist Board brochure *Motoring Wales,* Tregaran jewellery
is made from a mixture of Welsh gold (from Clogan mine)
and Irish gold.

'Irish' Golden Age Bluett (1994) writes: 'In Ireland the Golden
Age refers to the time between the seventh and the ninth
centuries, when the cultural currents brought in the Christian religion blended with Celtic traditions to produce great
results in the intellectual and artistic spheres. The Golden
Age was also a time of peace, relatively speaking.'

Irish golf, cradle of Holywood, Co. Down (Killanin, 1962). The
Irish name Mulligan is a golfing term which means a second chance for a golfer with a poor first drive (A. Booth and
M. Hobbs, *The Sackville Illustrated Dictionary of Golf,* 1987).
Similarly, Ireland has been described as 'the Mecca of Golf
in Europe' (www.golftravel.ie). In America, the nickname
'turf cutters' (derived of course, from the practice of the
Irish using peat as fuel) refers to 'drunk Irishmen working
as greenkeepers and on golf courses'.

Irish goose In mid-nineteenth century American slang, cooked codfish (Green, 1998). Perhaps it was coined by analogy to 'Bombay duck' (dried fish served at Indian restaurants). Yet the most probable origin of the phrase is perhaps by reference to 'Manx goose', i.e. herring (Moore, *et al*, 1924). The substitution of poultry names for fish can also be seen in 'Alaska turkey' (salmon – Green, 1998) and 'Norfolk capon' (red herring – Partridge, 1937), but a 'Norfolk turkey' is a native of Norfolk. 'Irish goose' is not to be confused with *Paddy's Goose* (Appendix 5). See also *Irish chicken, Irish dodo, Irish turkey*.

Irish Gothic With reference to tower houses (built between 1400 and 1650), Connolly (1998) writes that they were 'square or rectangular, with four storeys, in a style known as Irish Gothic [and] were commodious and ostentatious'. Morton (1930) said that, in contrast to the Irish Romanesque, which he loved, 'in Ireland Gothic was a transplanted sapling which never became acclimatised'; he in fact described this style not as Irish Gothic but as 'Celtic with a Gothic veneer' and not in keeping with true Irish architecture. See also *Irish Georgian*.

Irish gown A long Irish garment. An Amazon in Henry Burnell's novel *Land gartha* (1639) is described as wearing 'an Irish gown tucked up to the mid-leg' (Welch, 1996). See also *Irish cloak*.

Irish Grail A metaphor for something of extreme beauty which is marred by the cost incurred in obtaining it. With reference to 'the lovely face of Connemara', which Ó Faoláin (1941) laments is offset by 'the tragedy of mortal impermanence', the author postulates that this is like 'the Irish Grail', the search for which involves 'the mud and briers through which the generations have dragged themselves for one glimpse of Beauty.'

Irish Grand National Run at Fairyhouse Racecourse, near Ratoath, Co. Meath, in early April. See also *Irish Classics*.

Irish Grand Prix A race with horses, not Formula One cars! (Smith, 1991) One of the most famous Irish Grand Prix was held in the Phoenix Park between 1929 to 1931.

Irish grape Potato (Green, 1996). This has nothing to do with the so-called 'Scotch grape', which was supposed to be used to make Scotch whisky (Magee, 1980). See also *Irish apple*.

Irish gravy straining spoon Michael Newman refers to a unique Irish spoon, namely 'The great Irish gravy straining spoon – it has a detachable grid from top to bottom of the bowl – from which lumpy gravy was taken up on one side of the grid and clear gravy poured out of the other (*Cornwall Today*, May 1999).

Irish gray 1 A breed of fighting cock (Encycl. Brit., Vol. 5). No connection with a 'Scotch grey', which is a louse (Partridge, 1937). See also *Irish brown-red, Irish gilder*. **2** Irish gray is also a species of watermelon in America.

Irish grazier A breed of pig that became extinct in the late nineteenth century (listed by Mason, 1951 and also found in *Webster's*). See also *Irish greyhound, Irish landrace*.

Irish green 1 Or Connemara marble (OED). With reference to unique forms of marble found in Ireland, Connolly (1998) writes: 'There are many variations in texture and colour such as Irish green, yellow-green stones from Ballynahinch, and the tinted and striped masses from Lissoughter.' The 'Marble County' is the nickname of Kilkenny. **2** 'A deep green' (*Webster's*). **3** Irish green is also a primula, for which see *Irish green, old*. See also *Irish national colour*.

Irish green, old A rare variety of primrose, an *auricula* hybrid (see website of *American Primrose Society [Primulas] Seed List*).

Irish green bell *Molucella Irish green bell belirgrbe* is a type of flower, probably the same as a tall stalk-like plant with bell-shaped flowers from green bracts which is called 'bells of Ireland'.

'Irish' greenfinch Like the *Irish canary*, it has no relation to birds; rather the Irish greenfinch was 'one of the pope's Irish guard' in the mid-nineteenth century (Partridge, 1937). See also *Irish Battalion of St Patrick*.

Irish Green Flag Or usually just 'Green Flag'. The green flag with a harp that was once a rival for the *Irish Tricolour*. Even as early as 1642 an 'Irish harp on a green field' was flown on the 'frigot' [*sic*, frigate] of Colonel Owne Ro [*sic*] (see Ó Brógáin, 1998). It was later adopted by various groups throughout history such as the *Irish Volunteers*, the Land League, the *Irish Home Rule* movement, the *Irish Republican Brotherhood* and the *Irish Citizen Army* (to accompany their

'*Irish*' *Starry Plough*). Ó Brógáin suggests that 'the Green Flag will be the only serious candidate for the flag of a re-united Ireland.' See also *Irish ensign* or *Irish jack* and *Irish national colour*.

Irish greenhouse Street urinal (from the hexagonal green-painted iron public urinals in Dublin). This phrase is derived from the *Irish-English* vocabulary of Dublin (Share, 1997) rather than being an anti-Irish joke. On similar lines, because of the country's wet climate (and by analogy to the expression 'It's pissing down') or perhaps since one euphemism for toilet is 'bog', from the late seventeenth century, Ireland was nicknamed 'the Urinal of the Planets' (Partridge, 1937). Also the Irish-sounding 'donegan worker' in early-twentieth-century slang was someone who stole from toilets and wash-rooms (Partridge, 1950); the name derives from a word for toilet in archaic English slang, *dunnaken*, rather than an Irish name. Incidentally, in 1960s British slang the Irish name 'Mrs Murphy' meant a lavatory, as did the Welsh surname 'Mrs Jones' (Green, 1998).

Irish greening A Scottish variety of small, greenish-yellow apple which is sweet and ripens early. See also *Irish canary*.

Irish greenpaint finish Characteristic green paintwork used to decorate many pieces of Irish furniture (Kinmouth, 1993).

Irish greyhound A breed of pig, also called an *Irish greyhound pig*. See also *Irish grazier*.

Irish greyhound pig 'Long-legged, bony and coarse-haired' breed of pig in nineteenth-century Ireland (Connolly, 1998).

Irish grey partridge According to one Irish ornithologist, this is a distinct species of partridge in Ireland (www.the-coop. org). See also *Irish coal tit*.

Irish grip In a form of croquet, the Irish grip (as opposed to the Solomon grip, the pencil grip and the standard grip) is one way of holding the mallet (see www.members.fortunecity. com).

Irish Guards The fourth-oldest regiment of Guards, founded in 1902 after the Boer War to demonstrate the English appre-ciation of Irish regiments (see also *Irish Brigade* and *Irish Transvaal Committee*). Yet under the Stuart monarchs, the Irish Guards fought with James II against William III. They now comprise a battalion of the elite regiment, the Grenadier Guards (Encycl. Brit., Vol. 10). The Irish Guards are nicknamed 'the Micks' (see web article by Paul Hinckley: 'A Dictionary of Great War Slang').

Irish Guards Band In the Scouse dialect of Liverpool, this means 'a bunch of Scousers with harmonicas' (see website *Mersey talk9*).

Irish guardsman A soldier in the *Irish Guards*.

Irish guinea-man A ship full of emigrants (Partridge, 2000).

Irish Guinness Unlike the phrase *Irish stout, Irish Guinness* seems to be a tautology. Eagleton (1999), however, writes that 'Irish Guinness is ... thought to be superior to London-brewed Guinness' as it contains the 'magical ingredient', Liffey water.

Irish Guinness Oaks Famous horse event founded in 1963 and sponsored by Guinness. It is open to three-year-old fillies and run over 2,400 metres at the Curragh in July. See also *Irish Classics, Irish Oaks*.

Irish guipure lace A form of *Irish lace* used as a trim for dresses (Ballard, 1998).

Irish gut string harp, neo- The *Irish harp* of most harpers today, as opposed to the late nineteenth century neo-Irish harp (Vallely, 1999).

Irish Gypsies A misnomer used by some writers (e.g. Cole, 1973) to refer to the *Irish Travellers*. While Romany Gypsies and *Irish Travellers* have certain things in common, such as a nomadic lifestyle, itinerant trades and languages that are unintelligible to outsiders, *Irish Travellers* are not related to Gypsies. They do not have similar physiognomy, nor is the *Irish Travellers' Cant* related to the Romany Gypsy language.

H

Irish half-door Evans (1957) refers to 'the Irish half-door in contradistinction to the Dutch double-door'. The half-door kept animals out while letting light in. Here I can't resist mentioning MacHale's joke (1979): How do you recognise a submarine designed by a Kerryman? It's got half-doors.' Incidentally, the Irish-sounding names Rory O'Moore and Rosy O'Moore in rhyming slang both mean 'door' or 'floor' (see website *Rhyme Slang English to Slang Dictionary*).

Irish ham, boiled Made by boiling ham in *Irish stout*, brown sugar, cloves and a wisp of hay and then covering it with breadcrumbs (Sheridan, 1965).

Irish handball 'Irish handball has nothing to do with the soccer-like field sport played in mainland Europe. It's much more like fives or Basque *pelota* and looks a bit like squash played without a racket' (Bluett, 1994). As distinct from the sport exported to America by Irish immigrants, Day (2000) writes that on Easter Monday, 'Handball was popular, the Irish version being played with a gloved hand and a hard ball' by two or four players. Also called *Irish hardball*. See also *Irish rounders*.

Irish hanging table Or just hanging table (Ir. *bord crochta*). Also called a folding, falling or wall table (Kinmouth, 1993). It is basically a board suspended from the wall with a single foldable leg. It can be lifted to provide more space, in which case the underside may be painted.

Irish hardball A synonym for *Irish handball*. It is so called since, of the two types of balls used, the faster, the hard ball, is used only in Ireland (Bluett, 1994).

Irish hard shoes Shoes with tips and heels made of fibreglass, plastic or, rarely, steel, to make rhythmic tapping in *Irish step-dancing*. By contrast, ghillies are soft shoes worn by women for dancing (see website *Glossary of Irish Dance Words and Jargon*).

Irish hard-shoe step dancing Another name for *Irish step-dancing* because of the use of special hard shoes.

Irish hare 1 The native species of hare which has a smaller white tail than the non-Irish species. In Irish it is called simply *giorra* or 'hare' and the word 'Irish' is not used to qualify it; yet the non-native species is called *giorra gallda* or 'English hare'. Ó hÓgáin (1995) explains that 'The Irish word for hare (*giorra*) originally meant 'little wild one' or even 'little deer' ... the ancient Irish regarded the deer as a strange animal which consorted with otherworld beings, and they saw the hare in a similar light.' This power was possibly the reason why it was unlucky to meet a hare (Lady Wilde). It was also unlucky for a pregnant woman to see one, lest her child have a harelip, and unlucky to shoot one in case it was your grandmother's soul (Kavanagh, 1959). In fact, the superstition (also found outside Ireland) that a hare, when shot, could turn back into a hag or a witch, explains the confusion in *Irish English* between 'hag' and 'hare': for instance, in Ulster, a hare is the last sheaf of harvest (Macafee, 1996) elsewhere called a *cailleach*, i.e. 'hag'. Similarly, a blue hare was a witch who turned into a hare to steal milk (Bluett, 1994). **2** The recipe *ghiarrfhia Gaelach* made with hare, stock, flour, beef dripping, carrot, onion and turnip (Thomson, 1982). It is served with redcurrant jelly and forcemeat balls. Not to be confused with the recipe for *Irish rabbit*.

Irish harp 1 The special form of harp used in Ireland, a heavy wooden instrument with brass strings which rests on the left shoulder (Ir. *cláirseach*). So characteristic is the *Irish harp emblem* for the Irish that in America one nickname for an Irishman is a Harp or Harpy (RDGED, Vol. 3). **2** An Irish harp is also a long-handed shovel (Rawson, 1991). See also *Irish banjo, Irish fan, Irish spoon*.

Irish harp, high-headed An eighteenth century Irish harp with a straight fore-pillar, taller than earlier harps, with longer bass strings (Rimmer, 1969).

Irish harp, large Type of harp in use after the medieval *Irish harp* but before the *neo-Irish harp* (Rimmer, 1969).

Irish harp, large low-headed A harp used in the late-sixteenth and seventeenth centuries. It was larger than the *small low-headed Irish harp* and with more strings, as well as a soundbox, which was larger towards the treble (Rimmer, 1969).

Irish harp, neo- Very general term (used by Rimmer, 1969, and Ó hAllmhuráin, 1998) to refer to later evolutionary forms of the *Irish harp* from the early nineteenth century. They were of different sizes and some made by Egan were portable, yet 'all ... have a pedal-harp kind of soundbox with a flat belly and rounded or occasionally ribbed back, and all are strung with gut or nylon' (Rimmer, 1969).

Irish harp, small low-headed See *large low-headed Irish harp*.

Irish harp emblem The emblem of the *Irish harp* seen on many flags, including the *Irish Green Flag*. See also *Irish crowned harp*.

Irish harper Player of the *Irish harp*; the term has also occasionally been used to denote the craftsman who makes the instrument. The phrase 'Irish harper' is generally favoured over Irish harpist. The word 'harper' was seventeenth-century Irish slang for an *Irish penny* because the instrument was always featured on Irish coins (Partridge, 1937). Moreover, in *Anglo-Irish* the expression 'play the harp' encapsulates one Irish stereotype, namely 'to wander drunkenly, tapping the railings as one passes' (Green, 1998); it was so coined because of 'the supposed similarity of the railings to harp-strings'. The same stereotype can be seen in other words such as 'Rileyed' (i.e. drunk – Green, 1998). See also *Irish Bloody Mary, Irish piper.*

Irish Harrogate Because of the spa water, 'Swalinbar [Co. Cavan] was "the Harrogate of Ireland"' (Connolly, 1998). See also *Irish Bath, the.*

Irish harvest goddess So Latiaran is called, for whom see *Irish fertility goddess of spring.*

'Irish' harvest knot Or inside Ireland, just 'harvest knot'. A plaited straw knot or bow made at harvest time, especially in the north of Ireland. This knot is similar to the corn dolly of Britain and is sometimes exchanged as a love token. It is really a variation of the *cailleach* or hag made from twisted straw after the harvest. See also *Irish hare.*

Irish harvest time jig A dance, the name of which possibly derives from it being performed at the *meilseara* or harvest-home festival. It is in 6/8 time and is performed 'either in longways or quadrille ... with twice as many men lined up as women' (Leach, 1949). See also *Irish jig.*

Irish hat Or more commonly a *Paddy hat*, i.e. a toadstool, especially in Ulster (Macafee, 1996). See also *Irishette, Irish Kerby.*

Irish hawthornden A variety of apple first recorded in 1831 (NAR). See also *Irish canary.*

Irish hay-cart 'The Irish hay-cart is a specialised vehicle used for no other purpose; its low platform can be backed against the cock, which is then drawn on to it by a winding gear' (Evans, 1942). See also *Irish car.*

Irish haye A type of dance (also called *Irish hey*). Vallely (1999) writes: *'Haye, rinnce fada,* and *rinnce mór* are all three names used to refer to dance in old literature: *haye* was a chain dance.' See also *Irish jig, Irish reel, Irish trot.*

Irish heath *(Daboecia cantabrica).* A variety of heath *(Webster's).*

Irish heather wine Hughes (2000) refers to this seventeenth-century drink, which he believes was a forerunner of *Irish mist*.

Irish hedge chair In contrast to the English equivalent, for which the lathe is used just to turn the spindles and legs (which are joined by stretchers), 'Irish hedge chairs rarely exhibit these characteristics. Lathe work is highly exceptional and the legs are rarely linked by stretchers ... Irish hedge chairs ... have been wrongly assumed to have English origins' (Kinmouth, 1993). See also *Irish Windsor chair*.

Irish hedge school Or a 'fodeen' school (Wall, 1995, from Irish *fóidín* – a small sod). Often small huts built in the countryside under the protection of hedges where teachers (often priests) provided basic education for Catholic children. See also *Irish Christian Brothers*.

Irish hedge schoolmaster The teacher at an *Irish hedge school* (Adams, 1998).

Irish helot A helot was a Spartan serf. *Orellana or an Irish Helot* (1784–5) was a work by United Irishman and poet, William Drennan, lamenting the lack of political reform in Ireland. See *Irishmen, United*.

Irish hen dresser Also called a 'coop dresser'. An *Irish dresser* with a compartment at the bottom for keeping fowl inside the house in winter-time. It was the equivalent of the Welsh dog kennel dresser, which had a space for a dog below. For the relationship between animals and some rural 'small farm' homes, see *pig in the parlour Irish* (Appendix 4).

Irish Hereford Unlike other cross-breeds of cattle which are interbred with native Irish breeds (e.g. *Irish Aubrac* and *Irish Blonde d'Aquitaine*), this unique cattle cross, though Irish-bred, is different from any Hereford elsewhere! The distinction is that 'the Irish dairy farmer has long recognised the merit of using a Hereford sire on his Fresian dairy cattle. The black Hereford cross Fresian animal is always sellable at a premium price' (see the website *Irish Hereford Breed Society*). See also *Irish cow, old*.

'Irish' Herodotus 1 Geoffrey Keating/Seathrún Céitinn (c. 1580–1644), an Irish historian and poet 'primarily honoured as the Herodotus of Ireland' (Welch, 1996). **2** Standish James O'Grady (1846–1928), historian and novelist. 'He has been called father of the Irish literary revival and the Herodotus

and prose Homer of his country' (Boylan, 1998). See also
See also *Irish historians, the prince of; 'Irish' Homer*.

Irish hey A dance referred to by eighteenth-century travellers
(Breathnach, 1971; Ó hAllmhuráin 1998). A synonym of the
Irish haye. See also *Irish trot*.

Irish Hibernia A tautology, like *Irish Ireland,* but sometimes
used, for instance in Jerry Cohan's 'Irish Hibernia Show'
(mentioned by Vallely, 1999).

Irish High Commissioner James MacNeill was appointed Irish
High Commissioner in 1923 to represent the *Irish Free State*
in London. The prefix 'Irish' is often used (e.g. by Killanin,
1962). This post has no relation to the High Commission,
an ecclesiastical court set up to enforce Protestantism in
Ireland in the late sixteenth century.

Irish high cross A tall stone cross often associated with monastic sites. Most Irish high crosses date from the ninth or tenth
century and are often divided into panels on which biblical
scenes were carved. There is thus speculation that they
were sometimes used by priests to illustrate sermons during outdoor mass. Often the cross is mounted on a stone
base and at the top a circle is merged with the cross to form
a ringed cross. See also *Irish Cross.*

Irish high king (Ir. *ard rí*). The supreme king in ancient Ireland,
to whom all other petty kings or chieftains swore allegiance. See also *'Irish emperor'; Irish king, buggered for the want
of an; Irish king, uncrowned; Irish lord.*

'Irish' highland The 'highland Gaelach' dance done with one
boy and two girls (as opposed to the 'highland garbh' or
'rough highland', for couples) (Vallely, 1999). See also *Irish
haye.*

Irish Highlands The mountainous and hilly regions of Ireland
(Evans, 1957). See also *Irish Midlands.*

Irish hillsiders A synonym for *Irish rebels.*

Irish hint A very broad one (Green, 1996). See also *Irish whisper.*

Irish historians', 'the prince of Father Paul Walsh, SJ (1885–
1941), as he was called by Belgian medieval historian Pawl
Grosjean (cited in Four Courts Press' 2000 catalogue). Walsh
wrote over twenty books on Irish history, notably on medieval Gaelic Ireland. See also *'Irish' Herodotus.*

Irish hobelars A native breed of Irish horse requested by Edward I for his army (Smith, 1991).

Irish hobby A pedigree breed of horse which, according to Mason's list (1951), is from crossing an *Irish thoroughbred* or Connemara pony and an *Irish draught*. It is twelve to fourteen hands tall and was used by the Normans for warfare.

Irish hobby horse (Ir. *láir bhán*). A hobby-horse carried sometimes by the wren-parties (see *Irish wrenboys*) on St Stephen's Day. It has a movable jaw and is covered by a sheet. It is very similar to the Welsh hobby-horse (or *mari lwyd*) and Manx *leare vane* (Iorwerth Peate, *Folk Life,* Vol. 1, 1963).

Irish hoist 1 A kick in the backside (Rawson, 1991; Share, 1997). **2** A painful fall (Green, 1996).

Irish hold 'em Poker variation in which players must discard two of their four cards having seen the first three 'community cards'. For the rest of the game, the players use the five community hands and the two cards left in hand (see www.poker.com).

Irish hollow The word 'hollow' is generally used for 'describing an area of a town, usually combined with a reference to [the] poor or foreign groups [who live there]' (Green, 1998). An 'Irish hollow' refers to such a place in Ireland. See also *Irishtown*.

'Irish' Hollywood 1 As well as Hollywood in Los Angeles, there is Hollywood in Co. Wicklow and Holywood in Co. Down. See also *Irish golf, cradle of.* **2** By analogy to the booming Bollywood (Bombay Hollywood) of Indian cinema, Eagleton (1999) similarly talks of '*Paddywood*' (see Appendix 5) to describe the Irish film industry.

'Irish' Holy Mountain Croagh Patrick, Co. Mayo, on top of which St Patrick (see *Irish patron saint*) fasted. Actually called 'Ireland's Holy Mountain' (Morton, 1930; Killanin, 1962). On *Domhnach Chrom Dubh* (the last Sunday in July), the faithful walk to the summit or *cruach* and at the various 'stations', the pilgrims make seven *deiseal* (clockwise) circuits. See also *Irish Lourdes, Irish penal rosary, 'Irish' Sinai, 'Irish' Sugar Loaf, the.*

'Irish' Homer 1 Or Gaelic Homer. Madame de Stael described Ossian as the 'Homer of the North'. Ossian was the poet-hero son of Fionn Mac Cumhail. He is therefore associated with the Ossianic cycle (Fionn cycle) of heroic myths just as Homer is associated with the myths of the Greek heroes in *The Odyssey*. **2** Rumann Mac Colmain (d. 747). People in medieval times took the view that there were 'three poets of the world – Homer of the Greeks, Virgil of the Latin and Rumann of the Irish' (Ó hÓgáin, 1990). Similarly, the 'Scottish Homer' was William Wilkie (author of the epic 1753 poem *Epigonaid),* according to www.bibliomania.com; and the 'Welsh Homer' was Taliesin (Edwards, 1998). See also '*Irish*' *Herodotus*.

Irish Home Rule Term used mainly until the formation of the *Irish Free State* to refer to the desired autonomy of Ireland from British rule. Also in the late nineteenth and early twentieth centuries the term 'home rule' was used for *Irish whiskey* (Partridge, 1937). For similar idiomatic phrases, see '*Irish*' *Home Ruler*.

Irish Home Rule Party Or just Home Rule Party, see *Irish Parliamentary Party*.

'Irish' Home Ruler 1 A supporter of the Irish Home Rule movement. **2** In *Irish English*, 'Home Rulers' are stout bottles (Share, 1997). **3** In the same period, roast potatoes baked in London streets were also called Home-rulers since 'so many potatoes came from Ireland' (Partridge, 1937).

Irish hooley Party with Irish music, dancing and drink. The prefix 'Irish' is sometimes used. Green (1998) provides the word 'hoolihan', which may be connected, meaning 'to have a very good time' and derives it from an Irish surname and 'thus the stereotyped image of the riotous Irish', which from his description is closer in sense to 'hooligan'. Share (1997) believes that the word comes from the Hindu festival of 'Holi' (which he misspells 'hoolie') and was picked up by Irish soldiers in the service of the British Raj in India. See also *Irish babu, Irish soma*.

'Irish' hoper Or just 'hoper'. 'An Irishman who wishes he wasn't one' (Rawson, 1991). This expression was coined with reference to disadvantaged Irish immigrants in nineteenth-century America. It should not however be inferred that the Irish immigrant was anything but proud to be Irish: the phrase suggests his basic desire to gain American citizenship.

Irish hop jig Slip jig in 9/8 time. See *Irish jig*.

Irish horse 1 Corned beef (Partridge, 1937). Rawson specifies 'tough corned beef' (1991) or just any tough meat generally (OED). Kemp (1976) suggests that this expression (popular among sailors) was 'probably based on the belief ... that the Irish, being so poor, worked their horse much harder and longer than the English' and therefore the meat was tougher. **2** A drooping male private part (Share, 1997) and as such the opposite of the *Irish toothpick*. See also *Irish toothache*. **3** The Irish horse regiment; see for example Richard Doherty's *The North Irish Horse: A Hundred Years of Service* (Spellmount, 2003)

Irish horse harness The 'Irish horse harness (which had a harness of plaited straw) was still somewhat different from what was the norm on the continent and in England' (Smith, 1991). See also *Irish martingale*.

Irish horse racing, capital of The Curragh, Co. Kildare (Bernstein, 1980). See also *Irish capital*.

Irish hospitals 'As early as the 6th century, the Irish monks had established on the continent *Hospitalia Scothorum* (Irish hospitals)' (Encycl. Brit., Vol. 15).

Irish Hospitals Sweepstakes Or simply, the Sweeps. A long-distance gambling event based on the results of four well-known horse races; the money raised from selling tickets went to fund Irish hospitals. See also *Irish Classics*.

Irish Hudibras A lampoon by the Irish writer, James Farewell entitled *The Irish Hudibras Or The Fingallian Prince* (1689). It was a 'transversion', as Farewell claimed, of Virgil's *Aeneid* in which Aeneas goes to Fingal rather than Hades. Ó Suilleabháin (1967) called the work 'a mock *Aeneid*'. Yet Boylan (1998) calls *Eachtra Ghiolla an Amarrain* by Donncha Rua Mac Conmara (written c.1750) the mock *Aeneid*. See also *'Irish' Virgil*.

Irish hunter An Irish horse which is an *Irish draught* cross-bred with an *Irish thoroughbred* (Mason, 1951; Connolly, 1998). See *Irish carthorse, Irish cob*.

Irish hurler 1 Player of *Irish hurling*. Sometimes the prefix 'Irish' is used to distinguish hurlers from players of the very similar Scottish *shinty* (in north Antrim, hurling is called 'shinny' – see Law, 1998). **2** An *Irish whiskey* measure (Share, 1997). See also *Irish spirits measure*.

Irish hurling (Ir. *iomáin).* Like *Irish* or Gaelic *football,* it is played with fifteen members in each team and on a pitch of the same size. Players hold a four-foot *camán* or hurley (hence the Irish ladies' version of hurling called camogie). The *sliotar* or ball is hit with the hurley and a goal (three points) is scored if it goes under the crossbar. (Formerly five points were given for a goal if the ball was hit over the crossbar and just one point was given for hitting the ball underneath the bar.) Possibly the occasional aggression in the sport has given rise to the slang expression 'ground hurling', which means political in-fighting (see website *The O'Byrne Files Dublin Slang Dictionary and Phrasebook).*

Irish hurling ball The *sliotar* is made of horsehair in pigskin casing (from old Irish *liotar* = hair). See also *Irish hurling.*

Irish hurricane A flat calm (especially at sea) (Kemp, 1976; Share, 1997). Also called *Paddy's hurricane* (Green, 1996) or an *Irishman's hurricane* (OED). According to Partridge (1937), the real Irish nautical phrase for calm weather was 'straight up and down the mast'.

Irish Hussars, King's Royal The *Blue Hussars* – a unit of the British army whose members are good at horse-jumping.

Irish Hussars, Queen's Royal Formed part of Montgomery's 'Desert Rats' (see *Planet* 85, Feb/March 1991).

I

Irishian A person familiar with the 'Celtic language' or antiquities of Ireland (OED). It is more correct than the neologism, Irishologist.

Irishification Synonym of *Irishisation, paddification* (Appendix 5).

Irish illuminated manuscripts Sixth- to seventh-century illustrated religious manuscripts, of which the most notable are the *Cathach* (from Ir. *cath* = battle) of St Columba and the *Book of Kells,* which was written on 150 animal hides. See also *Irish School.*

Irish Impressionists The Irish artists who studied and painted in France and Belgium from the mid-nineteenth century to 1914 (hitherto such artists had generally gone to London and Rome). Among the great Irish Impressionists are Nathaniel Hone, Frank O'Meara, Sarah Purser, Edith Somerville and Helen Mabel Trevor; together, they created a distinct form of Impressionism. With special reference to the works of two Impressionists, Paul Henry and Sean Keating, Brady (2000) writes: 'The impact of the Irish Impressionists on Irish art was not the adoption of radical French styles but a greater concern with nationalism, which became an important part of the nostalgic, nationalistic imagery ... in the early years of the *Irish Free State.*' See also *Irish School.*

Irish inch An erect male private part (Green, 1998). No relation to the *Irish English* word 'inch', which refers to a long strip of level grassy land along a river (Joyce, 1910 – from Ir. *inis* = island; see also W. *ynys*). See also *Irish root, Irish toothache.*

Irishing 1 The special marking on the Sheltie dog (see *Irish spotting*). **2** Making Irish. In a review of the New Zealand Irish music group called Mickey Finn, the reviewer says that they sing 'Celt songs as well as Irishing other people's songs' (www.guitarnoise.com). See also *Irishing out* and *de-Irishisation* (Appendix 4).

Irishing gene The special white gene that contributes to *Irishing* (www.kyleah.com).

Irishing out In gambling (unlike 'welshing' – not paying a bet – perhaps derived from one whose surname was Welsh or Welch rather than the Welsh people), *Irishing out* means withdrawing while ahead and not staying on to lose everything (see webpage *RPGnet: The Inside Scoop on Gaming*). See also *Irish loo, Irish poker, Irish roulette.*

Irish Independence Party Founded in October 1977 by Frank McManus and Fergus McAteer. The party demanded British withdrawal from Northern Ireland.

Irish Industrial Exhibition Or the Great Industrial Exhibition, held in Dublin in 1853 and sponsored by William Dargan in an attempt to promote Irish products and innovations in technology. The exhibition building was inspired by Crystal Palace in London. Among the many exhibits was the Tara Brooch. Queen Victoria visited the exhibition and knighted the Cork architect, John Benson, who designed the building. See also *Irish International Exhibition.*

Irish Insurrection 1 The *United Irishmen's* Rebellion or 'the Ruction' of 1798 against the British government troops. The various Irish divisions, e.g. in Ulster (who joined late) and

Leinster, were not coordinated in their attacks. **2** As the insurrection of 1641 is sometimes called (Canny, 1989). This was directed against the English (and also Scottish) planters of whom 2,000 were killed. This provided Cromwell with the pretext for spiteful revenge, laying siege to Wexford and Drogheda in 1649.

Irish Interlaken Ó Faoláin (1941) said of Enniskillen: 'Somebody has called it the Irish Interlaken because of its position between the two great lakes of Upper and Lower Erne.'

Irish International Exhibition This event, which was held in Herbert Park, Dublin, in 1907, featured exhibits of Irish industries. It also included a pavilion (see also *Irish pavilion*) for British, colonial and foreign exhibits. It was visited by, among others, King Edward VII. See also *Irish Industrial Exhibition, Irish whiskeries*.

Irish Invincibles Or Irish National Invincibles or just 'the Invincibles'. An extremist group that broke away from the *Irish Republican Brotherhood* and was founded in 1881. The Invincibles were notorious for the Phoenix Park murders of the *Irish chief secretary,* Lord Frederick Cavendish and his under-secretary, Thomas Henry Burke, in 1882. One of the assassins, James Carey, turned Queen's evidence (not *Irish evidence)* and, as a result of his testimony, his accomplices were hanged. There were still some Invincibles left, such as Patrick Donnell (who shot Carey), but the organisation did not last very long after that. See *three cold Irish* (Appendix 4).

Irish Ireland Term coined by D. P. Moran which basically emphasises the Gaelic (as opposed to English-influenced) aspects of Irish culture and heritage. See also *Irish Hibernia.*

Irish Irelanders Supporters of D. P. Moran's philosophy of *Irish Ireland.*

Irish irregulars Or often just 'irregulars'. The anti-Treaty soldiers of the *Irish Republican Army* during the *Irish Civil War.*

Irishisation 1 Or *Irishise*. The correct word should be 'Gaelicisation', i.e. the 'making Irish' of something. The verb often has connotations of Anglo-Norman assimilation into Ireland (e.g. Connolly, 1998). See also *Irish than the Irish, more.* **2** Conversion of a bar into an *Irish pub*. Routledge, with reference to such a conversion in London, writes: 'The Nag's Head has become O'Neill's – a victim of the fake "Irishisation" of pubs across the country' (quoted in www.wordspy. com). The Irish themselves are usually the greatest critics of this *Faux Irish* (see Appendix 4) style, which misrepresents the true Irish institution. Note that the word 'de-Irishisation' means the opposite of 'Irishisation' (used with regard to British programmes in *Dáil Éireann*, Vol. 285, 30 October 1975). See also *Irishification, paddyfication* (Appendix 5).

Irishism 1 Also 'Iricism' or 'Hibernicism'. An Irish turn of phrase in English. **2** Some characteristic of the Irish. The word 'Gaelicism' is very rare but on similar lines we have the word 'Hibernianism' or 'Hibernicism' as distinct from the slightly derogatory 'Paddyism' (Green, 1996) and 'Mickism' (see Casey's article in *Books Ireland*, September 1999). **3** In the sense of *Paddyism* (see Appendix 5), it means 'excessive or exaggerated display of perceived Irish national characteristics' (see website *The O'Byrne Files Dublin Slang Dictionary and Phrasebook*). See also *Irishry*.

Irishist This neologism seems to mean 'racist' in the sense of anti-Irish. It was coined by an Irish football fan (not, however, a fan of *Irish football*) who at a match refers to the 'worst Irishist insults' from rival fans (www.geocities.com). See also *Irishest*.

Irish ivy A unique plant, the Latin name for which is *hedera helix canariensis*; there is also a subspecies of helix called helix Irish lace. See also *Irish bladderwort, Irish lace*.

J

Irish jack The *Irish ensign*. Incidentally, one etymology of the word jackeen ('Dubliner') is that 'Dublin was always seen as the most "English" city in Ireland by provincials and this was coined as a term of derision stemming from the English flag, the Union Jack, by adding the diminutive *-een*' (see website *The O'Byrne Files Dublin Slang Dictionary and Phrasebook*).

Irish jacket A type of garment. 'Another distinctive male dress item in late medieval Ireland was the Irish jacket. Of gilled and embroidered leather or of wool. It had a thickly plaited shirt, stand collars and *Irish sleeve*' (Connolly, 1998). For other entries on Irish clothes, see *Irish cloak*.

Irish Jailic Or just 'Jailic': Irish learned by nationalist prisoners in Northern Ireland, especially in Belfast's Long Kesh. The Irish name 'Kathleen Mavourneen' in Australian slang of the 1920s meant a three-year prison sentence (as well as a criminal – see Partridge, 1950; later the term referred to payment by instalments – see Share, 1997) and in French *envoyer à l'Irlande* ('to send to Ireland') means to smuggle items out of prison (Green, 1996). Liverpudlians have the expression 'as mad as a Mick in the nick', since 'in jail the Irish are stereotyped as being particularly beserk'. Similarly, in US prison slang, a 'mickey' (see also *'Irish' mick*) is a fellow inmate, from a 'stereotyping of the Irish as criminals' (Green, 1998). By contrast, the non-captive Irish also had some relation to prisons, as in pre-war American slang a 'mulligan' was a prison warder, since, as Green, 1998, noted, 'early prison guards, like early policemen, were often Irish'. See also *Irish progressive stage, Irish Siberia*.

Irish jambs In architecture, inclined jambs 'arranged so they lean inwards towards the centre of the opening' (see website *The Corpus of Romanesque Sculpture in Britain and Ireland: CRSBI Glossary*). A jamb is an upright side of an archway, doorway, window or other opening. See also *Irish Romanesque*.

'Irish jane' James Curtin uses this phrase to refer to an Irish sovereign (coin) in *The Gilt Kid* (1936) (quoted by Partridge, 1950). See also *Irish penny, Irish pound, Irish shilling*.

'Irish' jarvie 1 The prefix 'Irish' would only be used by non-Irish speakers for the 'jarvie' or driver of the *Irish jaunting car*. **2** The word 'jarvey' (also 'jarvis' or 'jervis') can also mean the jaunting car itself (Partridge, 1937). **3** It is also a verb meaning 'to drive the Irish car' (Partridge, 1937). **4** A waistcoat (Green, 1998), as waistcoats were worn by jarvie drivers.

Irish jaunting car A unique horse-drawn vehicle for two passengers who ride back to back sideways-on. It is also called simply an Irish jaunting or Irish jaunting cab as well as an *'Irish' sidecar* or *outside car*. The form 'Irish jaunting car' was preferred by Seamus Mac Manus (1869–1960) for his prize-winning article 'A ride in an Irish jaunting car' (published in the *Weekly Irish Times*, c. 1890). It is also favoured by other writers (Floyd 1937; Evans, 1957; Smith, 1988; and

Bluett, 1995). See also *'Irish' jarvie*. The reader may be surprised to find another synonym for this vehicle under the unlikely entry *Irish fart*.

Irish jay *(Garrulous glandarius hibernicus)*. A unique subspecies of the bird which is darker and duller than the British and Continental types. The crown is not so white and there is rarely a white patch below the eye. The word 'Jays' in Anglo-Irish refers to the Jesuits (Share, 1997).

'Irish' jazz Vallely (1999) writes: 'Micheál Ó Suilleabháin has his own style of piano playing and piano vamp, which he dubs Hiberno-Jazz.' See *Irish piano-style*.

'Irish' jewel Or rather the 'jewel of Ireland'. Morton (1930) quotes a Frenchman who believed that 'Ireland was the jewel of the west, that Kerry was the jewel of Ireland, that Killarney was the jewel of Kerry and that ... Innisfallen was the jewel of Killarney.' See also *Irish Sea, Jewel in the*.

Irish jig 1 (Ir. *port*) A popular Irish dance. Young, who travelled to Ireland in 1776–9, mentioned the Irish jig (cited by Ó hAllmhuráin, 1998). There are several variations; see *Irish haye, Irish reel, Irish trot*. **2** In Cockney rhyming slang, 'jig' means 'wig'. Yet sometimes the word 'Irish' alone means 'wig' (see www.probertencyclopaedia.com/slang, and also Appendix 1). For other rhyming-slang entries see *Irish lasses, Irish rose, Irish stew*. **3** A cigarette (Green, 1998). This is possibly another example of rhyming slang: 'cig' for 'jig'?

Irish jig, single An *Irish jig* in 12-8 time.

Irish johnnies A Scottish variety of medium-sized green apple that ripens early. See also *Irish canary*.

'Irish' John O' Groats Floyd (1937) draws the analogy between Malin Head, the most northerly part of Ireland, and John O' Groats, the most northerly part of Scotland.

'Irish' joint-eater The *Alp Luachra,* or invisible fairy, who eats all one's food (Briggs, 1976). The term is probably derived from the word 'athlukard' (from Ir. *earc luachra* = lizard, newt). It was believed that a lizard or newt, if swallowed, would cause wasting. 'The cure was to hang oneself upside down over a dish of bacon, which attracted it' (Share, 1997).

Irish joke 1 Usually the phrase refers to a racist and often trite form of 'joke' best described as an anti-Irish joke (MacHale,

1979, Christensen, 1996). Yet only the very cleverest of these jokes (i.e. those that are really adaptations of the *Kerryman joke)* have an authentic smack of *Irishness*. For the Americans (who also tell Irish jokes), the equivalent is the Polish joke, where the victim is a 'Polak'. In Greece, the equivalent is the 'Pontian' joke, in which the subject or hero is the Pontian Greek (or *Pontios,* as he is called in Greek), that is a descendant of those Greeks from the Black Sea region who fled to Mother Greece in 1922. Despite the Pontian's pristine wealth, his immigrant or refugee status in Greece was analogous to the Irishman's status in nineteenth-century America. Moreover, as the Irish rightly take exception to many 'Irish jokes', so in Greece (because of increased awareness of the Pontian genocide at the hands of the Turks, coupled with a growing interest in the rich Pontian folk heritage), there is also an acute sensitivity about such jokes. **2** An *Irish joke* uniquely encapsulates the Irish wit and Irish logic. The Kerryman joke is only one form of this joke, there are also Corkman and other jokes that tend to make fun of fellow Irishmen in a good-natured way. See also *Irish bull, Irish pub joke, Paddy and Mick joke.*

Irish juniper *(Juneperus communis hibernica).* 'A narrow columnar ornamental juniper that is a variety of the common juniper' *(Webster's).* See also *Irish dwarf pine, Irish mahogany, Irish whitebeam, Irish willow, Irish yew.*

K

Irish karne An old spelling of *Irish kerne* used by Derricke in 1581 (quoted by Mahon, 2000a): 'And with the mantle commonly the Irish karne do go.' See also *Irish mantle.*

Irish Keats Thomas Caulfield Irwin (1823–92), a poet from Warrenpoint, Co. Down. Irwin was a Romantic poet who wrote about nature. Fortunately his life was longer than that of the English poet John Keats (1795–1821), yet in his old age Irwin became mentally unstable, threatening to kill his neighbour. (Irwin was given the epithet 'the Irish Keats' by Richard Dowling in *Tinsley's Magazine,* quoted at www. pgil-eirdata.org).

Irish keeners F. S. [*sic*] recalls 'people called Irish keeners who were paid to cry at funerals' *(Ulster Folklife,* Vol. 8, 1962).

See also *Irish cry, Irish funeral howl, Irish wake, weep Irish* (Appendix 4).

Irish Kerby A phrase used on the west coast of America for a derby hat (Partridge, 1950). Also called an Irish Kirby. See also *Irish topper, Irish Walking Patch Cap.*

Irish kerne 1 A type of light-armed mercenary soldier. These soldiers were armed with just a sword and throwing darts and were usually grouped into very small bands (in fact the original Irish *ceithearn* means, literally, a band of such warriors). **2** The phrase 'Irish kernes' was used very broadly by the Cornish royalists as an insulting nickname for their Irish allies (who were not actually *kernes* as above) in the English Civil War (see Payton, 1996). The Irish retaliated by calling them 'Cornish choughs' (Payton, 1996), after the large black bird which is the symbol of Cornwall and which the Cornish believe to be the incarnation of King Arthur. Thackery wrote: 'I have seen hanging enough in merry England, and care not to see the gibbets of Irish kernes' (quoted by Christensen, 1996). See also *Irish bandit, Irish crow* and *Irish Feud, Cornish-.*

'Irish' Kerry blue A breed of terrier, usually called simply a *Kerry blue*. See also *Irish Glen of Imaal terrier.*

Irish key Kinney, in a review of Robert ap Huw's work, refers to two musical tunings for harp strings: *Cower gwyddelig dierth* ('strange Irish key') and *lledf gower gwyddyl* ('plaintive or oblique Irish key') *(Planet* 68, April/May 1988). See also *Irish harp.*

Irish kid stew According to Sheridan (1965), *Irish stew* was originally made from kid, not lamb.

Irish kilt As opposed to actual garments of Irish dress (see *Irish cloak* for these entries), there was never an *Irish kilt*. Danaher (1964) writes: 'The so-called Irish kilt is merely a copy of the Scottish kilt.' It has, however, been adopted by many patriotic Irishmen and sometimes appears as part of the men's *Irish dancing costume* (Robb, 1998), which may or may not have an *Irish tartan* design. Even though, by copying the costume of their fellow Gaelic Scots brothers, the kilt seems truly Celtic, many Irish people dismiss it as *stage Irish* (Appendix 4) rather than authentic Irish dress. Ireland's Cornish cousins have similarly tried to create their own

Cornish kilt, as have the Welsh, which never existed in history either. See also *Scotch Irish* (Appendix 4).

'Irish' kiltie One who wears a kilt (in a kilted army regiment rather than in the innovated pseudo-'national' dress). The word 'kiltie' can be used on its own. In the case of Ulster Protestants (for Ulster tartan, see the so-called *Irish tartan)*, the wearing of a kilt is perhaps consistent with their Scottish heritage (see *'Irish' plantations).*

Irish king 1 A rare yellow variety of the *paphiopedilum* flower. It is sometimes known by its full name of *Valime 'Irish King'* and is often used in combination with other *paphiopedilums* to make hybrids. **2** *Ard Rígh* ('Irish king') is also a type of trumpet daffodil.

Irish king, buggered for the want of an In NZ English slang, 'an often jocular elaboration of buggered, ruined, frustrated' (Orsman, 1997).

Irish king, uncrowned 1 Daniel O'Connell (1775–1847). Smith calls him 'the uncrowned king of Ireland' (1991). See also *Irish Dan*. **2** Charles Stewart Parnell (1846–91) is perhaps more often given this epithet (and was called this name by Timothy Healy). Similarly, Thomas Edward Ellis (1859–99), a prominent supporter of Welsh home rule, has been called 'the Parnell of Wales'. See also *Irish Parliamentary Party*.

Irish kiss A slap in the face (Rawson, 1991; Green, 1996). So-called because, throughout history, the Irish have often violently opposed foreign rule and so have been stereotyped as violent and brawling. This phrase has a few parallels: a Glasgow or Gorbals kiss is a head-butt (Green, 1998), which in Irish slang would be a 'loaf' (Share, 1997). Similarly, a Liverpool kiss is a blow to the mouth (Green, 1998). See also *Irish beauty; Irish wedding, to have danced at an.*

Irish knee harp Or Irish bardic harp. A small medieval harp that is rested on the knees while being played. See also *Irish harp*.

L

Irish Labour League A short-lived body founded in 1891 in Dublin by the National Union of Gasworkers (nothing to do with 'gas-house micks', for which see *'Irish' mick)* and General Labourers, who sought, unsuccessfully, to nationalise transport. Not to be confused with the Irish Labour Defence League, an amalgamation of trade unionists and left-wing *IRA* members that lasted for a short time in 1931.

Irish lace 1 Exquisite embroidery, such as Carrickmacross lace and Limerick lace. The various forms are often referred to collectively as 'Irish lace' (see OED). Not to be confused with *lace-curtain Irish* (see Appendix 4). See also *Irish flowerer, 'Irish' Frizzler*. **2** Spiders' webs (Green, 1996; Share, 1997). See also *Irish curtain, Irish draperies*. **3** A white variety of *tagetes filifolia* (a type of marigold). **4** A rare type of Japanese maple with 'lace' leaves. **5** There is also a subspecies of ivy called helix Irish lace (see *Irish ivy*). In Ireland, the expression 'to lace' also means 'to beat' (Ir. *léasadh* = flogging – see Ó Muirithe, 1997).

'Irish' ladderback chair Or simply 'ladderback chair' – so called because of its horizontal backrails, which resemble the rungs of a ladder. However, since the seats are invariably made of *súgán* (rope made of hay or straw), Kinmouth (1993) says they are often called *'súgán* chairs'.

Irish Lady (Modern Cornish: *An Arlothas Worthenack*). On the Cornish coast, there is a fantastic woman who 'appears on the rock called the Irish Lady and is ... tall, dressed in white and carries a red rose in her lips; her appearance warns of disaster at sea' (Weatherhill and Devereux, 1994)).

Irish lady's tresses A tall white orchid similar in appearance to another endemic species, namely 'O'Kelly's orchid'. In 1993, the Irish lady's tresses was featured on the Irish 52 pence stamp. See also *Irish bladderwort*.

Irish lake goddess The epithet of Murigen (CGG). Etymologically, her name may be related not to Morrighan the goddess of war and death, but to Morgan. (See also the Breton *Mari-Morgan* or 'water fairy', the Welsh *Môr* – sea and the Arthurian *Fata-Morgana* [It. *fata* meaning fairy and *Morgana* being a cognate of the Welsh *môr*]).

Irish lamb stew It seems a tautology to use the word 'lamb' here, since lamb (or mutton) is invariably used in *Irish stew*. Nevertheless, some writers, such as Joanne Smith (1995), use this form when writing for American readers who may be used to an Irish stew recipe with beef. See also *Irish beef stew, Irish kid stew*.

Irish lament Not only the keening and wailing (or *yllagone* from Ir. *olagón*) done by women *(Irish keeners)* at funerals but the actual dirges. Seán Ó Coileáin used the term in his article 'The Irish Lament: An Oral Genre' *(Studia Hibernica* 24, 1984–8). See also *Irish cry, Irish wake.*

Irish Land Acts Wynham's Act (1903) which encouraged landlords to sell their property, for which see *Irish Land Purchase Act;* and Birrell's Act (1909), a revision of Wynham's Act. There have also been other Land Acts in Ireland not usually called 'Irish': in 1870, 1881, 1885 and 1891, and in 1923 in the *Irish Free State.* The 1870 Act compensated tenants for improvements they had made to the land but did not protect them from eviction or rent increases. The 1881 Act introduced the '3 Fs' (fair rents, fixity of tenure and freedom of sale). Gladstone's 1885 Act gave tenants £5 million to buy property from their landlords rather than rent. The 1909 act, the Birrell Act, reintroduced payment by land bonds; and the Hogan Act of 1923 enabled the compulsory purchase of all land not yet dealt with under the previous acts (Hickey and Doherty, 1980).

Irish land bridge Term used by scientists to refer to a possible geographical land link between southern Ireland and the Iberian peninsula. One online article (www.stir.ac.uk) refers to a feature as being 'a good example of a postglacial relict which probably managed to move up the coast from the Mediterranean to Ireland just before the Irish land bridge was broken.' See also *Irish bridge, Mediterranean Irish* (Appendix 4).

'Irish' Land League Also called the Irish National Land League. This organisation was founded in 1879 and led by Michael Davitt against the landlords. The support of Parnell (see *Irish king, uncrowned)* as president gave the League impetus. Its goals were peasant ownership and reductions in rent. The League was outlawed in 1881 when executive members, including Parnell, issued a 'no rent' manifesto from Kilmainham Jail, urging tenants to withhold rent payments.

Irish Land Purchase Act, 1903 Induced landlords to sell their estates 'on 'favourable terms' to the state and enabled tenants to buy their farms by 'terminable annuities' (Encycl. Amer., Vol. 15). The term could also be applied to Birrell's

1909 Act. See also *Irish Land Acts*.

Irish landrace A breed of pig derived from the British or Norwegian breed (Mason, 1951). See also *Irish grazier, Irish greyhound*.

Irish Land War Term that refers to the peasant struggle for power between 1879 and 1882 as a result of evictions. Inspired by the '*Irish' Land League*, tenants demanded lower rents; moreover, evictions were both opposed and physically prevented as were any new tenants who replaced those evicted. The conflict was settled by the Kilmainhan Treaty (1882), which saw the release of prisoners, and by the Arrears Act of the same year which made concessions to tenants. See also *Irish Agrarian Rebellion*.

Irish language (Ir. *Gaeilge*) With Scots Gaelic and Manx (Gaelic), it belongs to the Goidelic (see also W. *gwyddel* = Irishman) branch of Celtic languages (see also *Irish Q-word*), as opposed to the Brythonic branch (i.e. Welsh, Breton and Cornish). The first known written form of the *Irish language* was ogham (which flourished from the third to the sixth centuries; see also *Irish alphabet*), yet this language, which was inscribed on standing stones, was very different from the *Old Irish* (see Appendix 4) that was to appear on the first manuscripts. The early foreign settlers in Ireland posed little threat to the language and indeed usually assimilated well (see *Irish than the Irish, more*). However, later settlers (see, for instance, the '*Irish' planter*), and their governments, tried systematically to eradicate the Irish language and culture. The *Irish Famine* was another serious blow to the language, as was the ensuing mass emigration, mainly of Irish-speakers (see *Irish diaspora*). Perhaps if independence had been achieved earlier and linguistic issues had not been overshadowed by more pressing political needs, the current *Gaeltachtaí* (for which see *Irish-speaking area*) would have been much larger. Yet even outside the *Gaeltachtaí*, Irish people are proud of the Irish language; most children learn it in school and most Irish people can 'get by' in *Gaeilge* with varying degrees of fluency. The Irish language has also contributed many words to the rich vocabulary of *Irish English*, as well as a few dozen words to standard English, such as *whiskey* (for which see *Irish loanwords*).

Irish-language Bill of Rights Phrase used with reference to some *Irish language* activitists who campaign for greater official status for Irish than for English in Ireland (*Carn* 102, Summer 1998).

Irish-language capital, the See *Irish capital*.

'Irish language enthusiasts' As the *Gaeilgeoirí* are described, as opposed to the normal native Irish speakers (Welch, 1996). The Irish word *Gaeilgeoir* refers to both an Irish-speaker and an Irish-learner. See also *Irish-speaking area*.

'Irish' lantern 1 More commonly *Paddy's lantern*, i.e. the moon (Orsman, 1997, and see Appendix 5). **2** The chapel of St John's Protestant Church in Kilkenny, which because of its many windows is called 'the Lantern of Ireland' (Killanin, 1962).

Irish lass No relation to either *Irish lasses* or the famous eighteenth-century racehorse, Irish Lass (alias Paidrín mare) (Brady, 2000). It is a rare variety of green *cymbidium* (the other *cymbidium* plant can be pink, white or red) and is sometimes called by its full name of *Lillian Fujimoto Irish Lass* (see the website for *Oak Hill Gardens Cymbidiums*).

Irish lasses On the west coast of America in the nineteenth century, rhyming slang for 'glasses' (i.e. spectacles) (Partridge, 1950). For other entries from rhyming slang, see *Irish jig, Irish rose* and *Irish stew*.

'Irish' latch-key A crowbar. So named because the *Royal Irish Constabulary* (alias the 'crowbar brigade' – no relation to the *Irish Brigade)* helped the 'crowbar landlords' by using their crowbars to break cottage doors in order to evict tenants (Partridge, 1937).

Irish Latin Or Bog Latin (named after the Irish bogs), Macalister describes it as the jargon of 'schoolboys in monastic schools' (1937), based on Irish rather than Latin.

Irish lavender Not lavender but a variety of heather.

Irish lays Heroic songs of the Fenian and Ulster cycles called in Irish *laoi*. Shields (1993) uses the prefix 'Irish'. See also *Irish come-all-ye*.

Irish lazy-beds Evans (1957) refers to 'Irish lazy-beds' as distinctive ploughed ridges, especially for growing potatoes. See also *Irish potato*.

Irish League, United Founded in 1898 by William O'Brien to get holdings redistributed to small farmers. Not to be confused with the *Irish National League*. Nor does it bear any relation to the Gaelic League *(Conradh na Gaeilge)*, which was founded in 1893 to revive the *Irish language*.

Irish Legion Established in 1803 under Bernard Mac Sheehy. It recruited many *United Irishmen* exiles to prepare for an invasion of Ireland with Napoleon. It disbanded in 1815 after the restoration of the French monarchy. John G. Gallaher wrote a book called *Napoleon's Irish Legion*. See also *Irish Martello tower*.

Irish legs Thick legs (Partridge, 1937). See also *Irish arms*.

Irish lemon 1 Potato (Green, 1996). 'Brave lemons' referred to new potatoes (Lover and Croker, 1995). For other synonyms, see *Irish apple*. **2** A type of *Erica stuartii* heather which is light purple, with bright lemon-coloured new foliage (see also *Irish orange*).

'Irish lemonade' Red lemonade, popular in Ireland.

Irish Lenin Michael Collins (1890–1922), soldier and politician. Because of his skills in evading the British, he was also nicknamed the Dublin Pimpernel (see also the *'Irish' Scarlet Pimpernel*). 'He was a sort of Irish Lenin. He took hold of a potentially revolutionary situation in Ireland and made it work' (Robert Kee, cited on www.genealogy.ie). See also *'Irish' Bonnie Prince Charlie; Irish king, uncrowned*.

Irish leprechaun Some writers use the prefix 'Irish' (e.g. White, 1976; Curran, 2000) to distinguish the leprechaun from other 'diminutive races' elsewhere. Traditionally, the leprechaun is dressed in a green suit (see *Irish national colour*) with shiny buttons, smokes a *dúidín* (see *Irish clay pipe*) and promises to find a crock of gold but usually vanishes before anyone can catch him. He is so closely associated with Irish folk culture that the word 'leprechaun' is used in America as a nickname for an Irishman. 'Leprechaun' probably means either 'shoemaker' (for which see *Irish brogue*) or pygmy *(lucharachán)*, and there are literally dozens of spellings and variant dialect forms of the word.

Irish leprechaun nation As Curran (2000) calls the nation of the *Irish leprechaun* with an overlord called 'the Grand Himself' and each 'Sept' (see *Irish sept*) led by a 'Himself'. See also *Irish Pooka*.

'Irish' lichen There are some endemic varieties of Irish lichen, e.g. *Zamenhofa hibernica* as well as *Porina hibernica*.

Irish Limerick 1 The five-lined rhyme (named after the Irish city), which begins with a line such as 'There was a young lady named ...' **2** *Hemerocallis Irish Limerick* or *Irish Limerick Daylily* is a rare type of flowering plant.

Irish Limousin Not a car but a type of cattle breed from North America. The prefix 'Irish' would only be appropriate for those calves born as a result of cross-breeding with native Irish breeds, however. There is an Irish Limousin Cattle Society in Clogheen, Co. Tipperary. See *Irish cow, old* for other cattle breeds.

Irish Lily, The A gold mine in Coolgardie, Australia – so called as in the late nineteenth century, Irishmen worked there (yet the greatest number of miners in other mines were Cornishmen).

Irish linen 1 Made from *Irish flax*, a 'fine, plain-woven, full-bleached linen cloth ... for shirts, handkerchiefs, blouses etc.' (Wilcox, 1969). The secret of this material lay in the unique beetling process used (the process of beating and pressing linen which, before water-powered beetling mills, was done with a wooden mallet); this gave the linen a special sheen. See also *Irish lace, Irish poplin*. For the epithet 'Linenopolis', see *'Irish' Glasgow*. **2** Irish linen is also a beautiful garden hybrid, the petals of which have 'a yellow-green halo'. It is fragrant and semi-evergreen.

'Irish lion of St Mark' A lion used in church architecture in Kerala, India, possibly called 'Irish' because it is fierce and pouncing, as opposed to the tamer lions that surround Nelson's Column in London, for instance (see K. George-Varghese's online article *Construction of Images in the Art of Early Christian Churches*).

Irish Lions The famous rugby team. By coincidence, *The Irish Lion* (1838) was a one-act farce by John Baldwin Puckstone with a loquacious Irish tailor who is mistaken for Thomas Moore. It has nothing to do with what has occasionally been called the *Irish Tiger*.

'Irish Literary Renaissance' Term used by Augustus Boyd as the title of his 1916 book. The phrase is often interchangeable with 'Celtic Dawn' or 'Celtic Twilight' (named after

W. B. Yeats' collection of writings in 1893). This literary renaissance or revival spans approx. the period from c.1890–
1922, i.e. concluding with James Joyce's *Ulysses*. Some of
the notable authors in this period were William Sharp,
George Russell, Lady Gregory and perhaps the most prominent, John Millington Synge. The language of the Irish
Literary Revival was Hiberno-English, yet many works are
inspired by Ireland's Gaelic heritage and are pervaded with
references to Irish mythology, folklore and history.

Irish Literary Revival, father of the See *Irish Revival, father of
the*. See also '*Irish*' *Herodotus*.

Irish literary revival, language of the As the Encycl. Brit. (Vol.
15) refers to the *Irish English* dialect 'Kiltartan' used by Lady
Gregory (1859–1932) in her writings. (The name is derived
from the district near her home of Coole Park in Co. Galway.). Not all Revivalist writers used this dialect, however;
other forms of *Irish English* were used, as well as fine standard English adorned with Irish words or allusions to Irish
mythology.

'Irish' liverwort A variety of bright to dark-green liverwort
(*Moerckia hibernica*) found also on the coast of Wales in
dune-slacks (see webpage *Mosses and Liverworts in Wales:
Moerckia Hibernica*). See also *Irish moss*.

Irish loanwords Irish words in standard English (as opposed to
in *Irish English*, which is extremely rich in Irish-derived vocabulary). The term is used by Stalmaszczyk (1997b), among
others, and refers particularly to those words which have
entered the English language, such as *brogue, poteen* and
shebeen. Even *Irish whiskey* is really an Irish loanword, despite the fact that it is now firmly established in English.

Irish local A wheelbarrow (Rawson, 1991; Green, 1996; Share,
1997). For synonyms, see *Irish baby buggy*.

Irish Local Government Act, 1898 This Act established county
councils in Ireland.

Irish logic Walter Nash describes Irish logic (used in the *Irish
joke*) as 'a capacity to jump huge gaps or engage in creative
paradox that is simultaneously foolish and wise' (McArthur,
1992).

Irish longhorn A dark red, brindled breed of cattle listed by
Mason (1951). Connolly (1998) writes: 'An Irish type of long-

horn was identified, particularly in midland counties. Robert Bakewell may have used some of these in developing
his famous breed.' For other cattle breeds, see *Irish cow, old*.

Irish longhouse A special type of Irish country house (so called
by Buchanan, 1961), yet sometimes the 'Irish' prefix is not
used. As its name suggests, it is very long; it has just one
storey and is found especially on the Aran Islands.

Irish longwool A breed of sheep previously common in Galway and Roscommon (Mason, 1951). Incidentally, the term
'rotten sheep' was applied to one who betrayed the Fenian
cause (Partridge, 1937). See also *Irish shortwool, Irish Texel*.

Irish loo 'Three-card loo played with five cards' (Parlett, 1992).
In Australian slang, Mulligans (the plural of the Irish name)
are playing cards (Simes, 1993). One way of cutting a deck
of cards is called *Paddy's poke* (for which see Appendix 5).
Moreover, the Earl of Cork is slang for the ace of diamonds –
the poorest card in the pack – just as the Earl of Cork was
the poorest nobleman in Ireland (Green, 1998). See also *Irish
hold 'em, Irish whist*.

Irish Loop The southern shore of Newfoundland, which is 'the
Irish cultural heart' (see website for *Newfoundland Tours*).

Irish lord 1 This term was used in the western states of America
in the 1940s for a fish. This fish was 'also called "bullhead"
or "devil fish" and refers to any of a variety of scalping from
the genus *Hemilepidotus*. The fish, large-headed and spiny
in appearance, is found mainly in Alaska waters' (Clark,
1996). *Webster's* also records this fish as being found in the
Bering Sea. See also *Irish fish, the; Irish pollan; Irish trout; red
Irish lord* (Appendix 4). **2** 'Lord of Ireland'. Title assumed
by King John. In 1541, Henry VIII changed Ireland from a
lordship to a kingdom. See also *'Irish emperor', Irish high king*.

Irish lough style A particular style of angling using wet-fly
tactics through summer and natural baits like grasshoppers
or daddy-long-legs placed in three wet flies on a floating
line' (see the website *Fishing on Lough Connculinn from the
Pontoon Bridge Hotel, Co. Mayo*).

Irish lough wet fly Also called an 'Irish wet fly' or 'lough wet
fly'. A fishing fly specially designed for the loughs, with a
floss tail and pheasant crest (see website *Luck of the Irish*).
See also *Irish shrimp fly*.

Irish Lourdes Knock, Co. Mayo, the centre of pilgrimage. Ó Faoláin writes that 'August is the best month to visit this Irish Lourdes, especially the fourteenth and fifteenth, the feast of the Blessed Virgin, or the twenty-first, which is the anniversary of the apparition which has made Knock famous.' Moreover, Purcell (1991) states that since 1879 Knock has been regarded as 'the Lourdes of Ireland'. The actual Lourdes in France has been a place of pilgrimage (and healing) ever since fourteen-year-old Bernadette Soubirous had visions of the Blessed Virgin Mary there in 1858. See also *'Irish' Canterbury, 'Irish' Sinai, Irish Thebaid*.

Irish low-back car 'The Irish low-back car ... is a light vehicle fitted with block wheels rigidly attached to a rotating axle' (Evans, 1957). See also *Irish car*.

Irish Loyal and Patriotic Union Organisation founded in 1885 to resist *Irish Home Rule*. Due to lack of support, it disbanded and in 1891 became the *Irish Unionist Alliance*.

Irish lubricaun Hazlitt (1905) prefixes the word 'Irish' to 'lubricaun', which is a synonym of *Irish leprechaun*.

Irish luck 1 Or often 'the luck of the Irish'. Extremely good luck (Green, 1996). But, as Jan Morris observes, 'The luck of the Irish is a wish more than a characteristic' (quoted by Brady, 2000). **2** Sometimes it is said sarcastically and means the opposite, i.e. 'bad cess' (Share, 1997) – a term which may derive from the 'cess' or exactions, a type of tax (see Connolly, 1998); or 'scran', another word for luck (as in 'Bad scran to you!' – Share, 1997). As Green (1996) observes, it 'also means good fortune, with the proviso that it can often be meant ironically, and implies a degree of unfairness'. In Ireland, luck is indeed often seen in the opposite aspect: Morton (1930), for instance, observed about horseshoes that 'Irish stud farms hang them the reverse way over the horse-boxes'.

Irish lurcher Not an actual breed but a distinct type and a good hunting dog. As opposed to British lurchers (usually greyhound and saluki crosses), the Irish lurcher is a greyhound and collie cross (to hunt hares) or a whippet and Bedlington terrier cross (to hunt rabbits). Other combinations in Ireland include the *Irish terrier* or wheaten terrier, found especially in the north. It is usually light brown, with either rough or smooth fur, and if from a deerhound will be very large (see website for *Gilford Terrier and Lurcher Club* and also www.geocities.com). For other dog breeds, see *Irish Glen of Imaal terrier*.

Irishly In an Irish way or manner (OED and *Webster's)*.

M

'Irish' Maffia Or rather the 'Murphia', which is 'A facetious name, a play on the word "Mafia" applied to a group of Irish broadcasters prominent in the UK in the 1980s' (Pickering, *et al*, 1991) and coined on similar lines to the 'Taffia' in Wales (Edwards, 1998). It reminds me of MacHale's joke about the Kerryman Mafioso who started a protection racket and 'threatened to beat people up if they paid him money' (1979). See also *Irish Gang, The; Irish Mob*.

Irish Magna Carta Or Magna Carta Hiberniae (see Connolly, 1998), literally the Irish 'Great Charter'. This was modelled on the original (English) Magna Carta in 1215 in which King John guaranteed the civil liberties of the barons, the freemen and the Church. The Irish version (once thought to be a contemporary adaptation written after the king's death in 1216, but now believed to be as late as the fourteenth century) is almost the same as the English with certain key words such as England and London, replaced with Ireland and Dublin.

Irish magnifying glass In Liverpudlian dialect, something that reduces the size of something else: 'It's an Irish magnifying glass: it makes everything look smaller' (see website *Merseytalk9*).

Irish mahogany The elder tree (Rawson, 1991; Green 1996). See also *Irish yew*.

Irish Mail 1 The train service between Euston and Holyhead in north Wales) which started in 1848. The name was officially adopted in 1929; since 1947 there has been both a day and a night service (Jackson, 1997). See also *Irishman* (Appendix 2); *Wild Irishman*(Appendix 3); and *Paddy train* (Appendix 5). **2** 'A three-wheeled or four-wheeled toy vehicle activated by a hand lever, somewhat on the principle of a manually operated railway hand car' (*Webster's*). **3** Potatoes (Partridge, 2000).

Irish malt-drying kiln Booth uses the term for the particular kilns used for *Irish whiskey*, which, unlike Scotch whisky, do not use peat (1995).

Irish malt whiskey Sometimes the word 'malt' is added (e.g. by Johnson, 1995, who says that, blended with French cognac, Irish malt whiskey becomes 'Celtic crossing').

Irishman See Appendix 2; for terms containing the word 'Irishman', see Appendix 3.

Irish man-of-war A barge (in late nineteenth–twentieth century Thames-side slang; see Partridge, 1937) and a synonym of *Irish battleship*. Portuguese man-of-war is a type of jellyfish of the genus Physalia. See also *Irish boat, Irish coracle, Irish two-boater*.

Irish manner Refers to ploughing with the horse's tail attached to the plough by *gads* (straw ropes) instead of a yoke or collar. Smith (1991) writes: 'There were several substantial reasons for ploughing like this in what was called by English writers the Irish manner, since much of the country where the practice occurred was hilly and the ground stony.' See also *Irish horse harness, Irish martingale, Irish plough*.

Irish mantle A unique Irish garment (OED) or *brat*, the length of which once denoted a person's social rank. Dunlevy writes that the Irish mantle was used 'both as a day cover and a night blanket ... it was never washed [and] retained both dampness and infection' (Ballard, 1998). Connolly (1998) also refers to the Irish mantle. The term exists in Welsh as *mantell werddonig* or *mantell Gwyddel/Wyddel* (GPC). See also *Irish cloak*.

Irish manuscript lettering As Ó hÓgain (1990) refers to the special style of letters of the Gaelic alphabet. See also *Irish alphabet, Irish typeface*.

Irish Maori In NZ English, a Catholic Maori (also called simply an 'Irishman' – see Orsman, 1997). New Zealanders also call a Catholic by the Irish-sounding name 'doolan' (Green, 1996). Irishman Frederick Edward Manning (1812–83) was nicknamed the 'pakeha Maori' ('pakeha' being Maori for 'white man' – see Boylan, 1998). On the subject of Irish–New Zealand connections, the acronym 'IRISH' (for 'Ireland Researching Into Southern Hemisphere') has been coined to describe Irish–Kiwi friendship, and 'KIWI' (for

'Kiwi Irish With Interest') connotes a half-Irish, half-New Zealander (see website *Acronyms Category Listing – People and Relationships: Nationalities and Races*). Also in New Zealand, an early non-British (especially Irish) Australian was called a 'shagroon' (from Ir. *seachran* = wandering – see Green, 1998).

Irish marathon 1 A relay race (Rawson, 1991; Green, 1996). **2** Protracted lovemaking (Share, 1997).

Irish marbled, Burnet A variety of *pimpinellifolia* (Scotch rose), for which see website *Peter Beals – Full collection listed by classification*.

Irish marriage bell Or 'Irish crystal marriage bell'. 'A traditional Irish wedding and engagement gift ... to be kept in their new home. The bell is to be rung when one partner is ready to "make up" ... Legend has it that the crystal-clear ringing of the bell will always bring an end to disagreement, as the lovers remember the sound of their wedding bells.' The Irish marriage bell was first made four hundred years ago in Galway (see website for *Island Ireland Marketplace Index*). For the bell called *Finn Faideach*, see *Irish patron saint*.

'Irish' Marseillaise 'Hold the Harvest', the poem by Fanny, the sister of Charles Stewart Parnell (see *Irish king, uncrowned*), was described by Davitt as 'the "Marseillaise" of the Irish peasantry' (Connolly, 1998). See also *Irish national anthem*.

Irish Martello tower Christensen (1996) uses the prefix 'Irish' for this squat circular tower on the Irish coast constructed to warn of a Napoleonic invasion (from Martello – a town in Corsica). See *Irish Legion*.

Irish martingale 'The Irish martingale is a favourite for racing. It consists of a short, four-inch piece of leather with two rings, through which the reins are inserted. There is nothing round the horse's neck nor connecting to the girth' (Peel, 1978). This is in contrast to the alternative running martingale and standing martingale, as well as another type which 'combines the running and Irish martingales into one' (Peel, 1978). A martingale is a strap passed under the horse's forelegs, fastened to its girth, bit and reins so that the horse's head is kept down. See OED. See also *Irish manner*.

'Irish' Mary Or rather 'Mary of the Irish' (Welch, 1996) or 'the

Mary of the Gael' (Ellis, 1987; Share, 1997), as St Brigid is often called. The full title is 'The Prophetess of Christ, the Queen of the South, the Mary of the Gael' (Killanin, 1962). She is the most important female saint in Ireland, although, of course, no Catholic would ever agree that she has anything like the position of the Blessed Virgin Mary. St Brigid may have had a more legendary than historical basis. She is celebrated on 1 February: one custom is to make a *cros* or *bogha bríde,* i.e. 'St Brigid's cross' (see also *Irish Cross*). Consequently, Bridget is a popular girl's name in Ireland and the diminutive form 'Biddy' has been used for 'the quintessential Irish girl' (Green, 1996). Hence the nineteenth-century term 'bridgeting', i.e. taking money from Irish girls for alleged political purposes (Partridge, 1937).

Irish Mason(ic) speech As Macalister calls the distinct jargon of Irish masons (1937), called *Béarlagair na Saor.* Unlike *Shelta* (see *Irish Travellers' Cant),* there is very little material of this language extant. According to Macalister, it was essentially the *Irish language* with Irish syntax and largely Irish vocabulary. However, in each sentence, usually just one Irish word was replaced by a jargon term: 'An Irish mason might say something entirely in Irish about a knife; only instead of *scian,* the Irish word for knife, he would say *glaidín'* (Macalister, 1937). See also *Irish English, Irish language, Irish Latin, Irish Travellers' Cant, Turkey Irish* (Appendix 4).

Irish May Day festival As Wall (1995) refers to *Beltane* or *Bealtaine.* This was the festival when the *Beltane* fire (see *Irish fire)* was lit; it was also one of the *Irish gale-days* and was the time when cattle were taken to the *buaile* or summer pasturage. A 'May bush' or hawthorn was brought into the house and a 'May ball' – a decorated *Irish hurling ball* – was given as a present (Danaher, 1972). May dew was collected early in the morning and kept in a bottle for its healing properties, and mayflowers (marsh marigolds) were sprinkled on the bush outside to deter the fairies (Kavanagh, 1959). See also *Irish gale-days.*

Irish mayfly An endemic insect species (Morton, 1961).

Irish mead Booth (1995) cites a ninth-century writer who referred to mead being made from hazelnuts rather than the more usual honey. See also *Irish heather wine.*

Irish mease 'The *Irish mease*, which was a measurement indicating a nominal 500 fish ... was roughly equivalent to half a cran [cran = a Scottish fishing measurement]' (*Folk Life* 29, 1990–1).

Irish medicine goddess As Airmed or Airmid is called. She helped her father, Dian Cecht, guard the well of healing.

Irish Memorial Erected in 1963 at Culloden Moor, near Inverness, Scotland, to honour the Irish allies who perished with their Highland brothers at the battle of Culloden (1746). It was the unfortunate advice of Prince Charles Edward Stuart's Irish ally, John William O'Sullivan, that exposed the fine Highland and Irish force to danger on Culloden Moor; the troops should perhaps have adopted the guerrilla tactics preferred by the prince's other adviser, Lord George Murray.

Irishmen, Chapel of the (W. *Capel Llan y Gwyddel*) Legend says that this building, located near the church of St Cybi in Wales, was built for the Irish Pictish king, Singi. Yet it is more probable that it had a connection with the Irish saints.

Irishmen of Islam The Moors of Morocco. The implication here being that the Moors' diminished social status after their expulsion from Andalucia, Spain in the sixteenth century was analogous to the Irishman's subservient status in the past. (see website *Brewer's Readers Handbook*). See also *Irish of South-Western and Western America, the; smoked Irishman* (Appendix 3); *Mediterranean Irish* (Appendix 4).

Irishmen, Pass of the (W. *Bwlch y Gwyddel*) A pass in Snowdonia, north Wales. One of the first references to this place was made by Pennant in 1778. There are several placenames throughout Wales which testify to the historical presence of their Irish cousins, e.g. *Nant y Gwyddel* (Irishmen's Valley) and *Pont y Gwyddel* (Irishmen's Bridge).

Irishmen, Penman of the United Sobriquet which Douglas (1936) gives to William Drennan (1754–1820), poet and United Irishman (see *Irish Helot*). He wrote on behalf of the United Irishmen's cause and his radical ideas attempted to influence the Volunteer movement. It was Drennan, in his poem, 'When Erin First Rose', who coined the phrase 'Emerald Isle'.

Irishmen, United Also called the Society of United Irishmen and the United Irish Society. This organisation was established in 1791 in Belfast (mainly by Protestants) and in Dublin (by Catholics); clubs later opened elsewhere. Its leaders, notably Theobald Wolfe Tone, were inspired by the French and American Revolutions. It sought parliamentary reform and the end of British rule in Ireland. General Lake's reactionary measures provoked the United Irishmen's abortive rising in 1798 which was ruthlessly suppressed. The movement soon broke out again, only to collapse completely after Robert Emmet's unsuccessful rising of 1803.

Irishmen's cottages (W. *Cytiau Gwyddelod*) In relation to clusters of these houses, Seymour (1971) refers to 'the many hut circles that dot the hills' in parts of present-day Dyfed in Wales. The author states that these constructions were built by both the Irish and the Welsh in the Iron Age. Perhaps it is slightly anachronistic to speak of 'Irishmen' and 'Welshmen' in this prehistoric era – but certainly these builders were their Celtic ancestors.

Irishmen's Walls (W. *Muriau'r Gwyddelod*) A place near Harlech, in north Wales.

Irish mermaid The 'merrow' (*mudhuacha*), which Briggs (1976) calls 'the Irish equivalent of mermaids'. The merrow is also known as a 'merra' in *Irish English* (Share, 1997). They live in *Tír fo Thoinn* ('the Land Beneath the Waves') and do not like humans. In an internet heraldic glossary, we read: 'The merrow is an Irish mermaid, the female is beautiful with webbed hands and fishes' tails but the male of the species is ugly, green with pig-like eyes' (see website *Precedents of Baldwin of Erebor*). See also *Irish water beings*.

Irish mether Kinmouth (1993) mentions 'the singularly Irish mether, a square-topped wooden drinking vessel' used from early historic times to the nineteenth century.

Irish Metropolis Dublin (see also *Irish capital*). It is also called 'the Metropolis of Ireland' (e.g. by Morton, 1930).

'Irish' mick Or just plain 'Mick', meaning an Irishman. This nickname (derived from the popular Irish name 'Michael') is almost as common as Paddy. Indeed, some expressions even combine the two names (e.g. *Paddy and Mick*, for which see Appendix 5). The word 'Mick' is quite rich in connotations (like the word 'Paddy'). For instance, a 'Mick' could refer to an Irish sailor or soldier (Partridge, 1937), whereas in American slang it means a road mechanic (Partridge, 1950). Moreover, due to the manual occupations pursued by the Irish immigrant, a Mick can also be a road labourer (Green, 1998). In Ulster, 'Mick' also means 'Catholic' (Share, 1997) – hence the 'Morning Mick' is the Belfast *Irish News* (read mainly by Catholic readers with nationalist sympathies). 'Mick Doolan' is similarly a New Zealand phrase for either a Catholic or an Irish immigrant (Green, 1998). Like a 'Murphy', a 'Mick' can also be a potato (Green, 1998 – and see also *Irish potato*). Another connection between the names 'Murphy' and 'Mick' can be seen in the expression 'Mickey Murphy Mickey Murphy', i.e. 'six of one and half a dozen of the other' (Share, 1997). Perhaps the most surprising meaning of 'Mick' is 'Englishman' (Green, 1998). (For this confusion of the Irish with other white people, especially on the part of African-Americans, see 'Paddy' in Appendix 5.) Sometimes the name is shortened further to 'Mic' or 'Mc' (for surnames, see *The Racial Slur Database*), or alternatively it is lengthened to other forms thereof, such as 'Micky' or 'Mickey'. According to historian Paul Hinckley, the *Irish Guards* were nicknamed 'the Micks' (see the website *Dictionary of Great War Slang*). Hinckley also states that the expression 'to take the mickey', i.e. to tease, derives from the word 'mickey', meaning 'louse'. In Irish slang, James Joyce also used 'micky' to refer to the male private part (quoted by Wall, 1995 – see also *Irish inch, Irish root*). Wall also gives the phrase 'micky dazzler', used by Sean O'Casey and other Irish writers to mean a 'lady killer'. Apparently in early-nineteenth-century police slang, working-class Irishmen were dubbed 'gashouse micks' (from 'gas', in the sense of talking or bragging – see Partridge, 1950). In Liverpool, a person's intelligence can be questioned by calling them 'as daft as soft Mick' (see website *Merseytalk9*). Also the Irishman's stereotyped supposed stupidity is seen in rhyming-slang phrases like *Paddy and Mick* (see Appendix 5), i.e. 'thick' (Green, 1998). Other rhyming-slang phrases include 'Mick O'Dwyer', i.e. 'fire' (Green, 1998 – see also *Irish fire*) and 'Micky Spillane', i.e. 'game', in Australian slang (from the novelist Micky Spillane – see Green, 1998). There is also a 'Mickey Finn' – a double drink, knock-out drops or a laxative (Partridge, 1950). Green (1998) calls it 'Mickey Flynn' – no relation to 'Brian O'Flynn' or 'Brian O'Linn', i.e. gin. The Canadian slang phrase 'Texas Mickey' means rye whiskey (Green, 1998). Other equations between 'Mick' or 'Mickey' and Ireland can be seen in the name 'Mickland' or 'Mickeyland' for Ireland (Green, 1996) – a parallel of 'Murphyland' (Green, 1998). (See also Teagueland, for which see *Irish Teague* and *Paddy Land* in Appendix 5). 'Mick' or 'Mickey' is also one of several nicknames of the *Irish terrier*. For other expressions that include the word 'mick', see *Irisher, Irish fortune, Irishism, Irish Jailic, Irish potato, Irish toothpick, Irish whisky, shanty Irish* (Appendix 4), *Paddy and Mick* (Appendix 5).

Irish Midlands As opposed to the English Midlands (and the industrial 'Black Country'), Evans (1942) writes that 'the Irish Midlands is a veritable black country, black with peat, not with the grime of coalfields'.

Irish mile (Ir. *míle mór Gaelach/Éireannach*) **1** 'The Irish mile (still in rustic use) is 2,240 yards' (Christensen, 1996), compared with the English mile of 1,760 yards. Similarly in Ulster, a lucky mile is 'a mile and a bit' whereas an 'old man's mile' is a short distance (Macafee, 1996). The phrase also exists in Welsh (i.e. *milltir Wyddelig*), where it is given as 7,720 feet. (GPC). **2** Metaphorically, an Irish mile is 'a country mile, i.e. a mile that twists and turns and thus seems much further' (Green, 1998). Similarly, a Welsh mile is a tedious journey more than a mile (Edwards, 1998); a Scots mile is 1,980 yards (Robinson, 1985); and a Cornish mile is 2,240 yards. See also *Irish acre, Irish perch, Irish spirits measure, 'Irish' yard*.

'Irish' milk Or rather 'mother's milk of the Irish', i.e. stout (Kearns, 1996). See *Irish stout*. See also *Irish wine*.

Irish mint A rare cultivar which is 'an improved selection of Leyland Cypress'. It has thick 'vibrant lighter green foliage' and is cultivated in America. It would be unlikely to thrive in Ireland since it 'prefers full sun' (see www.encore plants.com).

Irish mischievous spirit 1 As Jones (1995) calls the *cluricaun*, who is similar to the *Irish leprechaun*. **2** She also calls the *púca* by this name. See *Irish Pooka*.

Irish mist 1 The famous Irish drink, first made by D. E. Williams, the ingredients of which include *Irish whiskey,* heather wine and heather honey. See also *Irish heather wine.* **2** *Chamberlainianum 'Irish mist'* is a rare variety of orchid. Crossed with *Parishii Charles,* it makes the special orchid hybrid *keelingii.* **3** Irish mist is also a variety of *cryptanthus* (a type of plant with pinkish, spiky leaves) and is also called *Cryptanthus Irish Mist.* **4** There is also an orange or salmon-pink variety of rose called 'Irish mist'.

Irish mist or light goddess As the *ignis fatuus* is dubbed. For which, see *Irish fairmaid.*

Irish Mob As the American gangsters of Irish extraction have been called, e.g. by Dick Lehr and Gerard O'Neill in their book *Black Mass: The Irish Mob, the FBI and A Devil Deal.* This book was a result of research that began in 1988 on the *Irish Bostonian* brothers Jim ('Whitey') and Billy Bulger and their connection with their former schoolfriend, Irish FBI agent John Connolly. No relation to the *'Irish' Maffia.* See also *Irish Gang, The.*

Irish moiled A breed of cattle that is red or roan in colour but was formerly grey, dun, black or white (listed by Mason, 1951). It is so called from the Irish *maol* – bare or bald, i.e. 'polled' or hornless (W. *moel*). See *polled Irish* (Appendix 4). See also *Irish cow, old.*

Irish mojara (*diapterus auratus*)A species of fish found off the coast of Southern Florida. It is greenish or grey above and silvery below, not weighing more than a pound. See *Irish lord.*

Irish molly 1 A variety of a 'green striped yellow' medium-sized apple from Scotland (NAR). See *Irish canary* for other apple varieties. **2** A type of hybrid flower about which we have few details (see newsletter www.merriments.co.uk). It is probably the same as *Viola Irish Molly,* which has bronze-gold flowers.

Irish moon goddess An epithet of Re or Ri (CGG). The same source describes Sadb as the Irish moon goddess presiding over fertility. The latter was turned into a fawn by the Dark Druid – yet Fionn's hounds would not kill her.

'Irish' Moonlighters Sometimes the prefix 'Irish' is used, especially by the non-Irish. The Moonlighters attacked the property and animals of landlords who evicted tenants from 1879 to 1901. The protesters got their name from the threatening letters they sent, which were signed by 'Captain Moonlight'.

Irish moonshine Like 'the Connemara Doctor' and *Irish mountain dew,* Irish moonshine is a name for *poitín* (Johnson, 1998). See *Irish poteen.*

Irish moonshiner A maker of *Irish moonshine,* i.e. *Irish poteen* (see Steven McCaffery's article 'Sun Sets on Irish Moonshiners' in the *Irish News,* 8 November 1999).

'Irish' Moses In nineteenth-century verse, Daniel O'Connell 'assumed the messianic role proclaimed in traditional prophecy with the poets hailing him as the second Moses' (Welch, 1996). See also *Irish Dan; Irish king, uncrowned; Irish Solomon.*

Irish moss 1 (a) The sea plant *chondrus crispus,* which has a variety of names: carrageen or caragheen (from Ir. *carraigín* = little rock), sea moss, pearl moss, curly moss and jelly moss (Brady, 2000). (b) A similar red algae, *mastrocarpus stellatus,* from which carrageen is also made. Both forms of seaweed (particularly the first) are used to enhance the consistency of many Irish desserts. **2** In the West Indies (the Irish also settled in Montserrat – see *Black Irish* in Appendix 4), Irish moss refers to 'a popular drink with health-food enthusiasts ... believed to aid sexual prowess' (Allsopp, 1996). **3** The perennial *sagina subulara* (see webpage *Johannsens Greenhouses Perennial List).* **4** Another type of flower, *Irish moss soleirolia soleirolii.*

Irish moss, golden The perennial *sagina subulata aurea* (see website of *Johannsens Greenhouses Perennial List).*

'Irish' moss bag Or just 'moss bag'. A large burlap bag used to carry *Irish moss* (Pratt, 1988).

Irish-moss bleacher The person who bleaches the moss (see *Yahoo's Dictionary of Occupational Titles Index).* See also *Irish-moss operator.*

'Irish' mosser 1 Someone who harvests *Irish moss* (Pratt, 1988). **2** Or just 'mosser', a strong wind that brings *Irish moss* to the shore.

Irish-moss harvester One who uses a horse (see *'Irish' moss horse*) and a special drag rake to harvest *Irish moss* from the shore.

When harvesting from a boat, a longer pole rake is used (Pratt, 1988).

'Irish' moss horse Or just 'moss horse'. A horse used to harvest storm-tossed *Irish moss* to shore (Pratt, 1988).

Irish-moss operator A specialist profession of a person who treats the harvested *Irish moss* with chemicals (see *Yahoo's Dictionary of Occupational Titles Index*). See also *Irish-moss bleacher*.

'Irish moss' pudding Or 'sea-moss pudding', which is simply 'blancmange made by boiling Irish moss with milk' (Pratt, 1988).

'Irish moss' syrup What Fitzgibbon (1983) calls 'carrageen syrup', made with *Irish moss,* lemon rind and sugar, with optional *Irish whiskey* or brandy. This is not served as a dessert but is given as a cure for chest colds and coughs.

Irish mother goddess As both Buana (represented as a cow) and Caireen are dubbed. The spelling of 'Buana' is in question – she may be connected with Buanann, whom Ellis (1987) calls 'the mother of heroes' and who had a school for warriors. See also *Irish people, mother of the*.

'Irish' Mother Saint Or rather the 'Mother Saint of Ireland', as Hutton (1996) calls St Brigid, for which see *'Irish' Mary*.

Irish mountain dew Another name for *Irish poteen*.

Irish mountain goddess The epithet of Ebhlinne or Ebhlen. She gave her name to Slieve Eelim (Sliabh Eibhlinne) near Limerick. No relation to a woman of the same name whose kingdom in Ulster was built at such a low level that it was flooded, forming Lough Neagh.

Irish mousetrap The term refers to the 'choker mousetraps called "Irish" in English hardware catalogues from about 1810 to 1910' (Drummond, 1996–7). A few types are listed: the 'gnaw-thread Irish mousetrap', 'push-wire Irish mousetrap', 'bait-hook Irish mousetrap' and 'improved Irish mousetrap'.

Irish mouth-blown bagpipes Term used by Vallely (1999) to distinguish *Irish bagpipes* from *Irish elbow pipes*. See also *Irish Union pipes*.

'Irish' mudcrawlers Or sometimes just 'mudcrawlers'. Irishmen who came to Wales to escape the *Irish Famine*. Perhaps so called because many crawled on the mud of some river estuaries in order to reach the land (O'Riordan mentions the word in *Cambria*, May–June 1999). See also *Irish Pantry*.

Irish music Irish folk or traditional music.

Irish musket A club (Rawson, 1991). No relation to *Irish rifle*.

Irish Mussolini Thus James Curky, mayor of Boston 1914–18, 1922–6 and 1930–4 was dubbed by his opponents.

Irish mustard As opposed to hot English mustard, Irish mustard is more herby and does not refer to just one specific type but rather to various blends of mustard which are uniquely Irish. For instance, Lakeshore have made some distinct varieties with Guinness, *Irish whiskey*, horseradish and even honey.

Irish mutton Syphilis (Rawson, 1991). See also *Irish button*.

N

'Irish' narrowback Or (especially if used by Irish-Americans themselves) just 'narrowback'. This refers to an American of Irish extraction who, unlike his immigrant parents, had an easier life and so was without such a strong physique (i.e. a wide back) and was less capable of manual work (see Rawson, 1991). See also *Irish returnees*.

Irish Nation League Founded in Ulster after the 1916 Easter Rising to oppose any partition of Ireland. Its members were too few to have much influence. Not to be confused with the *Irish National League*.

Irish National Aid The word 'Association' is often added. This organisation was founded in 1916 after the *'Irish' Easter Rising* to raise money for families of imprisoned and killed *Irish Volunteers*. It amalgamated with the Irish Volunteers Dependants' Fund. Michael Collins (see *Irish Lenin*) was secretary of both organisations.

Irish National Alliance Republican organisation founded in 1894. It was more radical than the *Irish Republican Brotherhood* and had a military wing known as the Irish National Brotherhood. It dwindled after the turn of the century.

Irish national anthem The 'Soldier's Song' (*Amhrán na bhFiann*), written by Peadar Kearney, with music by Patrick Heaney, in 1907. It was adopted as the anthem of the *Irish Free State* in 1924. Up to 1914, J. D. Sullivan's 'God Save Ireland' (1867) was used. (This song was analogous with the English national anthem 'God save the Queen'). 'The Red Flag', writ-

ten by James Connolly, 'became the socialist anthem' (Boylan, 1998). Moreover, the Irishman Don Emmet (of Virginia)
wrote the Confederacy's anthem 'Dixie' (Vallely, 1999). See
also *'Irish' Marseillaise; Irish sportsmen, the national anthem of.*
Irish national brew As Guinness is called (Morgan, 1996).
Irish National Brotherhood See *Irish National Alliance.*
Irish national colour Green (see Connolly, 1998), because Ireland is so green. Ireland is even called 'the Emerald Isle'
(see also *Irish favourite)* and even 'the Green Isle' *(Brewer's).*
In the late nineteenth century one nickname for an Irishman
was a 'Greenlander' (Partridge, 1937). Despite its aptness,
bearing in mind Ireland's beautiful green landscape, Green
(1998) believes the name 'Greenland' was originally a mild
insult (since the Irish were believed to be 'green', i.e. naïve).
Similarly, because of the common persecution of Irishmen
and black people, the Irish were also known in America as
'green niggers' (Green, 1996 – see also *Irish wog, Black Irish*
in Appendix 4 and *sunburnt Irishman* in Appendix 3).
Michael Hopkinson very aptly entitled his book on the *Irish
Civil War* (1988) *Green Against Green.* Similarly, the 'Green
Army' were Jack Charlton's Irish soccer team's supporters
in the 1980s and 1990s (Share, 1997). The 'little green man'
is a small bottle of *Irish whiskey,* preferably Jameson's (see
website *Yahoo's Everyday English and Slang in Ireland).* Irish-
American schoolchildren practise the St Patrick's Day Pinch
(the custom of pinching classmates who do not wear green
on St Patrick's Day – see website *Marvelicious St Patrick's
Day Page).* Irish-Americans also dye the San Antonio River
in Texas green on St Patrick's Day; and on the same day the
Empire State Building is lit up with green lights. However,
'Saint Patrick's blue' is the saint's own colour. 'Green came
into use in the nineteenth century', according to Christine
O'Keefe (see website *Christine O'Keefe's St Patrick's Customs).*
Politically, green is used to denote Irish nationalism, as opposed to orange (of the Protestant 'Orangemen') or sometimes black (used by the Loyalist 'Blackmen'). See also *Irish
blue, Irish green, 'Irish' greenfinch, Irish Green Flag, Irish greenpaint finish.*
Irish national dancing costume Or *Irish dancing costume,* which
consists of the *brat* (cloak) and *léine* (tunic or shirt) influ-

enced by Irish rural costumes. Solo dance costumes are more elaborate, with Celtic motifs, *Irish lace* cuffs and collars, buckles on shoes, and medals worn to adorn the costume. The men's costume features knee breeches (formerly *Irish kilts)*, a crested *brat* and a tie (Robb, 1998).

Irish national day The seventeenth of March, or St Patrick's Day (see *Irish patron saint)*, which is important not only in Ireland but wherever Irish people live. According to Law (1998), it is celebrated on the seventeenth because 'a priest resolved the bitter dispute over whether Saint Patrick's Day should be on the eighth or ninth of March by simply adding the two dates together'. The seventeenth of March is called Green Ribbon Day (*Brewer's)* since a green ribbon is worn with a shamrock (see *Irish shamrock)* on this day.

Irish National Federation Anti-Parnellite organisation founded in 1891 when it seceded from the *Irish National League.* The federation later re-merged with the league, accepting John E. Redmond's leadership in 1900.

Irish National Foresters Or Irish National Foresters Benefit Society. Founded in 1877 in Dublin and open only to people who are Irish by birth or descent. Though it developed out of the English Ancient Order of Foresters, it is fully Irish. The uniforms consist of green jackets with epaulettes, white breeches, black boots, a green and black plumed hat and a dark tie with a crest.

Irish National Hunt Racecourse Punchestown, Co. Kildare, where the National Hunt Festival and International Horse Trials are held in April and May respectively. Brady (2000) similarly dubs it 'Ireland's premier National Hunt racecourse.'

Irish National Hunt Steeplechase Although steeplechasing (racing over fences) began in Co. Cork in 1752, English rules were followed in Ireland from 1864 until the Irish National Hunt Steeplechase Committee was founded in 1869. Irish horses have also been very successful in British racing. Interestingly, in the Irish game of 'Steeplechases', played at Christmas, obstacles such as books and cushions were placed on the floor to be stepped over by a person who was blindfolded (Killen, 1985).

Irish nationalism, the saint of Fred Ryan (1876–1913). He was given this name by his co-founder of the *National Democrat*, Francis Sheehy-Skeffington (Welch, 1996) because, through his writing (he was a social journalist and playwright), he championed the Irish cause.

Irish Nationality and Citizenship Act Act introduced by the Fianna Fáil government of 1935 under which Irish nationals were no longer regarded as British citizens.

Irish National Invincibles See *Irish Invincibles*.

Irish National League Inaugurated in 1882 by Charles Stewart Parnell, replacing the *'Irish' Land League*. It was declared illegal after incidents in 1887 and in 1891 fell apart after the divorce scandal involving Parnell (precipitated by Parnell's adulterous affair with O'Shea's wife).

Irish National Liberation Army Illegal paramilitary group formed from a left-wing offshoot of the official *Irish Republican Army*. In 1979, the INLA assassinated Conservative shadow secretary of state for Northern Ireland, Airey Neave and in the 1980s, some of its members were believed to be active in the killing of Protestants under the name of the 'Catholic Reaction Force'. In August 1998, they announced a ceasefire and issued an apology for the deaths they had caused.

'Irish' national poet Thomas Moore (1779–1852), who wrote *Irish Melodies* (1808–34), thus 'ensuring his place as Ireland's national poet' (Vallely, 1999).

Irish national tartan In addition to the thirty-two *Irish county tartans*, the House of Edgar in Scotland has created a so-called Irish national tartan. See also *Irish kilt, Irish tartan*.

Irish national trademark 'In 1906 the IIDA (Irish Industrial Development Association) registered an Irish national trademark, consisting of a Celtic motif inside a circle that contained the words *Déanta in Éirinn* (made in Ireland)' (Connolly, 1998).

Irish Naturalisation Act, 1784 This Act concerning Irish citizenship excluded Jews and was repealed in 1816.

'Irish' navigators A rhyming-slang phrase for potatoes from the rhyme of navigator with 'tater', i.e. potato (Partridge, 1937). In Ireland, the form *tattie* or *tatty* is more common, especially in Ulster (Share, 1997). The rhyme is not coincidental, since it implies 'the connection with the predominantly Irish navigators (i.e. navvies), builders of Victorian Britain's railways and canals, whose stereotype consumed many potatoes (Green, 1998). There is also the rhyme 'navigator Scot', i.e. 'potatoes all hot' (Partridge, 1937; Green, 1998). See also *Irish apple* for synonyms.

Irish necktie See *Irishman's necktie* (Appendix 3).

Irish nectar In Greek mythology, nectar was the drink of the gods. No less than three Irish drinks have been dubbed 'the Irish nectar': Guinness, Bailey's Irish Cream and *Irish whiskey*.

Irish Need Apply, No Notorious note added to many nine-teenth-century advertisements for jobs, especially in America (Morgan, 1996). See also *Irish riots, anti-*.

Irish Neo-Gothic Later development of *Irish Gothic*.

Irishness (OED). The quality of being Irish or of that which is Irish. Dr Conor Cruise O'Brien said: 'Irishness is not primarily a question of birth or blood or language; it is the condition of being involved in the Irish situation, and usually of being mauled by it' (quoted by Boylan, 1998). On similar lines, the opposition to Irishness is described as anti-Irishness (Gray, 1995).

Irish Nessie By analogy to the Loch Ness Monster in Scotland (popularly known as 'Nessie'), there is speculation that a sister monster may live in Lough Ree, Ireland. Recently, Scandinavian scientists have made underwater recordings in this lake. Attention to the Irish monster was first brought by three priests in 1960 'who said a large snake-like creature swam close to their boat ... it was then described as having an eighteen-inch long head with eyes, nose and ears rising out of the water' (see the website *Ananova: Irish Nessie*). This may have been one snake that St Patrick missed! See also *Irish Dragon*.

Irish nightingale 1 The sedge warbler, also called the Scotch nightingale or nightsinger (Swainson, 1886). **2** A frog (Green, 1996). The same as a Dutch nightingale, Cambridge nightingale, Cape nightingale and Fen nightingale. In Ulster, a frog is called a *Paddy frog* (see Appendix 5). **3** The 'Irish Nightingale': the famous Irish soprano Patricia Cahill (www. patriciacahill.com). Like the great *Irish Caruso*, her repertoire is mainly Irish ballads rather than opera pieces. Similarly, the 'Welsh Nightingale' was Edith Wynne (1842–97), the 'Cornish Nightingale' was Fanny Moody of Redruth and the 'Swedish Nightingale' was Jenny Lind (1820–87). See also *'Irish' Prima Donna*.

Irish noggin A wooden bucket with a vertical handle used to carry milk and porridge (but see also *Irish porridge*).

Irish 'No Rent' Manifesto Or just 'No Rent Manifesto' (some writers, e.g. Pascoe (1968) use the prefix 'Irish'). The manifesto, drawn up by William O'Brien in 1881, called on supporters of the *'Irish' Land League* to withhold rents because many tenants had been excluded from the *Irish Land Act* of that year. The document bore the names of Parnell, Davitt, Egan, *et al* and was declared illegal.

'Irish' Normandy 'Wexford, a country of gardens, has been called in the easy Irish way the Normandy of Ireland' (Floyd, 1937). See also *Irish Flanders, 'Irish' Garden*.

Irish Northern Aid Committee (NORAID) American-based organisation, founded in 1969, that gives financial support to families of killed or imprisoned republicans in the north. There has been controversy concerning allegations that NORAID's funds have also been used to finance the *IRA*.

Irish Not The *bata scóir* or tally stick. 'A stick on which a notch was cut whenever the child was heard to speak Irish, his or her punishment afterwards dependent on the number of notches' (Ó Giolláin, 2000). It is thus named by allusion to the equivalent 'Welsh Not' used throughout Wales in an endeavour to eradicate Welsh. Parry-Jones (1964) writes: 'There was also an Irish Not, or tally, on which was recorded the number of Irish words used during the day, at the end of which suitable punishment was administered.' Similarly, in the *Irish hedge school* a *súgán* collar (of hay or straw) was placed round the neck of a dunce (Wall, 1995).

Irish notation The ancient Irish system of musical notation, which used special symbols (Vallely, 1999). See also *Irish key*.

Irish nuirt 'An Irish nuirt is an amulet worn on the finger, or arm, a ring' (Hazlitt, 1905). No relation to the *Irish amulet*. Perhaps the term 'Irish nuirt' is derived from the Irish word *neart* (strength or power, the genitive of which is *nirt)*, as it would bestow power on the wearer. See also *Irish torc*.

O

Irish Oaks Just like the (English) Oaks, the Irish Oaks (or Oak Stakes) is a famous horse-racing event; it is held at the Curragh in July. The race, which was inaugurated in 1895, is run by three-year-old fillies over a mile and four furlongs. See also *Irish Classics*.

Irish oat cakes These are usually round and divided into farls (quarters) (Connery, 1997).

Irish Ocean The Welsh refer to the Atlantic Ocean as *Môr Iwerydd* or the Sea of Ireland. This is logical since it is an extension of *the Irish Sea*. Hence, in Welsh, the Atlantic Charter is *Siart(e)r Iwerydd*, i.e. the Irish Charter.

Irish octagonal plate A distinct form of eight-sided Irish ceramic ware.

Irish Octennial Act The 1768 Act limiting the duration of the *Irish parliament* (Foster, 1989).

'Irish' Odin 'The Irish counterpart of Odin was Donn Firinne, who is depicted as a horseman riding at a gallop through the sky followed by his troop' (Smith, 1991).

Irish Odyssey Ellis (1987) says of Mael Duin: 'He set out in a quest to avenge the death of his father. He took with him sixty warriors and his subsequent voyage has been considered as the Irish Odyssey.' See also *Irish Circe, Irish Ulysses, The*.

Irish Office Established in 1801. The Chief Secretary for Ireland would use the 'Irish Office' while in London. Abolished after the Anglo-Irish Treaty in 1921.

Irish of South-Western and Western America, the Mexicans (Green, 1996). So called since the Mexicans today are still exploited as the Irish were in the last century in America. They are given low paid, menial work, hence expressions such as Mexican promotion, for which see *Irish promotion*. See also *the 'Irish' Acapulco, Irishmen of Islam*.

Irishologist A specialist in Irish culture (www.albertaDirec tory.net). See also the more correct word *Irishian*.

Irish Olympics With reference to the *Tailteann* Games for athletic and artistic competition, which saw a revival in the 1880s, Connolly (1998) writes: 'Official planning for the Irish Olympics began in 1922.' (The Games were held in

1924.) The Tailteann Games originated from the old pre-Christian sport and cultural competition, *Óenach Tailten*, in Teltown, Co. Meath, held in honour of the god Lugh on 1 August.

Irish 1,000 Guineas A horse race held in May at the Curragh. It began in 1922 and is run over a distance of one mile by three-year-old fillies. See also *Irish Classics, Irish 2,000 Guineas*.

Irish openfield system As Evans (1957) refers to the 'rundale' system, whereby 'plots ... change hand periodically among co-partners by the casting of lots.'

Irish open frame settle Term used by Kinmouth (1993) for a settle, often with a tall, panelled back and invariably with a deep seat 'to double as a bed'. See also *Irish box bed, Irish settle-bed*.

Irish orange No relation to a 'bog orange' (i.e. a potato – see Partridge, 1937). The Irish orange is a variety of light-purple heather, *Erica stuartii*, with bright-orange foliage. See also *Irish lemon, Irishman's harvest* (Appendix 3).

Irish organ The *Irish Union pipes* are 'what some commentators called the Irish organ' (Ó hAllmhuráin, 1998). The word 'organ' is meant in the sense of 'instrument' (see also Modern Greek *organo* – a musical instrument or organ of the body).

Irish Otherworld Term used (e.g. in *The Celtic Pen*, Vol. 2, Issue 2, winter 1994–5) to describe the otherworld of *Emain Ablach*. This was 'Emain of the apple trees' (etymologically similar to Avalon), ruled by Manannan Mac Lir (see *Irish sea god*). This was only one of many otherworlds; others included *Mag Meall* (the Plain of Delight), *Tír na nÓg* (the Land of Youth – where people remained young), *Uí Bhresail* (a land supposedly off the west coast of Ireland). See also *'Irish' Atlantis*.

Irish outshot bed Or just 'outshot bed'. A semi-enclosed sleeping area near the wall. See also *Irish box bed, Irish settle-bed*.

Irish outside car Or just 'outside car'. According to Smith (1988), this is the American name for the *Irish jaunting car*.

P

Irish Pale 'The Pale' was the English-speaking (and English-influenced) area of Ireland, also called Galltacht (literally

area of the 'gall' or foreigner, i.e. Englishman). It is perhaps
from this word 'pale' that the Shelta word for English/
England derives, i.e. Palantus (Macalister, 1937).

Irish Palladianism Irish variation of the Palladian style of
architecture named after Andrea Palladio (1518–80); he
modelled the style on that of Vitruvius. See also *Irish
Georgian, Irish Gothic*.

'Irish' palm There is a variety of palm, the Latin name of which
is *Areca novo-hibernica Beccari* (see website *A List of All Palm
Species*).

Irish Pantry O'Riordan *(Cambria,* May–June 1999) says that:
'there were inns in parts of Wales with Irish pantries where
the Irish labourers were served their ale apart from the
local population. The remains of these can still be seen.'
See also *'Irish' mudcrawlers*.

Irish paradise An African violet hybrid.

Irish parliament 1 The obvious meaning is *An Oireachtas,* which
consists of two houses: the Dáil and the Seanad. **2** The Parliament (1692–1800) that existed after the Williamite victory
(excluding Catholics) until the time of the Act of Union of
1801 (Welch, 1996). **3** 'A noisy argument bordering on a
free fight' (Dickson, 1997).

Irish Parliamentary Party Also called the Home Rule Party and
the Nationalist Party. The Irish Parliamentary Party was
founded in 1873 by Isaac Butt but it was under the leadership of Parnell (see *Irish king, uncrowned)* that it became an
important political force, even managing to convince the
British prime minister, Gladstone, that *Irish Home Rule* was
a necessity. Yet Parnell's divorce scandal affected the British
Liberals' previously positive stance on Home Rule. Irish
Anti-Parnellites led by Justin McCarthy divided the party
in 1890. John Redmond tried to reunify the party in the
post-Parnell era but the new pressure of Carson's Unionists made complete Home Rule unlikely. The party seemed
tame in comparison with newer nationalists. Redmond did
not approve of the *'Irish' Easter Rising* and the party dwindled after the 1918 election, which was a victory for Sinn
Féin.

Irish parrot Unlike the *Irish canary,* it is a caricature of a parrot –
all green and smoking a green dudeen (see *Irish clay pipe),*

perched on the hat of a lady dressed in green and holding the *Irish Green Flag*. It was a popular postcard image of the 1920s (see www.theparrotsocietyuk.org).

Irish Party See the *Irish Parliamentary Party*.

Irish passage graves A category of neolithic tomb dating from c. 2,500 BC; Newgrange in Co. Meath is perhaps the finest example. See also *Irish wedge tombs*.

Irish pasture A faint or coma. Partridge (1950) tries to explain it thus: 'a faint imposes upon the gullible, no less green than are the lush green pastures.' There seems to be some confusion here with *Irish posture*.

Irish patchwork Type of Irish needlework that refers to three kinds: 'appliqué', 'mosaic' and 'log cabin' (Shaw-Smith, 1984). *Irish chain* is used as a border for this type of work.

Irish patience Variation of the card game, patience, in which piles of cards are completed by building up with alternate colours from Ace to King (www.solitaire-card-games.net).

Irish patron saint St Patrick (Ir. *Naomh Pádraig*; in *Irish Travellers' Cant* he is called *Stofirt* or *Stofrik* – see Macalister, 1937). St Patrick lived in the fifth century and, according to legend, was told to return to Ireland by the angel Victor. St Patrick is famous for destroying the idol Crom Cruach (to whom first-born children were sacrificed) and banishing the snakes from Ireland by ringing his bell, *Finn Faideach*. Hence it is to be expected that (apart from being the 'patron saint of toothaches'), he is principally the 'patron saint of snakebites' (see website *Patron Saints Index*). He is also known for using the *Irish shamrock:* hence the expression to 'drown the sham-rock', i.e. to drink a lot on the saint's day. Indeed, like his Cornish counterpart St Peran, St Patrick is associated with drink. From the seventeenth to the nineteenth centuries, the term 'St Patrick' meant the best whiskey (Partridge, 1937) and to 'drink at St Patrick's well' meant to drink *Irish whiskey* (Green, 1998). Moreover, St Patrick's pot (Ir. *pota Pádraig*) refers to a drink taken on St Patrick's feast day (Danaher, 1972). Other words and phrases are derived from the saint's name, for instance, Patrickmas is the season around his feast day (Macalister, 1937). On St Patrick's Day, a special St Patrick's cross is made (for which see *Irish Cross*). Moreover, the saint is so identified with Ireland that

'The Irish are sometimes called "Patrick's People"' (Dickson, 1997). The trite expression 'mother of St Patrick' is a blasphemous allusion to female genitalia (Green, 1998), which are also called 'mother of all saints' or 'mother of St Paul', implying in a vulgar way the human origins even of saints (see also *Irish fortune*). There are also countless toponyms derived from the saint's name (see also *Irish place-name lore*). Apart from St Patrick's Well (near Clonmel, Co. Tipperary), there is Croagh Patrick (the peak in Connaught from which St Patrick banished the snakes – see *'Irish' Sinai*) and St Patrick's Purgatory (a place of penance in Lough Derg, Donegal). Moreover, Alf McCreary's recent book on Armagh (where the saint established his main church) is entitled *St Patrick's City* (Blackstaff, 2001). See also *Irish Anthony; Irish Apostle; 'Irish' Mary; Irish patron saint, second.* See also Appendix 5 for phrases with 'Paddy'.

Irish patron saint, second Colum Cill (521–97). Together with Brigid (see *'Irish' Mary*), he is second only to St Patrick. He is often described as 'one of the three patron saints of Ireland, the others being Patrick and Brigid' (Welch, 1996). In fact, there are so many saints in Ireland that it has aptly been called the *'island of saints and sages/scholars'* (Wall, 1995). See also *Irish Anthony, 'Irish' Mary, Irish patron saint.*

Irish pattern The celebration of a local patron saint. It is similar to the Breton celebration 'pardon'. See also *Irish Lourdes, 'Irish' Sinai.*

Irish pavilion A pavilion exhibiting Irish culture, e.g. at the 1972 World Fair.

Irish peach No relation to *Irish apricot,* this is a variety of apple also called the Irish peach-apple from Sligo: 'skin greenish yellow flushed reddish orange with red streaks, dotted' (NAR). See also *Irish canary.*

Irish peach-apple See *Irish peach.*

Irish Peace Agreement The agreement reached in 1921. See *Irish Treaty, Anglo-.*

Irish Peace Harp As the Peace Harp of Ireland is also called. This is a giant wind harp based on the twelfth-century Brian Ború harp. Ron Konzak (famous for the Peace Pagoda he built in Bainbridge for Japanese Buddhist monks) has proposed to build this, on the advice of a Catholic nun, where it will stand on the border between Northern and Southern Ireland and where 'the winds from the north and the south play the same beautiful melodies' (see website *Peace Harp for Ireland*).

Irish peas Peas cooked with mint and butter (Sheridan, 1965).

Irish penal rosary Not a complete rosary but only a decade (i.e. ten beads). Therefore at the time of religious persecution, when Catholicism (and the use of the rosarsy) was illegal, this small version was 'easily concealed in hand or pocket, making secret prayer possible' (www.stcecilia-bainbridge. org). See also *'Irish' dark rosary*.

Irish penannular brooch 'A long pin with a large ring' (Encycl. Brit., Vol. 15). See also *Irish torc*.

Irish pendant Spelling preferred by some (e.g. Jeans, 1993) for an *Irish pennant*. Interestingly, in the same book Jeans refers to a shamrock knot with three loops. See also *Irish shamrock*.

Irish pennant 1 Loose ends of ropes hanging over a ship's sail (Partridge, 1937). Whilst *Irish pendant* also exists, the form 'Irish pennant' is preferred by the OED. **2** One source, apart from giving the above definition, adds that it also connotes an 'unwhipped rope end' (www.infoplease.com). **3** A pennant is a long, narrow flag. See also *Irish fashion, to take a reef in the,* and *Paddy Doyle* (Appendix 5).

Irish penny Due to the inferior value of Irish currency, this was a thirteenth of a shilling (not a twelfth, as in Britain). Hence one word for a penny was a 'thirteen' (Christensen, 1996). In Irish, it is called a *pingin,* and in Shelta or *Irish Travellers' Cant,* a *niuc*. The old pre-decimal Irish penny was also called a 'harper' (Partridge, 1937) because of the harp symbol, and it was called a 'wing', as the penny used between 1928 and 1971 featured a hen. A 'dee' was another name for an Irish penny because of the symbol 'd' used for 'pence' (see Wall, 1995, and Share, 1997) and it has also been called a 'clod' or a 'lop' in Cork (Share, 1997). During the *Irish Free State* period, the penny of 1928 had an *Irish harp,* not the king's head, on it, even though the king was still officially head of state. Incidentally, the British penny has been called in rhyming slang a 'Kilkenny' (see website *Rhyme Slang English to Slang English Dictionary*). See also *Irish jane, Irish pound, Irish shilling*.

Irish people, mother of the As Cesair, the granddaughter of
Noah, is dubbed. She advised her father, Bith (who was
denied a place in Noah's Ark), to build an idol; this idol
advised that a second ark be built. Cesair sailed for Ireland
in the second ark but later did not escape the Deluge. Only
her husband, Fintan, survived (by changing into a salmon –
see *Irish fish, the*).

Irish people, the aardvark of the As Eagleton (1999) describes
alcohol. The aardvark (Dutch 'earth pig') is the anteater of
South Africa. It buries its snout to devour ants as one metaphorically does with drink. See also '*Irish' chloroform*.

Irish People's Liberation Organisation New faction of the *Irish
Republican Socialist Party* founded in 1986 as a breakaway
group of the *Irish National Liberation Army*. In 1992, two
rival factions, the Army Council and the Belfast Brigade,
had an internal feud, leading to the imminent disbandment
of the *INLA*.

Irish perch An undefined measurement that was invariably
larger than the English perch of 5.5 feet. Douglas (1936)
believed that the English made 'specially spacious "Irish"
perches and acres to suit their greed.'

Irish pestilences The plague (*galar breac*), and fever that raged
in Ireland during the years 1519–25 and 1535–6 (Kohn, 1995).
See also *Irish ague, Irish fever, Irish Plague, the*.

Irish pewter measure Like a pewter jug and used to measure
alcohol (Sharkey, 1985). See *Irish spirits measure*.

Irish phantom funeral In Irish, a *crocharnaid* (from *crochar* = bier,
stretcher) is an omen of death. See also *Irish death coach*.

Irish Phoenix With reference to the phoenix (the fabulous Ara-
bian bird of the ancient world that burned itself every five
hundred years to emerge from its own ashes), even expert
Irish folklorists would be surprised to learn of an 'Irish
phoenix'. According to the website *The Harry Potter Lexi-
con: The Bestiary*, it is 'another name for the "augurey"': a
mournful-looking green and black bird which nests in bram-
bles; its cry (like that of the banshee – see *Irish death messenger*) foretells death.

Irish piano A till. (See also the Anglo-Irish slang 'piano' for a
cash register – RDGED, Vol. 3). Similarly, the slang term for
a till or safe without money was a 'John O'Brien'; an 'O'Sul-

livan' was underworld slang for a safe-breaker (Partridge, 1950). On similar lines, a 'Jewish piano' or 'pianola' is a taximeter or cash register (Green, 1998).

Irish piano-style 'Open sound of vamping of *tionlacan* (accompaniment)' (Vallely, 1999). See also *'Irish' jazz*.

Irish pig The phrase usually refers to one of the unique Irish breeds of pig (see *Irish grazier, Irish greyhound, Irish landrace*). As opposed to the pigs used to make Danish bacon, K. M. Harris writes that 'it was the Irish pigs that made the bacon good' (*Ulster Folklife*, Vol. 1, 1959). For the Welsh gypsies, 'Pig Land' was a name for Ireland, possibly because of the *Irish bacon* (Jarman, 1991). ('Pig Land' is not to be confused with 'Pig Island', i.e. New Zealand, as Captain Cook introduced pigs there – see Green 1998). In Scouse dialect, the phrase 'Irish cattle' means 'pigs'! See also *Irish bacon* and *Irish as Paddy Murphy's pig, as*.

Irish pigeon Or Irish pidgin. Incorrect name for Hiberno-English; for which, see *Irish English*.

Irish pike Weapon with a long shaft and iron head used in the *Irish Rebellion*. Joyce (1910) called it a 'croppy pike'; he describes it as having 'combined in one a long sharp spear, a small axe, and a hook for catching the enemy's horse-reins'. Christensen (1996) calls it a 'Fenian pike'. See also *Irish croppie, Irish pikeman*.

Irish pikeman As Christensen (1996) calls the *Irish rapparee*, an irregular soldier during 1688–92 (the word is actually derived from the Ir. *rapaire* = short pike). See also *Irish pike*.

'Irish' Pimlico Area of Dublin off the Coombe in the Liberties. The prefix 'Irish' was sometimes used by the British to distinguish it from the original Pimlico in London.

Irish Pipe Band Band of Irish pipers. The Royal Scottish Pipe Band Association is affiliated to it.

Irish piper Player of the *Irish bagpipes*. The Irish pipers previously had a military as well as a musical significance and were present at various battles, including the 1544 siege of Boulogne. They sometimes accompanied *Irish kernes*. 'The Irish Piper' (c.1846) is a famous painting by Alfred Fripp which hangs in the Bristol Art Gallery.

Irish Pipers, King of the The famous Irish piper Leo Rowsome (1900–70) (Boylan, 1998).

Irish pipes *(Na píopaí)*. As the *Irish Union pipes* are often called (e.g. in Patrick O'Farrell's *Pocket Companion for the Irish or Union Pipes* (1810).

Irish pippin Or Kerry Irish pippin. A variety of cider apple (see website www.cumminsnursery.com). See also *Irish canary*.

Irish pitscher The name refers to two distinct varies of apples: a golden-brown apple from Co. Sligo with a pink flush and a golden russet, and a small Scottish apple that ripens early and is greenish-yellow. See also *Irish canary*.

Irish place-name lore As Stalmaszczyk (1997a) defines *dinnseanchas*, an Irish word which means literally 'topography' but also, by extension, refers to a uniquely Irish branch of folklore dealing with the mythological and legendary origins of place names.

Irish Plague, the The offshoot epidemics of the bubonic plague that occurred in Ireland in 1348–50, 1574–6, 1604–5 and 1650–1 (Kohn, 1995). See also *Irish ague, Irish fever*.

'Irish' plankton There is a unique variety of plankton called *nitokra hibernica*, which has two subspecies: *bulgarica* and *hibernica* (see webpage *European Register of Marine Species)*.

'Irish' plantations A misnomer for settlement of English and Scottish planters, not Irish, in Ireland, mainly during the reigns of Queen Elizabeth I and King James I but also up to the mid-eighteenth century. See also *Irish Society*.

'Irish planter' An incorrect appellation for an English or Scottish colonist of the so-called *'Irish' plantations*. Brady (2000) uses the term with reference to Sir Walter Raleigh.

Irish planxty A (lively) harp tune usually written in honour of a patron. See also *Irish harp*.

Irish plasterwork The eighteenth-century stuccowork found on ceilings of buildings in the *Irish rococo* and neo-Classical styles (Brady, 2000).

Irish plough A primitive type of plough: the 'common' Irish plough of the eighteenth century as opposed to the early-nineteenth-century metal swing (or wheel-less) plough (Connolly, 1998). See also *Irish ard, Irish foot-plough, Irish spade*.

Irish pluggy A wheelbarrow (Green, 1998). For synonyms, see *Irish baby buggy*.

Irish plum Yet another synonym for a potato (see website *The Probert Encyclopaedia)*. This may, however, be an adaptation

of the original phrase 'Munster plum', also meaning potato.
See *Irish apple* for other synonyms.

Irish plunderer, wild As *Chambers* and Cochrane (1988) refer to
the *Irish rapparee*.

Irish point (OED) See *Irish point lace*.

Irish point lace Type of *Irish lace* which was once used to em-
bellish the gown for a trousseau (Ballard, 1998). A trousseau refers to 'the clothes (and sometimes household linen
etc) collected by a bride for her marriage' (*Chambers*).

Irish point to point No relation to *Irish point lace* but a cross-
country horse race. The first such race in Ireland took place
in Co. Cork in 1752 between two gentlemen. See *Irish Classics* for other horse-racing events.

Irish poker 1 According to Connor Callahan, the 'Irish Poker
Game' 'is set up similar to pinball ... but it uses small balls
that you actually hit with a pool cue which is hit up a ramp
that takes the ball to holes that have different cards on them.
The object is to hit balls 5 or 7 to the correct hole to make
the best hand' (www.gameroomantiques.com). **2** Irish poker
is also a type of card game with four cards and in which
jokers win (for the complicated rules of this game, see the
webpage *Irish Poker* by Joe Jemrosic on www.online-visions.
com). See *'Irish' backgammon* for other games.

Irish pollan A type of fish that has always been prized as a
valuable food source, particularly during the Irish Famine
and can be found in Loughs Neagh, Ree and Derg (Bluett,
1994). See also *Irish fish, the; Irish lord; Irish trout*.

Irish pompano A synonym of *Irish mojarra*.

Irish Pooka 'The Irish Pooka is much tougher and rougher than
friendly English Puck, who at his worst is only amusingly
mischievous, while the pooka can ... be frightening and
harmful in its exploits' (MacManus, 1959). The pooka is a
type of fairy who can also take the form of a goat. See also
Irish leprechaun, Irish water horse.

Irish Poor Law, 1838 Modelled on the English Poor Law of
1834 and based on Archbishop Whately's Report of the
Poor Inquiry, 1836. It tried to relieve the squalid conditions
of the poor and give them food. As Kinealy (1995) observes,
it differed from the English Poor Law in that relief was confined to the workhouse and 'no "right" to relief existed'.

Eventually a system of outdoor relief (to the poor outside the workhouse) was implemented through this law.

Irish poplin Wilcox (1969) describes Irish poplin, which French Protestant refugees brought to England and Ireland in the eighteenth century, as 'a ribbed fabric with fine silk warp and a heavy worsted filling used for dressed coats, suits, raincoats and ski suits'. See also *Irish flax, Irish lace*.

'Irish porridge' The Council of Valence condemned the treatise *De Predestinatione* (851) by John Scottus Eriugena by calling it *pultes Scottorum* (Irish porridge), a pun on his name. The word 'porridge' may have been used because the treatise was indigestable, like lumpy porridge.

Irish Port Or Port Erin, the nearest port of the Isle of Man to Ireland (Webber, 1987). See also *Irish Sea, Jewel in the*.

Irish posture A faked fainting fit, in order to shirk work (Green, 1996). See also *Irish pasture*.

Irish potato (*Solanum teberosum*) The common potato, as opposed to the sweet potato. In Irish, it is called simply *prata*; the phrase *prata na hÉireann* ('the Irish potato') is used only for the title of the nineteenth-century ballad (Donnelly, 1987). The potato is so closely associated with Ireland that often nicknames for both are related. For instance, an Irishman has sometimes been called a 'potato-eater' or 'potato head' (Green, 1996), and the Irish have been called 'potato people' (Eagleton, 1999). The name 'Murphy' could be applied to both an Irishman and a potato (Green, 1998). Thus a person called 'Murphy' was nicknamed 'peeler' (one who peels potatoes) (RDGED) and 'Murphyland' is Ireland (Green, 1998). Similarly, 'spud' is a name for both the potato and an Irishman (Green, 1996; RDGED, Vol. 3). In Ireland the 'spud' is also the throwing line behind which players in *Irish skittles* must stand (Law, 1998). Similarly, the Irishman has been called a 'spud-nigger' (see *Irish wog*). Other Irish-associated nicknames of the potato include 'Mick' and 'Dono-van' (Rawson, 1991), as well as 'bog oranges' and 'Munster plums' (see *Irish apple* for other synonyms). They are also called 'navigators' (because, according to Green, 1996, many nineteenth-century Irishmen worked as navvies; yet it is really rhyming slang: 'navigator Scot' = 'potatoes all hot'). Talking of 'taters' or 'tatties', in American slang an Irish child has been called a 'tater tot'. See *Irish cobbler, Irish Home Ruler, Irish queen, Irish red.*

Irish potato, the birthplace of the Or 'birthplace of the Irish white potato'. Epithet of the Titicaca Plateau in the Andes, situated 10,000 feet above sea level, where the Aymara Indians developed the *chuño* or freeze-dried potato (www.sunspiced.com).

Irish potato bread As *boxty* is described (Brady, 2000). The Ulster equivalent is 'fadge'.

Irish Potato Famine Term some writers (e.g. Curran, 2000) prefer for the *Irish Famine.*

Irish potato famine fungus The fungus *phytophthora infestans (Mont.) de Bary,* from North America (see work by Alice M. De Jarnett at www.aibs.org).

Irish potato of all, the hottest As Eagleton (1999) calls Northern Ireland, even the name of which is a bone of contention. See also *Irish Revolution, the Second.*

Irish potato soup Made with potatoes, garlic, mace, thyme, bay leaf, parsley and chives (Sheridan, 1965). Blake adds chopped mint to this recipe (1971).

Irish potato stuffing Special stuffing of potatoes, onions, chopped goose liver, butter, thyme, sage, salt and pepper (Sheridan, 1965). It was prepared to accompany Michaelmas goose or duck on 29 September (it was once common for the poor to be given a goose at Michaelmas).

Irish poteen Home-made *Irish whiskey,* often distilled illicitly. As Partridge (1937) observes, it was called 'plain whiskey', as opposed to the customed drink, which was called 'the king's whiskey' or 'parliament whiskey', as well as 'the native' (Share, 1997). Illicit whiskey is also called 'the quare stuff' (see website *The O'Byrne Files: Dublin Slang Dictionary and Phrasebook).* Irish poteen is also called 'the real stuff' (Share, 1997) – not to be confused with 'the real thing', i.e. Scotch whisky (Green, 1998). The Scottish equivalent of poteen is 'peat-reek', i.e. 'illicitly distilled (Scotch) whisky' (Green, 1998). Moreover, the hated exciseman, who would try to prevent the distillation of poteen, was called a 'gauger' (see webpage *Glossary of Irish Whiskey Terms).* Curran (2000) says that 'leprechaun' poteen was very sweet but would rob men of their senses.

Irish pot still 1 Type of *Irish whiskey* (Magee, 1980). **2** The still used in making this whiskey.

Irish pot still whiskey 'The term "Irish pot still whiskey" requires that the spirit be distilled in the state [in Ireland] solely in pot stills, from a mash of cereal grains normally grown in the state' (Magee, 1980). See also *Irish whiskey*.

Irish pound Twelve-thirteenths of a pound sterling, in Irish called a 'punt' (and since, of course, replaced by the euro). See also *Irish penny*. A 'sky diver' (i.e. 'fiver') meant an Irish five-pound note (also called a 'nun with a price on her head' – Share, 1997 – as the five-pound note featured Mother McAuley). A 'Joyce' was an Irish ten-pound note; a 'Danny boy' or a 'score' was a twenty'; a 'walrus' or 'nicker' was a fifty-pound note; and a 'ton' was a hundred-pound note (see website *Yahoo's Everyday English and Slang in Ireland)*. A 'monkey' was 'five hundred Irish pounds' (see website *The O'Byrne Files Dublin Slang Dictionary and Phrasebook)*, although the same phrase was used outside Ireland by stockbrokers to mean 50,000 (Partridge, 1937). See also *Irish jane, Irish penny, Irish pound, Irish shilling*.

Irish praying stick Also called 'prayer stick', a stick which has three series of five notches (for illustration see Sharkey, 1985). Sharkey writes, 'On Patten Day crowds of country people congregated at the nearest shrine to pray ... using notched prayer sticks.'

Irish press bed The cupboard bed ('press' = cupboard). A tall cupboard which stands against the wall. It has two doors which, when opened, reveal a fold-down bed that can be lowered. During the day, to save space, it is pulled up again inside the cupboard. See also *Irish box bed*.

'Irish' Prima Donna Catherine Hayes (1825–1861), a soprano who was actually called the 'Hibernian Prima Donna', which is the subtitle of the eponymous biography by Basil Walsh. Hayes was born in poverty in Co. Limerick and gained fame among audiences in Paris, Milan, London and New York. According to Green (1998), in Australian slang a 'Catherine Hayes' is a drink of claret, sugar and nutmeg (named after either the singer herself or a namesake 'who murdered her lover following a drinking bout'). See also *Irish Caruso, Irish nightingale*.

'Irish' private jaunting car Or simply 'private jaunting car'. An *Irish jaunting car* for private use. The driver's seat is further back than on the standard jaunting car and the seats are better-upholstered. This car was designed by Christopher Killinger and displayed at the Dublin International Exhibition of 1865 (Smith, 1988).

Irish Professional People Living in England, New A category of Irish, the abbreviation for which is 'NIPPLEs' (Eagleton, 1999).

Irish progressive stage Prison system established by Sir Walter Crofton in 1854. This system had four stages: solitary confinement, hard labour, training and release on licence. Also called the *Irish system*. See also *Irish Jailic, Irish Siberia*.

Irish promotion 1 As a synonym of *Irish rise*, a reduction in pay (Partridge, 1937) and, by extension, demotion or dismissal (Green, 1996). The OED also gives the form 'Irishman's promotion'. Likewise, a 'Mexican promotion' or a 'Mexican raise' is 'a better job but one that brings no increase in salary' (Green, 1996). **2** Erection (Green, 1996). **3** Onanism (Share, 1997). See also *Irish wedding*.

Irish pronunciation, received 'A rhotic accent and the prestige pronunciation of Radio Telefís Éireann. It is closer to R.P. than other varieties of Irish speech and is favoured by middle-class speakers of Anglo-Irish' (McArthur, 1992). See also *Irish English*.

Irish pub An important institution found not only in Ireland but abroad that sells Irish drinks like *Irish stout* and *Irish whiskey* and has Irish-style decoration: 'Critical to the Irish pub is décor – hard benches, stressed pine furniture, caustic-dipped and worm-perforated, package ornaments that include obsolete and valueless book-club editions, household and farmyard utensils' (Vallely, 1999). See also *Irishisation, Irish theme bar*.

Irish pub joke A sub-category of an *Irish joke* usually told in – and invariably about – an *Irish pub* or drinking.

'Irish' Puffin Island The Puffin Island in Co. Kerry, as opposed to the Puffin Island just off Llandudno in north Wales.

'Irish' pug Actually the proper name is 'Mere's pug', which is a type of moth: a subspecies of *Eupithecia intricate*, or *ssp.-hibernica*. See also *Irish annulet, Irish Tinkers*.

Irish Pugin, the Referring to Killarney, Co. Kerry, Killanin (1962) records that St Mary's Cathedral (built 1842–55) was constructed: 'by Augustus Welby Pugin (spire and nave completed by Ashlin and Coleman of Dublin); interior decoration designed by J. J. McCarthy, the Irish Pugin.' Pugin (1812–52) was a famous English architect and designer.

Irish punch See *Irish whiskey punch*.

Irish punchmarks Special distinguishing marks on eighteenth-century *Irish silver*. For instance, the Dublin hallmark was a crowned harp *(Antique Collecting,* 21).

Irish punt The *Irish pound*.

Q

Irish Q-word Eagleton (1999) writes that in Ireland: 'there is nothing ... of any significance whatsoever beginning with the letter "Q". Irish scholars have written books and held conferences on why this is so, and the government has offered a £20,000 reward to anyone who can discover an interesting Irish Q-word.' Eagleton also mentions the theory that an eighteenth-century Dublin man invented the word 'quiz' to win a bet. Certainly in *Irish English* (see Share, 1997) there are several words beginning with 'Q' (see, for example, the word 'quilt' in *Irish quilt*). Although there is no letter 'Q' in the *Irish language,* Celtic scholars have long described the relationship between Irish (and the other Goidelic languages, i.e. Scots Gaelic and Manx) and Welsh (and the Brythonic languages of Breton and Cornish) as Q and P respectively. In this linguistic classification (explained in a very readable way by Ellis, 1985), the actual Irish Q-word is a word with the similar plosive letter 'C' (or 'G'), which often corresponds to a cognate (a word derived from the same root) P-word (or B-word) in Welsh. Here are a few examples of such words:

English	Irish	Welsh
head	ceann	pen
five	cúig	pump
son	mac	mab (or 'ap' before names)
tree	crann	pren (i.e. wood)
every	gach	pawb
worm	cruimh	pryf

Irish quarters Pub game in which you spin a quarter (of a dollar) and try to finish a pint of beer before it stops spinning. See also *'Irish' backgammon*.

Irish queen 1 Variety of potato. See also *Irish apple, Irish cobbler, Irish red*. Incidentally, one nickname for Queen Victoria was the 'famine queen', as the *Irish Famine* occurred during her reign. **2** 'Irish queen' is also a variety of cucumber from New England.

Irish queen of the fairies The epithet of Brí (CGG), who died of a broken heart as her father Midir the Proud would not let Liath, the man she loved, meet her. See also *Irish fairy queen*.

Irish queer Sean Ó Faoláin says: 'An Irish queer is a fellow who prefers women to drinks' (quoted by MacHale, nd). The derogatory word 'queer' is not commonly used though, Dubliners use the slang word 'fag' and in Limerick the word is 'steamer' (see website *Barking Lizards: Limerick/Dublin Slang*). 'Steamer' is also apparently used in Cork (see website *Bazzers, Steamers and Mebs: A Rough Guide to Cork Slang*). By coincidence, like the word 'fag', 'steamer' is a word for a cigarette (from Shelta 'stima' = pipe – see Share, 1997). See also *'Irish by birth but Greek by injection'*, as well as the second meaning of *Irish dip*.

Irish Question, the Usually means the *Irish Home Rule* question. Neil Evans, with reference to the way in which Irish patriots influenced their Celtic cousins, writes that 'In the nineteenth century the Irish Question created Welsh and Scottish questions on its coat-tails' (*Planet* 80, April/May 1990).

Irish quilt 'Irish quilts generally do not include a wadding or filling layer, but are of two layers of fabric. These two layers are usually joined by quilting stitches, which are worked all over the bed cover in a chevron or wave pattern' (see Ballard, a). This is not to be confused with the word 'quilt', as used in *Irish English*, which refers to a coward (Kavanagh, 1959) or an old woman, rascal, or timid, effeminate man. It also, when used as a verb, means 'to run away' (Share, 1997). See also *Irish patchwork*.

R

Irish rabbit By allusion to Welsh rabbit (toasted cheese on toast), Ayto (1994) has coined a similar name for the Irish version which includes onions, gherkins, vinegar and herbs. No relation to *Irish hare*.

'Irish Race' What 'Fine Gael' (the name of a conservative Irish political party) means in Irish.

Irish Race Conventions The Irish-American republican organisation, Clan na Gael, staged the first Irish Race Conventions in New York in March 1916 to appeal to American patriots to lend their support and funds to the Irish cause. It was here that the *Friends of Irish Freedom* were founded.

Irish Racing, the Headquarters of For this see *Irish Classics, Home of the*.

'Irish' rag-and-louse In the Northamptonshire dialect of English, an Irish labourer, due to his poor living conditions and exposure to the elements, was called an *'Irish' rag-and-louse* (Grimes, 1991).

Irish Railroad Municipal bus line (in the United States) used mainly by Irish commuters (Green, 1996). See also *Irish Channel*.

Irish Railways, Father of the Epithet of William Dargan (1799–1867), who in 1831 started the Dublin-to-Kingstown line (Connolly, 1998). See also *Irish Mail; Irish roads, king of the; Irishman* (Appendix 2).

'Irish' rake moss *Irish moss* that has been raked from the boat. More often it is called simply rake moss (Pratt, 1988).

Irish Rangers, Royal A regiment of the British army formed in 1968 from a merger of the Royal Ulster Rifles and Royal Ulster Fusiliers. In 1922, it merged with the UDR (Ulster Defence Regiment) to form the Royal Irish Regiment (Hickey and Doherty, 1980).

Irish rapparee The term refers mostly to the dispossessed Irish Catholic landlords who, after their dispersion by Cromwell, turned to plunder and revenge. Often called simply 'rapparees' but some writers use the prefix 'Irish' (e.g. William Carleton in his 1850 novel, *Redmond Count O'Hanlon, the Irish Rapparee*). Réamonn Ó hAnluain, i.e. Redmond O'Hanlon (1640–81) led a band of fifty outlaws and robbed English planters. He had a birthmark of a broken cross – indicative of his impending 'martyrdom'/early death. He was shot by his foster brother Arthur O'Hanlon for a £200 reward. See also *Irish bandit, Irish pikeman, Irish rogues, 'Irish' Wild Geese*.

Irish rat In a separate entry on the 'Irish rat', Knowles (2000) writes: 'According to legend, Irish rats could be killed or driven away by rhyming.' Interestingly, in Shakespeare's *As You Like It* (Act III, Scene ii), Rosalind says: 'I was rimed since Pythagoras' time, that I was an Irish rat.' Here she is alluding to the Pythagorean doctrine of the transmigration of souls; the word 'rimed' again reflects the belief that rats were killed in this way. Moreover, for some unknown reason, in Liverpudlian dialect an (Irish) Catholic was called a 'rat catcher' (see website *Merseytalk9*, and for other Liverpudlian phrases about the Irish see *Irish cattle; Irish Guards Band; Irish magnifying glass; Irish submarine, to make sails for an; Irish takeaway*).

Irish rebel One who took part in the *Irish Rebellion* or indeed in any uprising. In the eighteenth and nineteenth centuries he was nicknamed 'red shank', since his legs were often reddened from exposure to the elements (Share, 1997). (No relation to a 'redneck' which means a 'culchie' – see website *The O'Byrne Files Dublin Slang Dictionary and Phrasebook*).

Irish Rebellion There have been several revolts or uprisings in Ireland on various scales, yet this term is applied mainly to: **1** The 1641 Rebellion, when, mainly in Ulster, Irish lords and peasants massacred planters (see *Irish planters*). **2** The Irishmen's Rebellion of 1798. See *Irishmen, United*.

Irish red 1 A hair colouring lighter than ginger and not quite as fair as titian or strawberry blond. It is so called because many Irish people have this subtly 'red' type of hair. Taking this to its extremes, the website *The Racial Slur Database* traces the nickname 'clown' for Irish and Scottish people to 'a stereotyped image of Irish people: bushy red hair, a large red nose (from excessive drinking) and colorful clothes, often with plaids.' See also *red-headed Irishman* (Appendix 3). The colour red features in several phrases connected with the Irish. There was the 'red shank' (for which see *Irish rebel*), as well as a 'redneck' (an Irish immigrant and in Lancashire a Catholic – Green, 1998 – yet in Ireland it is used in the sense of 'culchie' – see Share, 1997). **2** A darker type of lager, e.g. Killian's Irish Red lager. **3** Irish reds are a variety of potato. See also *Irish cobbler, Irish queen*. **4** 'Irish Red' is also a type of plant: *Mammillaria elongata.*

Irish red and white setter A sub-breed of the *Irish red setter* which is really white with red patches, often symmetrical, on the face (see website *Dogdaze designs*).

Irish red deer Ó hÓgáin (1990) alludes twice to the 'native Irish red deer', the type of deer found in Ireland. Not to be confused with the extinct *great Irish deer* or *Irish elk*.

Irish red grouse Apparently among a group of Irish specialists, an Irish subspecies of red grouse is being considered as distinct. Yet the differences between the two types of bird are extremely subtle and would be noticed only by expert ornithologists: the colour variations are hardly discernible and there is interbreeding with the British species. (By contrast, non-Irish forms of coal tit and dipper are extremely rare in Ireland.) See also *Irish coal tit.*

Irish red setter Alternative name for the *Irish setter.*

Irish redstreak A variety of apple first recorded in 1831 (NAR). See also *Irish canary.*

Irish red terrier A synonym of the *Irish terrier.*

Irish reef See *Irishman's reef* (Appendix 3). (*Webster's* records both forms).

Irish reel (Ir. *cor*). An Irish dance in 4/4 time. Law (1998) says: 'A considerable number of the best-known Irish reels are Scottish in origin.' No connection with the Irish expression 'reel foot', which means 'a deformed foot ... thought to be induced by walking in pregnancy over a grave' (from Ir. *reilig* = grave – see Ó Muirithe, 1997). See also *Irish haye, Irish jig, Irish trot.*

Irish Reform Association Founded in 1904 and organised by the Fourth Earl of Dunraven to campaign for limited devolution (i.e. not complete Home Rule). It was opposed by unionists.

'Irish' Regent Street See *Irish Bond Street.*

Irish Regiment, Royal See *Irish Rangers, Royal.*

Irish reinette A variety of medium-sized apple from north-west England which is 'yellowish green with dull brownish red flush and large russet patches' (NAR). See also *Irish canary.*

Irish Remonstrance The 'loyal formulary of Irish remonstrance' drafted in 1661, stated that Irish Catholics should acknowledge Charles II as their king (Connolly, 1998).

Irish Renaissance Term used by some (e.g. Richard Fallis as the title of his 1947 work) for the *Irish Literary Renaissance*.

Irish Repealers Followers of Daniel O'Connell who sought repeal of the union of Great Britain and Ireland. See also *Irish king, uncrowned*.

Irish Republic Or 'Republic of Ireland' or simply 'Ireland' (Éire), as the modern state of Ireland has been called since Easter Monday 1949, as opposed to the *Irish Free State*. In Northern Ireland, some Irish nationalists still prefer to call it the South, the Free State or the Twenty-six Counties (as opposed to the Six Counties of Northern Ireland). Note that three counties of the province of Ulster (Cavan, Donegal and Monaghan) are not part of Northern Ireland but the Republic.

Irish Republic, American Association for the Recognition of the Organisation founded by Éamon de Valera in 1920 and nicknamed 'Growl' (Share, 1997). See also *Irish Freedom, Friends of; Irish Northern Aid Committee*.

Irish Republican Army (IRA) 1 The IRA was founded at the time of – and played a key role in – the fight for the early Irish Republic. From the inception of the *Irish Free State,* the IRA was bitterly opposed to the Treaty, which included partition; it was this opposition that led to the *Irish Civil War*. **2** The name 'IRA' has also been used by a group active in the last few decades that seeks a united Ireland (i.e. the Provisional IRA and its factions). It is perhaps no coincidence that the eras of both the original IRA and the current IRA have been called 'the Troubles'. The IRA's struggle has been directed mainly against Unionist/British rule in Northern Ireland. The organisation's frequent use of violence has been criticised not only by equally violent Unionist sectarian groups but also by the majority of moderate, peace-loving Nationalists and Unionists alike. The IRA has also suffered a great deal of internal opposition, leading to the emergence of the various factions listed below, not to mention the fellow nationalist INLA (Irish National Liberation Army).

IRA, Continuity (CIRA) Extremist group that split from the *Provisional IRA* in 1995. From September 1998, only this group and the *Real IRA* remained active.

IRA, Official (OIRA) Term given to those who remained in the *IRA* when there was an internal division and the *Provisional IRA* was formed. The group has been mainly inactive since its 1972 ceasefire.

IRA, Provisional The more extreme members of the *IRA* founded the Provisional IRA to continue their armed struggle; the comparatively more moderate *IRA* had accepted the cease-fire. In American slang the term 'Provo' (used by people who perhaps don't know what it means) refers to any Irish-man (as did the name 'Fenian' – see the website *The Racial Slur Database*). Another shortened form of this term is Pro-vie or Provvie (Green, 1998).

IRA, Real A splinter group which did not accept the IRA cease-fire. The group is notorious for the 1998 bombing in Omagh, in which 28 people were killed.

Irish Republican Brotherhood (IRB) A revolutionary group that stemmed from Fenianism and was founded in 1858 by James Stephens. An early name for this group was the *Irish Revolutionary Brotherhood;* members referred to it as 'the Brotherhood', 'the Society' or 'the Organisation'. The IRB was organised under 'centres', with captains and sergeants, and their oath swore 'allegiance to the Irish Republic' (yet it was not until 1949 that the words 'Irish Republic' were officially used). In 1867, their abortive rising was a great blow to the movement, as was the existence of the rival *Irish Home Rule* movement, with the IRB being overshad-owed by Parnell. The organisation later came to prominence once more in the *Anglo-Irish War;* their cause was shortly afterwards to be channelled by Bulmer Hobson into that of the *Irish Volunteers,* with which the IRB co-existed for a short period.

Irish republicanism, the father of Theobald Wolfe Tone (1763–98), a *United Irishman* 'widely regarded as the father of Irish republicanism' (Brady, 2000; see also 'Tone is a founding father of modern Irish republicanism', Connolly, 1998). Like Parnell (see *Irish king, uncrowned),* Tone is another example of a great Irish patriot who came from a Protestant family background. Tone was sentenced to death for his part in the *Irish Insurrection*, but slit his own throat in prison. See also *Irishmen, United*.

Irish Republican Movement, birthplace of the So de Valera called Belfast in his 1933 broadcast to America (cited by Douglas, 1936).

Irish Republican Socialist Party Founded in 1974 and considered to be the political wing of the *Irish National Liberation Army* (as Sinn Féin is to the *IRA*). Its main aim is to bring about a united, thirty-two-county socialist republic, and it has criticised the *IRA* ceasefire.

Irish RM The Resident Magistrate (during the British administration in Ireland). Edith Somerville and Martin (Violet) Ross wrote a book called *Some Experiences of an Irish RM* (1899).

Irish returnees Term used by Arrowsmith (2000) for Irish people who return to the 'Old Sod' after emigrating. In Munster, the word 'narrowback' refers to 'a person of Irish parentage born in America, especially one who returns to Ireland to live' (Share, 1997). See also '*Irish*' *narrowback*.

Irish Revival 1 Welch (1996) refers to: 'The fourteenth-century period known as the Irish Revival, characterised by the adoption of Irish customs by the great Anglo-Norman families.' See also *Irish than the Irish, more*. **2** With reference to Yeats, Synge and Lady Gregory, whose 'concern to use Gaelic material as the basis of a revitalised Irish literature in English has encouraged the alternative label Anglo-Irish Revival' (Connolly, 1998).

Irish Revival, Anglo- See *Irish Revival*.

Irish Revival, father of the Standish James O'Grady (1846–1928), historian and novelist, was thus dubbed by Yeats (Foster, 1989). His epithet is sometimes 'the father of the Irish literary revival' (Boylan, 1998).

Irish revivalist Term usually applied to those Irish literary pioneers, Yeats, *et al*, whose work constituted the *Irish* or *Anglo-Irish Revival*.

Irish Revolution 1 The Irish were always revolting against the English. Yet this term refers usually to the most serious and well-coordinated revolts, such as the *Irish Rebellion*. **2** Morton (1930) used this term to refer to the *Anglo-Irish War*.

Irish Revolution, the Second With reference to Northern Ireland and the Troubles, Townsend writes that 'the dramatic change [historical change brought about by intense political activity] ... may indeed be thought of as a second Irish revolution' *(Irish Studies Review*, Vol. 8, No. 1, April 2000).

Irish Revolutionary Brotherhood An early name for the *Irish Republican Brotherhood*.

Irish Revolutionary Republican Brotherhood See previous entry.

Irish Rhine 'The Blackwater from Cappoquin to Youghal is almost delightful enough to make one forgive the guide books for calling it the Irish Rhine' (Ó Faoláin, 1941).

'Irish' ribbonists The name 'Ribbonmen' was first recorded as a synonym of the *United Irishmen* in 1811. Like their predecessors the Defenders and the Whiteboys, the Ribbonmen were staunch Catholics and believed in egalitarianism and Irish independence. They protested against tithes (See also *Irish Tithe War)* and sought to protect the rights of tenant farmers. Their methods included sending threatening letters to landlords (see also *Irish Moonlighters)*, maiming cattle, burning crops and even killing landlords and their representatives.

Irishrie Misspelling or old spelling of *Irishry*, for instance in the Encycl. Brit. (Vol. 15). The plural, 'Irishries', is more common. Macalister (1937), for instance, talks of 'the Irishries of Liverpool.'

Irish rifle 1 Small comb (Partridge, 1937). **2** Fingers (Green, 1996). Similar to the term 'Welsh comb'. Other ethnic equivalents include 'German comb' (the hand) and 'Scotch louse trap' (a comb) (Green, 1998). A similar expression is the nineteenth-century Anglo-Irish one 'What the Connaught men shot at', i.e. nothing (Partridge, 1937). See also *Irish musket*.

Irish ringfort (Ir. *ráth* or *lios)* A special type of mound structure. The prefix 'Irish' is often used, for instance in the title of Matthew Stuart's book *The Irish Ringfort* (1997). In popular superstition, it is believed that these ancient forts are inhabited by the fairies. Indeed, the word *lios* in particular has the connotation of 'fairy mound', and in Irish there is a link between 'fairy' and 'fairy mound' (both *sí*) as Irish fairies live in such mounds.

Irish riots, anti- Morgan (1996) refers to 'anti-Irish riots' in nineteenth-century America. These began in 1834 with the burning of the Ursuline convent in Charlestown, Massachusetts. Similar riots followed in Philadelphia and Louisville; while in Lowell and Lawrence, Massachusetts, fires were started in Irish neighbourhoods. The anti-Irish feeling was essentially inspired by anti-Catholic sentiment; this is why Irish Protestants tried to disassociate themselves from the Catholic Irish by calling themselves *Scotch-Irish* (Appendix 4). See also *Irish Need Apply, No.*

Irish rise Or more rarely 'Irishman's rise' (OED). **1** A reduction in pay; a synonym of *Irish promotion* (Partridge, 1937). **2** Detumescence (Share, 1997). **3** Erection (Green, 1996). In this final meaning, other Irish-sounding synonyms are used, e.g. with reference to the granite mountains of Co. Down, 'Mountains of Mourne' (rhymes with 'horn' – see Green, 1998). See also *Irish toothache.*

Irish Rising, United See *Irishmen, United.* See also '*Irish' Easter Rising.*

Irish Riviera 1 'New York's shore at Far Rockaway, for example, was known as the "Irish Riviera"' (Morgan, 1996). **2** For Bostonians, the Irish Riviera was also the coastal stretch of 'the South Shore from Nantasket Beach as far south as Sandwich in the Uppa cape' (see website *Wicked Good Guide to Boston English*). See also *Irish Bostonian.* **3** Glengariff and the coast around Garnish Island, of which (with reference to the area's dramatic beauty, not its thriving tourist industry) Morton (1930) declared 'this is the Riviera of Ireland!'.

Irish Road Dodd (1972) refers to 'the Irish Road leading to Holyhead' in north Wales: there has always been some kind of a ferry service from Holyhead to Ireland. See also *Irish Mail, Irish Way.*

'Irish' road bowls An Irish game played with a twenty-eight-ounce iron ball (or 'bullet', hence the game is also called bullets), which two players throw along a stretch of road usually about three miles long. In the last century, it was played all over Ireland but is now found mainly in Counties Armagh and Cork. See also *Irish skittles.*

'Irish' road fever Or in Ireland just 'road fever' – so called as the 1847 fever 'was carried down the roads by people fleeing from the more stricken counties in the west' (Kee, 1980).

See also *Irish fever*.

Irish roads, king of the Charles (Carlo) Bianconi (1786–1875).
Bianconi was an Italian immigrant who came to Ireland in
1802 and in 1815 started his first horse-drawn car service in
Co. Tipperary, and later a network of open-topped cars
('Bians') from Dublin. His sobriquet comes from the title of
the book by M. O'C. Bianconi and S. J. Watson, *Bianconi,
King of the Irish Roads* (1962). See also *Irish jaunting car; Irish
Railways, Father of the*.

'Irish' Robin Hood 1 Ned Kelly. Peter Carey's historical novel
True History of the Kelly Gang (2001) is reviewed (online) by
Anthony Quinn, who uses the title for his review 'Robin
Hood of the Outback'. The title of the article reflects Carey's
new treatment of the Irish-Australian outlaw, presenting
him not as a mere robber but, according to Quinn, as 'a folk
hero and freedom fighter, a defiant exemplar of Irish-Aus-
tralian cussedness in the face of colonial oppression'. **2** The
Irish Chicagoan gangster Bugs Moran (for whom see *Irish
Gang, The*). Similarly, the Welsh Robin Hood was Twm Siôn
Cuti (Edwards, 1998) and the 'Robin Hood of Scotland'
was Robert McGregor or Rob Roy. See also *Irish Rob Roy*.

'Irish' Rob Roy Morton (1930) described the Irish heroine Grace
(Granuaile) O'Malley as 'a kind of feminine Rob Roy of
Ireland'. O'Malley (c.1530–c.1603) was a legendary female
pirate of Connacht who was frequently in conflict with the
English Crown. The original Rob Roy was Robert McGregor (1671–1734), the Scottish outlaw hero. By analogy, See
also *'Irish' Robin Hood, 'Irish' Walter Scott*.

'Irish' rock chopper Or simply 'rock chopper', yet the word
'Irish' could be prefixed for impact. 'Rock chopper' is Australian slang for 'the original Irish immigrants, who were
mainly convicts and, as such, condemned to hard labour'
(Green, 1998). By extension, it means 'Catholic' (rock chopper = RC = Roman Catholic). See also *Irish Catholic, White*.

Irish rock 'n' roller, the first Rory Gallagher (1948–1995), guit-
arist, singer and songwriter, who sold over 30 million records in the 1970s. Brady (2000) uses this epithet.

Irish rococo As Boyce (1985) observes, the eighteenth-century
style of furniture known as Irish rococo was later called
Irish Chippendale.

Irish rogues A name for *Irish rapparees*.

Irish Romanesque An architectural term used to describe such masterpieces as the doorway of Clonfert Cathedral and Cormac's Chapel at Cashel. More rarely, it is also called 'Hiberno-Romanesque' (Fleming, *et al*, 1966). See also *Irish Georgian*.

'Irish' Romeo and Juliet Aillinn (granddaughter of the king of Leinster) and Baile (son and heir of Buain of Ulster). 'Ulster and Leinster were deadly enemies and here we have an embryonic Romeo and Juliet tragedy' (Ellis, 1987). A malevolent stranger told Baile that Aillinn could not attend their lovers' tryst as she had died (in reality she had been prevented by the warriors of Leinster). On hearing this, Baile died of grief; the same stranger then told Aillinn of Baile's death and she died of a broken heart.

Irish root 1 Penis (Partridge, 1937), also called 'Micky'. No relation to *Irish tree*. See also *Irish inch, Irish rise, Irish toothache*. **2** A potato (Green, 1998). For synonyms, see *Irish apple*.

Irish rose 1 The endemic species of wild rose *rosa hibernica* discovered by naturalist John Templeton in 1795 near Holywood (Boylan, 1998). **2** Nose (in rhyming slang), especially the red, bulbous nose of a drunkard (RDGED, Vol. 3; another Cockney rhyming-slang term for nose is 'I suppose'). Incidentally, according to Green (1998), the expression 'to pay through the nose' derives from the ninth-century practice of the Danes of splitting the noses of Irish people if they did not pay the 'nose tax' [a tax levied per head of population] . Similarly, a 'Tokyo rose' is also a nose (Green, 1998). See also *Irish snipe*. For other rhyming-slang entries, see *Irish jig, Irish lasses, Irish stew*. **3** 'A stone for throwing' (Green, 1998). See also *Irish bouquet, Irish confetti*. **4** A pattern of *Irish crochet*. **5** (Wild) Irish Rose is a pattern for a bedspread. **6** A variety of the pinkish heather, *erica*.

Irish Rose Pageant, Miss Beauty contest for Irish girls in Texas, held on St Patrick's Day (Smith, 1995). See also *Irish beauty, Irish colleen*.

Irish rosepoint Or Youghal lace, which is 'fine flat needlepoint' (Ballard, a). See also *Irish lace, Irish point lace*.

'Irish' rossie Female *Irish Traveller* (from Ir. *rásaí* = vagrant).

Irish rothling A variety of apple, also called *Irlandischer rotling*

and popularly known as 'Sam Young'. See also *Irish canary,
Irish russet*.

Irish roulette Unlike Russian roulette (with one bullet in the
chamber of the revolver), Irish roulette is played with one
CD. 'Every time a song from your CD is played, you must
finish your drink before the song ends.' The penalty for not
finishing the drink is to consume a shot of tequila (www.
barmeister.com).

Irish rounders 'Irish rounders is a bat-and-ball game similar to
softball ... played nine a side. There are four bases each
thirty yards apart. The batter stands at home base and attempts to hit the ball thrown by the server from a mark
twenty yards away' (see the website *Robert Encyclopaedia of
Sport*). See also *Irish handball*.

Irish round tower The prefix 'Irish' is often used (e.g. by Bernstein, 1980). A unique pencil-shaped tower which in Irish
is called *cloightheach* or 'bell house' (from teach = house
and clog = bell) suggesting its monastic use. It is also believed that the round tower was used as a treasury; its five-
storey height meant that it could be defended against Viking
attacks (Connolly, 1998).

Irish rug (See also W. *brethyn Iwerddon* or *Iwerddonig*) Not a car-
pet but a garment like a cloak (Logan, 1986). See also *Irish
cloak*.

Irish rundale system See *Irish openfield system*.

Irish russet A variety of apple (NAR). Perhaps identical to the
Irish rothling, popularly known as 'Sam Young'. See also
Irish canary.

Irish Russian Cocktail of vodka, kahlua, cola and Guinness.
Incidentally, the phrase 'retreat from Moscow' referred to
'the exodus from England to Ireland by the better-off that
followed the Labour landslide of 1945', i.e. tax exiles (Green,
1998; the phrase is derived from Napoleon's retreat in 1812).

Irishry 1 The Celtic (i.e. Gaelic) people in Ireland, as opposed
to the Englishry. John Milton wrote of 'The whole Irishry
of rebels'. **2** Area where Irish people live (either in or outside Ireland). **3** 'A term for Irish character or nationality or
an Irishism' (McArthur, 1992).

S

Irish Salisbury With reference to Salisbury, the city in southern England famous for its cathedral, Morton (1930) referred to Dundalk as an 'Irish Salisbury'. This is because of the market town's impressive pro-cathedral dedicated to St Patrick. See also *'Irish' Athens*, *'Irish' Salisbury Plain*.

'Irish' Salisbury Plain Or rather 'the Salisbury Plain of Ireland', as Morton (1930) dubs the Curragh. The Salisbury Plain is a large area of open country in southern England famous as the site of Stonehenge. See also *Irish Salisbury*.

Irish salmon Not a fish (see *Irish fish, the*) but rather a type of *Erica* heather with dark salmon-coloured buds (cultivated in Burncoose Nurseries, Redruth, Cornwall).

Irish saloon Term used by Morton (1930) to refer to a traditional rural *Irish pub*.

Irish sauna See *Irish bath*.

Irish saxifrage An endemic plant found chiefly in the Burren (Brady, 2000). See also *Irish bladderwort*.

Irish scale As David C. Daye refers to the distinct musical scale of the *Irish Union pipes* (see website *The Famous Penny-Chanter*). Unlike the bagpipes, the Irish Union pipes can play a complete upper octave.

'Irish' Scarlet Pimpernel Monsignor Hugh O'Flaherty (1898–1963), papal diplomat and rescuer of prisoners of war. The epithet is derived from the true story of his life told by J. P. Gallagher in *The Scarlet Pimpernel of The Vatican* (filmed in 1983 as *The Scarlet and The Black,* starring Gregory Peck). For the Dublin Pimpernel, see the *Irish Lenin*. The 'Scarlet Pimpernel' was the hero of Baroness Orczy's 1905 novel of the same name; the scarlet pimpernel flower was used as an emblem by this elusive hero, who rescued aristocrats from the guillotine.

Irish School Generally the term refers to the school of painting that includes Sean Keating, Sean O'Sullivan, Leo Whedan and Maurice Mac Gonigal (Encycl. Brit., Vol. 15). See also *Irish Impressionists*.

Irish scorpion (Ulster English) rove beetle or devil's coachman (Macafee, 1996). In Ulster, it is also called a 'gellick', a 'kee-rog' or a 'Judas Iscariot' (Macafee, 1996).

Irish Scot A Scot of Irish origin. Originally the word 'Scot' (Lat. *Scottus*) was applied to the Irish. See also *Irish porridge*. The reverse situation also occurs: Gaelic-speaking Scottish Highlanders have been called 'Irish' (Robinson, 1985). The identification between the Irish and the Scots (since they have a common Gaelic ancestry) can be seen in terms like *Scotia Magna* or *Scotia Major*, meaning Ireland (see website *Brewer's Readers Handbook*). See also *Irish Gaelic, Irish Walter Scott, Scotch Irish* (Appendix 4).

Irish screwdriver A hammer (Share, 1997). Also called a 'Paddy rammer' (see Appendix 5). Likewise, Birmingham, French, Jewish or Yiddish screwdrivers are also hammers (Green, 1996) as is a 'Chinese screwdriver' (for which see *Paddy* in Appendix 5). For other jocular names for tools, see *Irish banjo*.

Irish Sea, the The large body of water separating the east coast of Ireland from Wales, the north of England and Scotland. See also *Irish Channel; Irish Ocean; Irish Sea, Jewel in the*.

Irish Sea, Jewel in the The Isle of Man, or Mannin. Brown dubs it thus in the preface to his book *Douglas: The Premier Guide to the Isle of Man* (1995). See also *'Irish' jewel, Irish Port, Irish Summer*.

Irish sea god As Manannan Mac Lir is often called (Loomis, 1949; Dixon-Kennedy, 1997, calls him the Irish sea deity). He ruled the sea from Emain Ablach (see *Irish Otherworld*) in *Tír Tairngire* ('the Land of Promise'). He could change shape and drive across the sea in his chariot. He fathered both divine and human children and his storms destroyed the Milesian fleet. The Isle of Man (Mx *Mannin*) is named after him . See also *Irish craft gods, Irish sea goddess*.

Irish sea goddess So Muireartach is called (CGG). She captured the Cup of Victory from the Fianna. When the Fianna recaptured it, she killed many of them, until Fionn Mac Cumhaill slew her. See also *Irish lake goddess, Irish sea god*.

Irish Sea Zone With reference to the (Welsh-speaking) area of Welsh culture along the west coast of Wales, Dodd (1972) talks of 'the cultural community of the Irish Sea Zone.'

Irish seal fairy So the *róane* is called (Ir. *rón* meaning 'seal'). The *róane* is, like the selkie in Scotland and Orkney folklore, a creature that lives as a seal, but can take human shape when ashore. In some versions of its legends, a mortal can marry a female roane if she hides her sealskin when she discards it on the beach. See I*rish mermaid.*

Irish seat 'French horse-racing fans call any snags that occur during the race *banquettes irlandaises* (literally 'Irish seats', in slang)' (Green, 1996). Not to be confused with *Irish chair.*

Irish septs Literally 'sevenths', an old division of Ireland. The adjective is 'septal'. See also *Irish fifth, Irish leprechaun nation.*

Irish Self-determination League (of Great Britain) Founded in 1919 to support Irish independence and the cause of Sinn Féin, with P. J. Kelly as president. The League, which aimed to keep Irish culture alive for the Irish in England, organised classes for *Irish music* and the *Irish language.*

Irish set-dance (Ir. *damhsa seit)* **1** The type of tune for a dance, which may be in 2/4 time or occasionally in 9/8, often with the first part doubled. Often the music for this dance is played by a special set-dance band with fewer musicians than the traditional *Irish céilí band* and with electronic amplification. **2** A dance which is a set of quadrilles danced to Irish music but combining French and Irish dance steps (Vallely, 1999).

Irish settle-bed 'The Irish settle-bed has a wooden section that is hinged at the bottom, which swings out and downward to form a box-bed' (Brady, 2000). In Canada it existed as the 'Murphy bed' (not a nickname but a term named eponymously in 1959 after the manufacturer, W. L. Murphy – who may well have been Irish – see Barber, 1998). See also *Irish box bed, Irish open frame settle.*

Irish setter (Ir. *sotar rua)* A beautiful breed of dog unique to Ireland that has a smooth, silky coat and a chestnut colour. It is also called the *Irish red setter,* and one rare variety is the *Irish red and white setter.* See also *Irish blue terrier, Irish foxhound, Irish terrier, Irish water spaniel, Irish wolfhound.*

Irish seven-course meal 'A potato and a six-pack' (Morgan, 1996). See also *Irish boiled dinner, Irishman's dinner* (Appendix 3), *Irishman's four-course meal* (Appendix 3).

Irish seven step An Irish dance (Thurston, 1954).

Irish shaggy mantle As the *Irish mantle* is sometimes called (*Journal of the Manx Museum,* Vol. 5).

'Irish' Shakespeare Richard Brinsley Sheridan (1751–1816) playwright (and son of Thomas), was described by Leigh Hunt as 'a Shakespeare without a heart' (Encycl. Brit., Vol. 15). See also *Irish Dickens, 'Irish' Homer, Irish Keats, Irish Voltaire*.

Irish shamrock (Ir. *seamróg*, possibly a diminutive form of *seamair*, e.g. *Seamair Mhuire* = Mary's clover) One of the most important symbols of Ireland and a popular decoration on Irish-related products, not only because it is green (see *Irish national colour*) but also because St Patrick (see *Irish patron saint*) used its three leaves to teach the doctrine of the Holy Trinity. Even today, to 'drown the shamrock' means to drink a lot on St Patrick's Day. As an emblem, the shamrock has been used in *Irish Volunteer* flags, badges for Irish regiments in the British army and for the *Royal Irish Constabulary*, and on the logos of the Irish Tourist Board and Aer Lingus. In legend, shamrock with healing properties would grow on the spot where a *fíorláir* ('true mare', i.e. the seventh filly born, without a colt born in between) fell at birth (Ó hÓgáin, 1990). In Ulster, 'shamrock tea' is weak tea (perhaps as it tastes as though it has been made using only three leaves – Share, 1997). Bernstein (1980) talks of a 'shamrock curtain' leading to the Gaeltacht (for which see *Irish-speaking area*). There is also a type of knot called a shamrock knot (see *Irish pendant*). Moreover, in slang usage the word 'shamrock' can mean a policeman (see *Irish clubhouse* for connections between the Irish and the police), as well as a mixture of *Irish whiskey* and *Irish stout* (Green, 1998). Someone on the internet with a rather perverse sense of humour has given a new meaning to the word shamrock – namely an Irishman's private parts (www.urbandictionary.com – and see also *Irish inch*). Indeed, on the internet, new terms are continually being coined, such as the facetious 'IRISH' ('ignorant rogues in shamrock highlands' – see the webpage *Acronyms Category Listing* – but see also *Irish rogues*).

Irish shave 1 No shave at all (Green, 1996). It is analogous to the 'Jewish shave' – applying talcum powder instead of shaving (Green, 1998). See also *Irish wash*. **2** Defecation (Share, 1997).

Irish shawl 'The Irish shawl evolved from the Kashmir and Paisley shawls fashionable in the early nineteenth century. It changed in style in Ireland through the decades until in the twentieth century it was the black shawl worn principally by widows' (Connolly, 1998). A working-class female street vendor (who often wore a shawl) was called a 'shawly'. See also *Irish cloak*.

'Irish' shebeen The prefix 'Irish' is often used (e.g. by Malcolm, 1998). An illegal drinking house, often just a two-roomed shack. The word derives from the Irish *'síbín'*, which means both illicit whiskey and the place where it is served.

Irish shift Also 'Irish switch'. In American usage, an unethical 'shift' or 'switch' in political policies to suit one's own ends (Green, 1996; Share, 1997).

Irish shillelagh 1 A cudgel used in *Irish faction fights* (see also *Irish stick-fighting*). The prefix 'Irish' is often used; 'shillelagh' derives from an oak forest in Co. Wicklow of the same name. Synonyms are a 'Tipperary lawyer' and a 'Dublin dissector' (Share, 1997). Also a police truncheon in the USA was once called by the Irish surname 'Callahan' (for which see *Irish clubhouse)*; the Irish surname 'Kennedy' meant a stick, poker or blow with a poker (Partridge, 1950). **2** The shillelagh is not only a weapon, however: it can also be used as a walking stick. Perhaps one reason for the shillelagh's appeal is that it is ideally made of blackthorn, and hence, according to Kavanagh (1959), it is a good defence against the fairies. See also *Irish toothpick*.

Irish shilling Twelve-thirteenths of an English shilling, since thirteen Irish pennies made an English shilling; the Irish shilling was thus called a 'thirteener' (Share, 1997; see also the 'Manx shilling', which was 'fourteen pence English' – Moore, 1924). Possibly due to this lower value, the Irish phrase 'he isn't the full shilling' was coined to refer to someone who is mentally deficient (see Ó Muirithe 1997). Due to the bar or stroke symbol for the shilling it was also called a 'bar' (Wall, 1995), as well as a 'hog' or 'mint-hog' (Share, 1997). Note that the 'Saxon shilling' was payment for Irish recruits who enlisted in the British army in the First World War (Share, 1997). This phrase seems to be derived from the 'king's' or 'queen's shilling' (given to newly enlisted British troops – see *Brewer's*). See *Irish penny*.

Irish ship (Ir. *long Éireannach*) Well-known Irish waulking song (sung by women when waulking cloth, i.e. soaking, beating and shrinking it). In this song, each woman in turn names her sweetheart/husband (Dwelly, 1988).

Irish shirt 'The Irish shirt is probably derived from the tunic of the early historic period ... Irish shirts were said to take thirty-five yards of linen, which may account for their distinctively full sleeves. By the sixteenth century they were frequently dyed saffron' (Connolly, 1998). Incidentally, in nineteenth-century English slang the word 'milltag' meant 'shirt' – a word derived from the *Irish Travellers' Cant* term 'melthog' (Green, 1998). The Irish word is *léine*, for which see *Irish national dancing costume*. See also *Irish cloak, Irish sleeve*.

'Irish' shore moss Or just 'shore moss'. 'Irish moss as harvested at the seashore after it has been washed up by a storm or as dropped from a drag rake' (Pratt, 1988). See also *Irish moss*.

Irish short bow An ancient weapon. Lighter than the English longbow, but arrows could not be fired as fast using it. There was also an Irish longbow.

Irish shortbread A variation of the famous Scottish shortbread, but made with both plain (i.e. wheat) flour and cornflour, as well as butter, of course. See also *Irish eggs*.

Irish shorthorn A breed of cattle (Mason, 1951). The horns of this breed were obviously shorter than those of the *Irish longhorn*. See also *Irish cow, old*.

Irish shortwool A breed of sheep, a synonym of which is Wicklow Cheviot, since it is a cross between the Wicklow mountain breed and the Cheviot of the Scottish-English border (Mason, 1951). See also *Irish longwool*.

Irish Showjumping Derby Important equestrian event held at Millstreet in Co. Cork (Smith, 1991). Not the same as the *Irish Derby*, which is a race. See also *Irish Classics*.

Irish shrimp fly A whole category of fishing fly for anglers in the loughs. These flies include 'Curry's red shrimp' and 'Bann special shrimp'. Incidentally, a 'glister of fish hooks' means 'a glass of *Irish whiskey*' (Green, 1998). See also *Irish lough wet fly*.

Irish Shrove Tuesday buns Buns with a filling of heavy cream, cake or macaroon crumbs and icing (Cole, 1973).

Irish Siberia With reference to writer Máirtín Ó Cadhain (1906–

70), Welch (1996) writes: 'because of his republican activities, Ó Cadhain spent most of the war years ... in what he
called the Irish Siberia, the Curragh Internment Camp,
where he read widely and wrote.' See also *Irish Jailic, Irish
progressive stage*.

'Irish' sidecar Or just 'sidecar' (but the prefix 'Irish' is often
used); for which see *Irish jaunting car*. Also called an 'outside car' or 'outsider'.

Irish sidewalk (American usage) Street or avenue. Also called
an *Irishman's sidewalk* (Rawson, 1991; Green, 1996), as the
supposedly gullible Irish immigrant would not know the
difference between a street and a sidewalk, according to
Green. It is reminiscent of the Kerryman who saw a sign
that read 'KEEP DEATH OFF THE ROAD', 'so he drove his car up
on the footpath' (MacHale, 1979).

Irish Sign Language (ISL) A completely distinct form of sign
language for the hearing-impaired which is not mutually
intelligible to signers using British Sign Language, as it dif-
fers in letters, vocabulary and syntax. It is interesting that
some British signers who are Catholic, often use a form
which is much more similar to ISL (with ISL word and
initialised signs reflecting the Irish manual alphabet) since
they have been taught by Irish monks.

Irish silver 1 Silver that comes from Ireland. See also *Irish
punchmarks*. **2** Fake silver. Logan (1986) quotes a report of
1456 referring to the importing to England of: 'silver plate,
broken silver, bullion, and wedges of silver, made of the
great chippings of the coin, of our sovereign Lord the King,
by his Irish enemies, and English rebels, within the said
land, by which the said coin is diminished and greatly im-
paired, and the Irish silver called Reily's increase from one
day to another.' The term is thus analogous with 'German
silver', which means something fake, especially a nickel
alloy (Green, 1998). In 1934, Pádraig MacGreine referred to
a unique device for cheating used by *Irish Travellers* called
a 'gladar box', in which one pretended to make silver coins
by using solder (Gmelch, 1977). **3** Irish silver is also a variety of erica (heather). See also *Irish diamond, Irish gold*.

'Irish' Sinai Or rather 'Ireland's Sinai', as Morton (1930) refers
to Croagh Patrick, where an annual pilgrimage takes place.

See also *'Irish' Holy Mountain* and, for the mountain's association with St Patrick, *Irish patron saint*.

Irish single jig Type of *Irish jig* in 6/8 or 12/8 time. See also *Irish double jig*.

Irish single whiskey Refers to the quick old pot-still process of single distillation, as opposed to the proper triple distilled Irish whiskey. See also *Irish pot still whiskey*.

Irish Sisters of Charity Order founded in 1816 by Catholic convert Mary Aikenhead (1787–1858) at the invitation of Archbishop Daniel Murray. See also *Irish Dames of Ypres*.

Irish six-hand reel A category of *Irish reel* rather than an actual dance (Thurston, 1954).

'Irish' skittles Irish version of the game, in which the skittles are thrown rather than knocked over. Played in parts of Counties Down, Fernanagh and Cavan. Two teams compete to knock over standers (five vertical sticks out of a target which is five feet tall) with the skittles. See also *Irish road bowls*.

Irish sleeve With reference to seventeenth-century fashion, Connolly (1998) writes: 'The Irish sleeve evolved about this time ... Worn by both sexes, it was a band of woollen fabric which stretched from the shoulder along the arm and was secured by buttoning or tying at the cuff. This allowed the display of the voluminous linen sleeves of the Kirtle and the Irish shirt.' See also *Irish cloak, Irish jacket*.

Irish slide car A small farming vehicle for carrying light loads. 'Although the Irish slide car is always pulled by a pony, it may be noticed that the Swedish slide car, used mainly for carrying hay, is often man-hauled' (Evans, 1957). See also *Irish low-back car*.

Irish smith god Goibhniu. See *Irish craft gods*.

Irish smut As the important Southdown sheep was called in New England. 'These "native sheep" were called Irish or English Smuts and were descendants from the old English Southdowns' (see www.wildwnc.org).

Irish snipe (Amer.) The avocet bird (*Webster's*). Because of this bird's distinctive beak, in Ulster dialect a 'snipe' is a person with a long nose (Share, 1997). See also *Irish rose*.

Irish Socialist, the first William Thompson (1775–1835) 'The first Irish Socialist, the forerunner of Marx' (Connolly, 1998).

A rich merchant and landowner who gave very generous leases to his tenants – much to the disgust of other land-owners! He was a writer and believed in feminism and the cooperative movement.

Irish Socialist Federation Group in New York similar to the *Irish Socialist Republican Party*.

Irish Socialist Republican Party Group founded in 1896 by James Connolly. It lacked support, however, and when Connolly emigrated to America in 1903, William O'Brien reorganised the party and it became the *Socialist Party of Ireland*.

Irish Society Organisation founded during the reign of King James I to expand the interests of London companies in Ireland. It developed the Ulster plantation and controlled customs and fisheries in Derry. It was prosecuted in 1635 for financial mismanagement but in 1658 Cromwell re-turned the confiscated plantation to them. In 1952, the Irish society disintegrated when its last asset (Foyle Fisheries) was sold. See also *'Irish' Plantation*.

Irish Society, United Another name for the Society of United Irishmen, for which see *Irishmen, United*.

Irish soda bread Bread made with bread soda (i.e. bicarbonate of soda) instead of yeast. The special taste of Irish soda bread comes also from the soft flour and the inclusion of butter-milk; if possible, it is also best baked on the traditional 'pot stove'. See also *Irish American soda bread, Irish brown soda bread*.

Irish soda cake, sweet Similar to *Irish soda bread* but with more of a cake consistency and the addition of nutmeg, currants and lemon rind (Cole, 1973).

'Irish' Sodom In Liverpudlian dialect, Dublin is called 'Sodom on the Liffey' (see website *Merseytalk9*). Perhaps the phrase was coined (by people who may never even have visited the city) in order to tease the Irish population of Liverpool. Sodom was the evil city destroyed by God in the book of Genesis. See also *Irish capital*.

Irish soft-coated wheaten terrier See *Irish wheaten terrier*.

Irish (solanaceae), (Miller) Type of chilli cherry peppers – used in Tabasco sauce – of which there are two varieties: *capiscum anuum v. cerasiforme* and *capiscum anuum v. conoides*.

Irish sole (Ir. *sol Gaelach*) Large fillet of sole prepared with mushroom stuffing, lemon juice, vinegar, salt and pepper (Thomson, 1982).

Irish Solomon Cormac Mac Art, who, like Romulus and Remus (the twin founders of Rome) was stolen by a she-wolf and raised with her cubs (as was St Albeus, for whom see *Irish werewolf*). Cormac was an early Christian who was very wise in his judgements. 'His great wisdom caused him to be called the Irish Solomon' (Matthews and Matthews, 1998). The 'Scottish Solomon' was King James VI of Scotland (who was also King James I of England, 1603–25 – see website www.bibliomania.com). See also *'Irish' Moses*.

Irish soma An ancient unknown hallucinogenic plant. With reference to the Sanskrit word *soma* (an intoxicating juice used in ancient Hindu ceremonies), Peter Lamborn Wilson in his online article 'Ploughing the Clouds: The Search for Irish Soma' examines the theory that the Indians took *soma* from the Irish. For other Irish-Indian connections, see *Irish babu*, *Irish Gandhi* and *Irish hooley*.

Irish spade With reference to the 'loy' or heavy potato spade (Ir. *laí*), Evans (1957) writes: 'The Irish spade is much more than a gardening tool: it was and still is ... an implement for field cultivation and for cutting turf ... The Irish spade is not a digging implement, it is essentially a ridge-maker or hand plough ... The Irish spade is more specialised and more primitive than the common-or-garden English spade.' Sharkey (1985) adds: 'The Irish spade differed from the English not only in its narrow, bent blade but ... in the way it was put to use. The Irish dig with the right foot, the English with the left.' This is probably why an (Irish) Catholic is called a left-footer (Green, 1996). In *Irish Travellers' Cant*, a spade is a 'naper' (Macalister, 1937). See also *Irish two-eared spade*. For jocular names for the spade or shovel, see *Irish banjo*, *Irish fan* and *Irish harp*.

'Irish' spalpeen The prefix 'Irish' does not need to be used. The 'spalpeen' (Ir. *spailpín*) was a seasonal hired labour or migratory farm labourer. See also *Irish tatie howker*.

Irish-speaking area In Irish, the term *'Gaeltacht'* (or more correctly, the plural form *na Gaeltachtaí*) refers to the areas where Irish is the first language, e.g. Donegal, Galway, Kerry, Cork,

Waterford, west Belfast (the only urban Gaeltacht). Each area has a slightly different dialect of the language. Outside these areas is the 'Galltacht' or English-speaking area. There are also some areas described as the *'Breac-Ghaeltacht'* (lit. speckled or dappled Gaeltacht) or what O'Farrell (1980) calls the *'Leath-Gaeltacht'* (half-Gaeltacht) where both English and Irish are in everyday use . There is also the term *'nua-ghaed-healtacht'* or 'newly created Irish-speaking district' in an English-speaking area (see MacLysaght, 1979). See also *Irish Pale*.

Irish spiced beef Beef prepared with shallots, bay leaves, cloves, mace, peppercorns, allspice, thyme, brown sugar and molasses. The beef is marinated for about a week and is then tied up with red ribbon and holly in butchers' shops around Christmas time (Sheridan, 1996).

Irish spice dresser An *Irish dresser* usually made of pine with many separate small compartments (instead of deep, spacious shelves) for storing different spices, herbs and cooking ingredients (see webpage *Glenmore Antique Irish Pine*).

Irish spirits measure These are more generous than the British measures: 'The standard Irish spirits measure is two and a half fluid ounces to the glass or four "half-ones" to the gill, which is five fluid ounces, or one quarter to a pint"' (as opposed to the English measure, which is six drinks to the gill – see Magee, 1980). Or in metric language, 35 millilitres (in contrast with 28 in Scotland and 23 in England – see Booth, 1995). Apart from standard measures, there were some other Irish drink measures that were popular but not legal, such as a 'pony', which was an Irish spirits measure of stout (as Con Murray recalls – see Kearns, 1996) and also a 'tailor' which was three-quarters of a pint (Kearns, 1996). In Canada, a 'Mickey' is half a bottle of liquor (Barber, 1998). Also, a 'baby Power' could be called a measure since it is a miniature bottle (the amount of a glass) of (Powers) *Irish whiskey* (Share, 1997). A 'crapper' is half a glass of whiskey. For other units of measurement, see *Irish acre* and *Irish mile*. See also *Irish tot*.

Irish spoon A spade or shovel (Green, 1996). Also known as an *Irish banjo, Irish fan* and *Irish harp*. 'Spoons' is also the name for a long single piece of wood (not particularly resembling spoons) divided at the top to make a tapping sound as a simple percussion instrument to accompany *Irish music*.

Irish sporthorse A breed which is also called an *Irish hunter* (Mason, 1951). An *Irish warmblood* originally from an *Irish throroughbred* and an *Irish draught*. See also *Irish cob*.

Irish sportsmen, the national anthem of With reference to the song which begins 'For rambling, for roving, for football or sporting', Redmond (1979) writes: 'The Cork ballad ... is accepted as virtually the national anthem of Irish sportsmen, some might say it is the bottle hymn of the republic.' See also *Irish national anthem*.

Irish spotting Or *Irishing*, refers to the characteristic white markings on the neck, chest, underbody and legs of the Shetland sheepdog (for a detailed explanation of the *Irishing gene* responsible, see www.kyleah.com).

Irish sprigging White hand-embroidered decorative *Irish linen* for tablecloths and other items. See also *Irish lace*.

Irish spring 1 Variety of pulmonaria (a type of flower), of which new foliage is unique mint-green appliqué. **2** A type of green soap. **3** A hardy dormant plant with bronze apricot blend and green throat, the flowers of which develop a pinkish tan. **4** A variety of yellow exhibition flower.

Irish springer A cross between an *Irish water spaniel* and an English springer. See also *Irish Glen of Imaal terrier* for Irish dog breeds.

Irish spring moss Also 'spring moss' (Pratt, 1988) or 'spring Irish moss'. *Irish moss* that is harvested in the spring.

Irish springtime A delicate pattern of *Irish crochet* (Weiss, 1985).

Irish spurge Sharkey (1985) gives a good description of this lethal plant: 'Irish spurge, known as *bainnicin* was collected, placed in a sack and pounded so that no poisonous juices escaped. When hurled into the water, all life for a hundred yards in either direction fell victim to the poison in a matter of minutes and the fish came floating to the surface, dead.' For entries on other Irish plants, see *Irish bladderwort*.

Irish square dance A dance performed by the 'Biddies' on St Brigid's Eve (January 31) in Killarney (Hilliard, 1962). For other dances, see *Irish haye*. See also *'Irish' Mary*.

Irish St Anthony See *Irish Anthony*.

Irish St Leger One of the *Irish Classics* which began in 1915. It is run at the Curragh in September by three-year-olds over a distance of a mile and six furlongs.

Irish Staffordshire bull terrier Breed listed on the website www.edreid.co.uk. Perhaps it is a cross between an Irish and a Staffordshire bull terrier. See also *Irish Glen Imaal terrier* for other Irish dog breeds.

Irish staple, the As the *Irish potato* is described (e.g. by Cole, 1973), meaning that it is the staple food of the Irish.

Irish stapple thatch Way of thatching a roof using clay (Buchanan, 1961). Incidentally, for an unknown reason (possibly the hairstyles – see also *Irish glib*) in the seventeenth century, one nickname for an Irishman was a 'thatched head' (Partridge, 1937). See also *Irish thrust thatch*.

'Irish' Starry Plough The prefix 'Irish' is used occasionally by non-Irish people to refer to this flag, which was devised by George Russell and William H. Megahey originally for the Irish labour movement. The flag features the stars that form the Plough (see also *Irish plough*) with a sword on a green ground. It was adopted by the *Irish Citizen Army* and was first flown in 1914. In the *'Irish' Easter Rising*, it was flown from the Imperial Hotel. See also *Irish ensign, Irish flag, Irish Green Flag, Irish Tricolour*.

Irish step-dance stage show As Vallely (1999) refers to the spectacular production of *Lord of the Dance* with Michael Flatley and Riverdance featuring *Irish step-dancing*. In fact, 'Riverdance' can mean commiting suicide by jumping into the River Shannon (see website *Everyday English and Slang in Ireland*). See also *Irish Dance, Lord of*.

Irish step-dancing A rhythmic form of dancing performed either solo or in a group by men or women, in which leg movement predominates. It is often danced to the music of an *Irish jig* or *Irish reel*. The music chosen may also determine the type of footwear used: for instance, *Irish hard shoes* are worn to add a tapping beat to certain dances, such as the hornpipe and treble reel, whereas lighter jigs call for pumps.

Irish stereotype, stage A name used (e.g. by Welch, 1996) for the *stage Irishman* (see Appendix 3).

Irish stew (Ir. *stobhach Gaelach*) **1** According to Ayto (1994), 'the name Irish stew ... first turns up in 1814, in Byron's *Devil Drive*: "The Devil ... dined on ... a rebel or so in an Irish stew".' This delicious meal, which is just as popular with foreigners as with the Irish, needs no description. Yet there is controversy as to whether carrots should be included. Perhaps even some Irish cooks who use lamb (rather than beef) may not know that Irish stew was originally made with kid (Sheridan, 1965). The predominant role of the *Irish potato,* sometimes more plentiful than the portions of meat in this dish, may have its origins in the times of Ireland's former poverty, when meat was scarce. Similarly, 'Mulligan's stew' is a stew made of whatever is available (Green, 1996) and 'mulligan' is a name for Irish stew (RD GED, Vol. 3). Yet 'when materials for "mulligan" are not to be had', it is called by tramps 'combination stew' (Partridge, 1950). Another Irish-English word for stew (with any meat, not necessarily lamb or beef) is 'potash' (from Fr. *potage).* 2 In rhyming slang, 'Irish stew' means 'true', as does 'two eyes of blue' (RDGED, Vol. 3). It is the phrase 'bonnets so blue' which means Irish stew (Partridge, 1937). For other entries from rhyming slang, see *Irish jig, Irish rose. Irish stew* also means 'blue' (Green, 1998). See also *Irish blue.*

Irish stew pie Irish stew with a slightly thicker juice and a pastry crust (Allen, 1994). In early nineteenth-century London, *Irish stew* was called 'Frenchpie' (Partridge, 1937). For more Irish-French connections, see *Franco-Irish* (Appendix 4).

Irish stick-fighting Fighting with a cudgel or an *Irish shillelagh,* not usually in individual combat but between rival gangs. In the last century, several such gangs existed, such as the 'Shanavests' and the 'Caravats'. In early-nineteenth-century slang, a *Paddy-row* was a row in which 'sticks supply the place of fists' (Partridge, 1937) and *Paddy quick* meant 'stick' or 'thick' (see Appendix 5). See also *Irish faction fights.*

Irish stitch Refers to Irish embroidery or crochet work (OED). See also *Irish crochet lace, Irish work.*

Irish stoat Often it is confusingly called an *Irish weasel* but some writers (e.g. Bluett, 1994) prefer the term *Irish stoat.* Like the *great Irish deer* and the *Irish hare,* it is a distinct subspecies *(mustela erminea hibernica)* and its Irish heritage gives it some distinct characteristics. Ó hÓgáin (1995) writes: 'The Irish stoat *(easóg)* is usually referred to in Hiberno-English as a "weasel". These animals are also thought to have human characteristics, organising their affairs annually and even holding funerals for their dead. To meet a weasel when setting out on a journey was a bad portent but one could avoid the bad luck by enquiring after its health and address- ing it as *a bheainín bheag uasal* ("a little noble woman"). Its spit was believed to be poisonous ... An *Irish stoat* was be- lieved to steal coins; it was unlucky for a person to steal from its nest.' See also *Irish hare*.

Irish stout Dark beer, the most famous brands being Guinness, Murphy's or Beamish. It is called affectionately by such names as 'the black stuff', 'brown gargle' (Share, 1997) or 'Liffey water' (as Guinness is brewed in Dublin, which is on the River Liffey). So strongly is stout (and especially Guinness) associated with the Irish that Colin Bowles cites a facetious definition of the Irishman as 'a simple machine for converting Guinness into urine' *(The Wit's Dictionary,* 1984). See also *Irish wine*.

Irish stout cake Or 'Murphy's Irish stout cake'. Made with raisins, currants, sultanas, glacé cherries, mixed peel, ground almonds, mixed spice and *Irish stout* (Johnson, 1995).

Irish Stroker, the Valentine Greatrakes (1628–83), the Puritan divine who carried out exorcisms from fairies (Curran, 2000) and served in Cromwell's army. He was so-called because he removed fairies from fairy-struck victims by stroking the victim.

Irish submarine, to make sails for an In Liverpudlian dialect, an expression denoting a futile and ludicrous act (see web- site *Merseytalk9*). See also *Irish half-door*. The submarine was in fact invented by an Irishman, John P. Holland (1841– 1914) (Newby, 1987).

Irish sugar bowl Bowl made of silver with three legs. See also *Irish silver*.

'Irish' Sugar Loaf, the The mountain in Co. Wicklow (as opposed to the one just outside Abergavenny in south Wales or the one in Rio de Janeiro). See also *'Irish' Holy Mountain*.

Irish Summer An episode in Welsh history (called in Welsh *Haf y Gwyddyl*), when in 1193 Rhodri ab Owain Gwynedd re- turned – with Manx assistance – having been expelled by his nephew from Anglesey (Stephens, 1986). It is called 'Irish' Summer since Manxmen were regarded by the Welsh as

ethnically Irish. Indeed, 800 years ago, before the different
forms of Irish Gaelic and Manx Gaelic evolved, they would
have been very similar.

Irish summer flan Made with raspberries, redcurrants, fresh
cream and figs with an oatmeal and flour pastry (Ross, 1997).

'Irish' Sunday Or rather 'Gaelic Sunday'. Sunday 4 August 1918,
when the GAA organised games with 100,000 players, without permits, refusing to pay the British entertainment tax.
(Healy, 1998).

Irish Sunday Closing Act, 1878 Act put forward by Thomas
William Russell which closed public houses at 9pm on Sat-
urday and Sunday. The aim was to curb drunkenness.

Irish sun god 1 As Crossley-Holland (1997) calls Dagda, for
whom see *Irish father god*. **2** As Lugh is called (CGG). See
also *Irish god of light*.

Irish sun goddess The epithet of Gillagriene (Gislla Greine)
(CGG). Her mother was a sunbeam and her father a mortal. See also *Irish sun god*.

Irish swaddies In the pre-*Irish Free State* years, the militiamen
in the service of the British army. Unlike the 'British Tom-
mies', they were recruited from the local Irish population
(Ó Faoláin, 1941).

Irish sweat house See *Irish bath*.

Irish Sweeps 1 A shortened form of the *Irish Sweepstake*, for
which see *Irish Hospitals Sweepstakes* (OED) **2** A variety of
African violet.

Irish Sweeps Derby Important horse-racing event held at the
Curragh in June and run by three-year-olds.

Irish sweeps sport Like *Irish Sweeps*, this is another rare hybrid
of the African violet.

Irish Sweepstake Synonym of *Irish Sweeps* (OED).

Irish sweetness A crimson lake variety of rose (Brett, nd).

Irish swigman A synonym used by Green (1996) for *Irish toyle*.

Irish switch Synonym of *Irish shift*.

Irish sword dance As Alford (1962) refers to the dance performed
by the *Irish kerne*. It is apparently very similar to the Mata-
chin sword dance on the continent. Alford writes that 'the
name of "Matachins" ... denotes a sword dance with the
traditional beheading of the leader.' See also *Irish haye*.

Irish Symphony 1 The name of Sir Arthur Sullivan's (1842–

1900) *Symphony in E Minor* (1864). **2** The subtitle of Sir Charles Villiers Stanford's (1852–1924) *Symphony No. 3 in F Minor*. **3** A 1904 composition by Sir (Herbert) Hamilton Harty (1871–1941) based on Irish folk songs (Kennedy, 1980).

Irish system 1 Term that refers to the distinct fingering system and chanter of the *Irish bagpipes,* as opposed to the Scottish system for the Highland pipes (see www.bagpipeworld. co.uk) **2** A synonym of the *Irish progressive stage (Webster's)*. Not to be confused with the *Irish English* word 'system', meaning a mixture of porter and Guinness, also called a 'half-in-half', a 'patent' (in Galway) and a 'predom' (in Cork) (see Ó Faoláin, 1941). See also *Irish Siberia*.

T

Irish takeaway (Liverpudlian) An abortion clinic (see website *Merseytalk9*).

'Irish' tally stick See *Irish Not*.

Irish tambourine 1 With reference to Allen MacMidhna, fairy musician of the *Tuatha de Danann,* Rose (1998) writes: 'He possessed a magic *tuinpan* (an *Irish tambourine)* or harp, on which he played so enchantingly that all who heard it were lulled to sleep.' **2** Vallely (1999) explains that in Sligo/Roscommon: 'The *bodhrán* is referred to as a "tambourine", and older models have jingles attached.' See also *Irish frame drum* and *What Paddy gave the drum* (Appendix 5).

Irish tandem, drive (Ulster) To go on foot (Macafee, 1996). On a similar note, 'Pat and Mike' is rhyming slang for 'bike' (Green, 1998, and see also 'Paddy' in Appendix 5). See also *Irishman's ride* (Appendix 3).

Irish tart Type of dessert-cum-drink made with strawberries, chocolate sauce and ice cream but with added *Irish poteen* (see webpage for *Knockeen Hills Irish Poteen).* No relation to the famous 'Tart with the Cart', as the statue of Molly Malone at the foot of Grafton Street is known (Share, 1997).

Irish tartan In relation to the innovated *Irish kilt* used sometimes in the male *Irish dancing costume,* Robb (1998) writes that the kilt colours were 'commonly of saffron (a colour outlawed in Ireland by King Henry VIII) or green.' Hence the *Irish kilt* is usually plain, yet occasionally the colours saffron and green (sometimes with black or cream) have been added to produce a tartan. Law (1998) also refers to an 'Ulster tartan' of red, green, yellow and black. See also *Irish county tartans, Irish national tartan*.

Irish tatie howker In Ulster and Scots usage, a potato-digger – a seasonal (Irish) potato-harvester in Scotland. See also *'Irish' spalpeen*.

Irish tatting fern (*Athyrium felix femina frizelliae*) A species of fern that grows up to a metre in height. See also *'Irish' fern*.

Irish TB Short for *Irish thoroughbred*.

Irish tea The Irish are great drinkers of 'scald' (Share, 1997), 'char' or 'Rosie Lee' (as they call tea in Irish slang). Yet the so-called 'Irish tea' is not the tea the Irish normally drink but a beverage of *Irish whiskey, Irish breakfast tea*, sugar, cloves and a cinnamon stick. See also *Irish coffee*.

Irish tea cake Made with dried fruit, soaked in tea with brown sugar, chopped walnuts and glacé cherries: 'a cross between a brack and a fruit cake' (Campbell, 1997).

Irish Teague 1 A Teig, Taig or Teague refers to an Irishman or Catholic and is said to be derived from the Irish proper name 'Tadhg'. Yet the similar word 'Tad' (which also means 'Irishman') is probably derived not from this name but from 'Thady' (Thadeus) (Partridge, 1950). By extension, 'Teagueland' (from the title of John Dunton's book published in 1698) is Ireland, and a 'Teaguelander' is an Irishman (Green, 1996 – see also *'Irish' mick* for 'Mickland' or 'Mickeyland' and Appendix 5 for *Paddy Land).* Moreover, from the word 'teague' is derived 'Tykes' or 'Tikes', 'the Australian Catholics' name for themselves' (Partridge, 1937). Green (1998) also argues that the word 'dogan' or 'dagun', which also means an Irishman or Catholic, derives from the word 'Taig' – but it could also be from the surname 'Duggan'. **2** 'The Irish Teague' was the alias of one William Maguire, an *Irish buffoon* (see Ó Ciosáin, 1998).

Irish Temperance, Apostle of Fr Theobald Matthew (1790–1861) is so dubbed by Douglas (1936). Non-conformist friends asked Fr Matthew (known for his work among the poor) to lead their temperance society. In 1838, he pledged total abstinence and, as a result of his campaign, not only drinking, but also crime, was reduced.

Irish tempo That which is relaxed, slow and 'laid back', like the stereotyped Mediterranean *'mañana'* style. Ó Faoláin, for instance, spoke of 'that Irish tempo of a civilised dawdle' (1941). Patrick Kavanagh said something along the lines of: 'The Irish language has ten words that mean *mañana*, but none of them conveys quite the same sense of urgency.'

Irish Tenant League Established after a conference in August 1850. It sought 'the three Fs' (fixity of tenure, fair rents and freedom of tenants to sell their interest in a holding).

Irish terrier (Ir. *madra gearr*) An Irish breed of terrier with a rough, wiry, reddish coat. It is probably from this beautiful Irish breed (and not from the popular Irish name 'Terry', as Partridge [1950] suggests) that in early-nineteenth-century slang a 'terrier' was an Irishman. This dog has also been called the *Irish red terrier*. See also *Irish water spaniel, Irish wolfhound*.

Irish Texel Breed of sheep first imported into Ireland from Texel Island, Holland, in 1964. In the strictest sense, however, only offspring of Texel rams (whose genes produce leaner meat) with native Irish ewes could really be termed 'Irish Texels' (see the webpage of the *Irish Texel Sheep Society*). See also *Irish longwool, Irish shortwool, Irish smut*.

Irish than the Irish, more (Lat. *Hibernis ipsis Hiberniones*). **1** As the Norman invaders of Ireland were described, since they adopted Irish ways completely. The phrase is also rendered 'more Irish than the Irish themselves' and was 'apparently coined in its Latin form by Francis Plowden' (Connolly, 1998). **2** The Germans living in Ireland at the time of the Second World War. Ó Faoláin (1941) wrote: 'there is hardly a town in Ireland where you will not meet a German name ... Many of these intermarry, stay here, and become as of old *hibernior hibernicis ipsis*.'

Irish theatre A military guardroom (for detaining military prisoners) (Partridge, 1937). Green (1996) suggests that this is 'presumably alluding to the likelihood of finding Irish soldiers incarcerated there.' See also *Irish clubhouse*.

Irish Thebaid Glendalough, a once-important ecclesiastical site associated with St Kevin (see *Irish Anthony*) which Morton (1930) refers to as 'this little ruined city – an Irish Thebaid'. Thebaid was the centre of Christian monasticism from the third century and was situated in the valley of the Upper

Nile (and was so called after Thebes, the capital of that area). See also *'Irish' Canterbury, Irish Lourdes, 'Irish' Sinai*.

Irish theme bar Referring to the admiration for things Irish in Australia, Vallely (1999) writes: 'Following a 1996 Guinness Irish pub promotion campaign, the many Irish theme bars that opened ... hosted everything from traditional sessions to "covers" of Irish rock groups.' See also *Irish pub, Irishisation*.

Irish theme pub Synonym of *Irish theme bar*.

Irish thoroughbred A pure-blood Irish horse. One nickname of Co. Kildare is 'the Thoroughbred' or 'Thoroughbred county' since Kildare is famous for its horses. See also *Irish cob*.

Irish thrust thatch A type of roof thatching alluded to but not explained by Buchanan (1961) and mentioned in connection with *Irish stapple thatch*.

Irish Tiger The term 'Celtic Tiger' is more common to refer to Ireland's economic boom of the late 1990s and early 2000s. Since the term applies specifically to Ireland rather than her Celtic sister nations, however, many call the phenomenon the 'Irish Tiger' (see the article *Irish Tiger: Parody of Ireland's Emerging Materialism* at www.geocities.com). Eagleton (1999) uses the phrase 'Emerald Tiger'. Not to be confused with a 'green tiger', which was South African slang for a ten-rand note (Green, 1998). See also *Irish Lions*.

Irish Tinkers 1 A synonym for the more popular term *Irish Travellers* but favoured by some, e.g. George Gmelch (1977) and Wiedel and O'Fearadhaigh (1976) as a title of their books. It can have a slightly pejorative tone but is not as insulting as the word 'knacker' which can be used as an insult for a Traveller (see website *The O'Byrne Files – Dublin Slang Dictionary and Phrasebook*). Other Irish nicknames for Travellers include Buzzies and Minks (see website *Everyday English and Slang in Ireland*) as well as 'White' Moths (see Website *Irish Trivia*) since by profession most were actually 'white' smiths (working with tinned or white iron) and they would have been often heard saying the word 'moth', i.e. 'girl' in Shelta. **2** The Irish Tinker is also a beautiful breed of horse that, like the *Irish draught*, is a very sturdy horse and capable of pulling the Irish Tinker's caravan (see *Irish caravan*). A synonym of *Irish Traveller horse*.

Irish Tinkers' Cant A term synonymous with *Irish Travellers' Cant*.

Irish tin whistle (Ir. *feadóg stáin*). The 'Irish' is usually prefixed, e.g. McCullough's *The Complete Irish Tin Whistle Tutor* (1976). It is not to be confused with the *Irish pipes* as it is a type of little flute. The Tuatha De Dannans used a primitive version of the *Irish tin whistle* to make people sleep. See also *Irish bagpipes, Irish flute, Irish harp* and *Irish tambourine*.

Irish Tithe Act Or Rentcharge Act of 1838, in which landlords, not tenants, were made to pay tithes. The Act converted the tithe payment into a rent charge which was three-quarters the amount, payable to the government twice a year. The tithe farmer and tithe proctor were also abolished, so direct confrontation was removed.

Irish Tithe Strike As Pascoe (1968) refers to the *Irish Tithe War*.

Irish Tithe War Refers to the campaign by tenants against tithes (1830–3). See also *Irish Tithe Act*.

Irish toil (toyle) One of the sixty-four categories of rogues (i.e. thieves and swindlers; no relation to *Irish rogues*) listed in *A New Canting Dictionary* in 1725 (Partridge, 1950).

Irish tonsure The outmoded early Celtic Christian tonsure (the shaved part of the head) from ear to ear; similar to the Druid tonsure (called *airbacc Giunnae*) as opposed to the Roman tonsure on the crown of the head (Ellis 1987).

Irish toothache 1 Priapism (Partridge, 1937). For the same meaning the Irish sounding name *Colleen Bawn* was used (as was *Marquis of Lorne*) to rhyme with 'horn' (Green, 1998). **2** Pregnancy (Green, 1998) and abbreviated to *ITA*. Other Irish phrases for pregnant include 'up the duff', 'up the flue', 'up the pole' or 'in the family way' etc. Other ethnic combinations have been used to denote pregnancy also, e.g. Egyptian flu (Green, 1998). See also *Irish reel*. **3** Sexual intercourse. By contrast, Mexican toothache (also Mexican foxtrot/twostep) is diarrhoea (Green, 1998).

Irish toothache, to give a hot poultice for the (Of a woman) to have sexual intercourse (Green, 1998). See also *Irish toothache*. It should be noted that before these phrases were dubbed 'Irish', as far back as the the sixteenth century, 'having an aching tooth' already meant to desire sexually (Green, 1998). So rather than reflecting supposed Irish characteristics or stereotypes, the label 'Irish' may have been merely prefix-ed to already existing phrases to insult the Irishman!

Irish toothpick 1 Pickaxe (Green, 1996). In late nineteenth cen-tury west coast America 'mad Mick' meant pick (Partridge, 1950). See also *Irish banjo* for other tool names. Similarly, an Arkansas toothpick, California toothpick and Harlem tooth-pick all mean a knife (Green, 1998). **2** Erection (Green, 1996). See also *Irish rise, Irish root, Irish toothache*. **3** Without the prefix 'Irish', the plain word 'toothpick' in the mid-nine-teenth century referred to 'an Irish watchman's shillelagh' (Partridge, 1937). See also *Irish shillelagh*.

Irish topper Tall green hat with black band and buckle worn by the *Irish leprechaun*. See also *Irish Walking Patch Cap*. Not connected with the *Paddy hat* (Appendix 5) which is not a hat.

Irish torc Newman (1981) writes that the *Irish torc* was: 'a type of massive torc made of gold in Ireland during the late Cel-tic period. The largest known is more than 1.5m long and weighs more than 765 grams; it is said to have been worn over the shoulder and across the breast.' A torque/torc was a necklace with a twisted band (from Lat. *torquere* – to twist). See also *Irish nuirt*.

Irish tories 1 Originally the word *'tory'* (from Ir. *tóraithe/tóraí* – pursuer, raider) was a synonym of the *Irish rapparee*. Some writers like Cosgrave (c.1740) prefix the 'Irish', e.g. in his *A History of the Most Notorious Irish Tories, Highwaymen, and Rapparees*. **2** Later the word came to refer to the political party with a Jacobite minority who were loyal to James and defended the Church against Protestant dissent. By extension, in American slang the word 'Tory' is one nick-name for any Irishman in general (see website *The Racial Slur Database* – which attributes the origin of this 'from the Irish Tory Island, a noted haven for bandits and pirates'). See also *Irish Toryism*.

Irish Toryism As distinct from English Toryism (Conservativ-ism): '*Irish Toryism* ... was not Jacobite or even pro-Stuart; It stood for hard-line Protestantism, with ... a cynical view both of Hanoverianism and of the intentions of the English Government' (Foster, 1989). See also *Irish tories*.

Irish tot Quarter of a gill (of *Irish whiskey*) (Newby, 1987).

Irish touchstone 'Basalt, the stone which composes the Giant's Causeway' (http://onlinedictionary.datasegment.com). The touchstone or Lydian stone was a siliceous stone used to test gold or silver by the streak left on it when rubbed against those metals. See also *Irish diamond, Irish gold, Irish green, Irish silver*.

Irish tower house Rectangular tower with four or five storeys for fortified private residence (fifteenth-seventeenth century) usually enclosed by a bawn (Ir. *babhún* – walled enclosure). The word 'Irish' is often prefixed. See also *Irish Gothic, Irish round tower*.

Irishtown 1 An area of Dublin, so called as in 1454 the Irish were ordered out of the city by the English authorities and they assembled in an area to the east towards the coast (see Bennett, 1991). The existence of areas dubbed 'Irishtown' in several Irish cities may point in some cases to a former system like apartheid in which Irish people were confined to a particular area outside the city. **2** An area of Limerick: 'The older city falls into three principal parts: English Town, on King's Island in the Shannon, Irish Town, on the mainland to S.E., and Newton Pery, to the S.W. of Irish Town' (Killanin, 1962). **3** An area in Co. Mayo where a meeting was held to establish the *Land League* in 1879. **4** A section of Kilkenny. **5** Generally, Irish Town is an Irish area in foreign cities outside Ireland, e.g. in Cleveland, and is often synonymous with 'shanty town' (see *shanty Irish* – Appendix 4). On a similar note, Cork and Dublin were two names for the Irish area of New York (Green, 1996). Indeed Cork could also be used for an Irishman (Green, 1998). See also *Irish Bostonian, Irish diaspora*.

Irish toyle 1 Or toyle. A beggar/travelling peddlar. In 1562, John Awdeley wrote: 'An Irish toyle is he that carieth his ware in hys walellet, as laces, pins, poyntes and such like. He useth to shew no wares until he have his almes' (Partridge, 1950). **2** By the eighteenth century, the meaning of *Irish toyle* had changed to that of a thief. Grose writes that the Irish toyles were: 'Thieves who carried about pins, laces, and other pedlars' wares, and under the pretence of offering their goods for sale, rob houses' (Share, 1997). See also *Irish fakirs*.

Irish traditional button accordion A popular instrument for *Irish music*. See, for example, David C. Hanruhan's book, *The Box: A Beginner's Guide to the Irish Traditional Button Accordion* (1988). The 'Irish' indicates not only the distinct variation of this accordion but also the style in which it is played.

Irish Transvaal Committee Founded to support the Boers in the Boer War (1899–1902) between the English and Dutch-descended Boers in South Africa. John MacBride's (1865–1916) Brigade of 500 Irishmen fought alongside the Boers. John MacBride was Maud Gonne's husband and was executed in 1916 for his part in the 'Irish' Easter Rising. See also *Irish Brigade*.

Irish Traveller horse For which, see its synonym *Irish Tinker*.

Irish Travellers The most appropriate and popular name for an interesting group of people also called *Irish Tinkers* and sometimes, mistakenly, *Irish Gypsies*. The term *Irish Travellers* is almost universally accepted, e.g. it is used by writers such as McCann, Ó Síocháin and Ruane (eds) in their *Irish Travellers, Culture and Ethnicity* (1994, Belfast). Irish people themselves do not prefix the word 'Irish' but refer to them simply as Travellers; literally, those who 'travel', i.e. walk (Share, 1997). They are mainly Catholic and attach great importance to the family and their community. See also *Irish caravan*, 'Irish' rossie, *Irish Travellers' Cant*.

Irish Travellers' Cant Or Irish Traveller Cant, the language or jargon of the *Irish Travellers* which is called Shelta/Sheldru, Gammon, The O(u)ld Thing (Partridge, 1937) or Minker's Torri. Apart from their physiognomy, their language distinguishes them from the actual Gypsies or Rom and so the appellation *Irish Gypsies* is incorrect. It is interesting that *Irish Travellers' Cant* is rich in vocabulary taken from the *Irish language*; many Irish words have been transformed: e.g. *laicin* is girl (Ir. *cailín* – see *Irish colleen*) and *rodas* is door (Ir. *doras*). However, the syntax that connects these words in sentences is English rather than Irish. Most probably 200 years ago there would have been an even richer (Irish-derived) vocabulary and (like *Irish Masonic Speech*) the syntax may well have been closer to that of the *Irish language*. See also *Hisperic Irish* and *Turkey Irish* (see Appendix 4).

Irish travelling man Term used (e.g. by Ó Muirithe, 1999) as a synonym of Irish Traveller.

Irish Travelling People Synonym of *Irish Travellers* used by some writers, e.g. Rottman, Tussing and Wiley in *The 1981 Census of the Irish Travelling People* (1984, Dublin).

Irish treasure A unique hybrid of African violet.

Irish Treaty, Anglo- (1921) Treaty which concluded the *Anglo-Irish War* or *Irish War of Independence*. It was signed in London by the Irish delegation which included Arthur Griffith and Michael Collins (see *Irish Lenin*), while de Valera remained at home. Apart from accepting the limited constitutional status of what was to be the *Irish Free State*, the delegates' greatest difficulty was to agree to any partition. Lloyd George displayed his own personal ambition as well as a callous disregard for the lives of his British soldiers when he threatened to resume war. The delegates chose to avoid the shedding of any more Irish blood and to secure the imminent chance of at least partial independence. It is probable that the delegates hoped (as many still do) that this Treaty would be just a stepping stone to the complete independence of a united Ireland. The Treaty was unpopular in both countries: in Britain, Lloyd George's coalition was ousted in 1922, while in Ireland there followed the tragic *Irish Civil War*. Collins was killed shortly after the Treaty, in 1922. See *Irish War of Independence*.

Irish tree Ó Giolláin (2000) refers to modern *Gaelic Irish* (see Appendix 4) culture as the 'Irish tree' with new 'bark', i.e. English influence. Similarly, Loreto Todd describes English in Ireland as 'a grafted tongue, an English foliage on an Irish stem, still nourished by an Irish root' (quoted in *Books Ireland*, October 1999).

Irish Tricolour The Irish national flag with the three colours: green (representing the Irish Nationalists – see also *Irish Green Flag*), orange (for the Unionists) and a central band of white (representing the peace between the two). Law (1998) says that 'in 1972 an Irish Tricolour was placed on the moon by Apollo 17 astronaut, Eugene Cernan'.

Irish triplets Birth of three children in three successive years (Rawson, 1991). See also *Irish twins*.

Irish triple pipe Type of early *Irish pipe* (the instrument) depict-

ed on the tenth century Cross of the Scriptures at Clonmac-
noise, Co. Tipperary. See also *Irish bagpipes*.

Irish trot A dance popular in the London Theatre in the 1720s
perhaps derived from the French Hay (see also *Irish haye/
hey*) (mentioned by Ó hAllmhuráin, 1998).

'Irish' Troubles 1 Violent period from the *'Irish' Easter Rising* to
the first years of the *Irish Free State*, i.e. 1916–22. **2** The
Northern Irish problem, especially since 1969.

Irish trout The gillaroo (from Ir. *giolla rua* – red fellow) a subspecies of trout found particularly in Lough Melvin, Co.
Fermanagh is described by Cochrane as an 'Irish trout with
thickened muscular stomach' (1988). Another endemic fish
in some lakes like a sea trout is *sonaghan*. See also *Irish fish,
the; Irish lord; Irish salmon*.

Irish turf spade See the *Irish spade* for this tool. See also also
Irish two-eared spade. As turf or sod was so precious, the
Irish diaspora sometimes affectionately refer to Ireland as
The Old Sod (see McArthur, 1992).

Irish turkey 1 Corned beef and cabbage (Partridge, 1950) the
same as *Irish cabbage*. Similarly for an old Irish Christmas
roast 'mock goose' would be made with beef steak (Killen,
1985). **2** (army slang) Hash (Rawson, 1991). **3** In nineteenth
century slang, 'turkey' meant an Irish immigrant (Green,
1998). No relation to *Turkey Irish* (see Appendix 4) but see
also 'Turks' in *'Irish' Turks*.

'Irish' Turkish bath Christensen describes the Irish-English
word *clochaun* or stone sweat house as 'the Irish version of
the Turkish bath' (1996). See also *Irish bath*.

'Irish' Turks Green (1996) writes 'Irish immigrants have more
usually been known as Turks' in the British slang of the
Teddy Boys (i.e. rock 'n' rollers of the 1950s). The stereotyped fierce Muslim Turk was feared even in Irish folklore
(e.g. on 5 January when the housewife pounds the Christmas loaf three times on the door repeating that famine
should leave the house and go to the *tír na d-Turcach* or
'country/land of the Turks' – Danaher, 1972). Yet, Rawson
suggests that the analogy with the Irish may not be from
the actual Turk but from the word *torc* or wild boar (1991).

Irish tweed Tweed (a textile of rough speckled wool) has been
woven in Ireland for six centuries and has been popular

for its warmth and waterproof quality as well as its beauty. The term 'Irish tweed' refers especially to tweed from Connemara or Donegal. Harnett made a poetic description of 'The old hills, now made of Irish tweed' (quoted by Christensen, 1996).

Irish twins By analogy to *Irish triplets*, Green (1998) seems to have coined this phrase which means 'two siblings born within a 12-month period'.

Irish twist An Irish lilt or pronunciation, especially when speaking English (Killanin, 1962).

Irish two-boater An Irish immigrant to Prince Edward Island (Canada). 'Since they reached Prince Edward Island via Newfoundland, hence requiring two vessels to complete the emigration journey from "the old country", they have been referred to as Irish two-boaters' (Pratt, 1988). See also *Irish battleship, Irish boat*.

Irish two-eared spade 'To this day the Irish two-eared spade is distinguished from the English spade by having iron footplates' (Evans, 1957). See also *Irish spade*.

Irish 2,000 Guineas One of the *Irish Classics* which, since 1921, has been run at the Curragh over a distance of a mile by three year olds. See also *Irish 1,000 Guineas*.

Irish two-touch A term derived from the style of Irish players especially in American soccer. Len Oliver in his online article *The Ethnic Legacy in American Soccer* with reference to 'soccer's public sense of differing styles' alludes to 'the Irish two-touch, shot-on-goal approach'. See also *Irish football*.

Irish typeface So Rhodri Pugh refers to the Gaelic letters of the *Irish alphabet* which have also been adopted and adapted for Welsh, e.g. with an incised 'd' (i.e. a 'd' with a line through it, as in Icelandic) to represent the Welsh 'dd', pronounced as 'th' in 'then' etc. (*Cambria*, spring 2002). See also *Irish manuscript lettering*.

Irish Typhus and Dysentry Epidemic Not one but several epidemics in Ireland: 1708–10, 1718–20, 1728–30, 1740–1, 1817–8, 1836–40, 1846–50. See also *Irish ague; Irish fever; Irish Plague*.

U

'Irish' uilleann pipe A synonym of the *Irish Union pipes*.

Irish Ulysses, The In mythology, the quest of Art, High King, for the beautiful Delbchaem, made him 'an Irish hero and voyager similar to Odysseus' (CGG). See also *Irish Odyssey*.

Irish Unionist Alliance Founded in 1891 in Northern Ireland and dominated by landlords who demanded preservation of the union. Its main aim was to disseminate propaganda against *Irish Home Rule*.

Irish Union pipes Bellows-blown pipes which, according to Vallely (1999), began to evolve from the *Irish bagpipes* in the early eighteenth century and by early nineteenth took their present form. There are three drones, a chanter as well as keyed melody pipes, which can be used to accompany the melody with harmony. It has a more versatile range than other bagpipes. Even though it is not blown, it is a type of bagpipe and many expert musicians/ethnomusicologists, e.g. Vallely, regard it as such.

Irish Universal Suffrage Association Founded in 1841 in Ireland, the association was a type of Chartism (a movement seeking electoral rights for the working class, which began in Newport, South Wales) (see Connolly, 1998).

Irish University Act (1908) This Act did not disestablish Trinity College but gave the same status to the university colleges of Dublin, Cork, Galway and Belfast. See also *Irish College*.

Irish up, to get one's Lose one's temper (Partridge, 1937). The stereotyping of the Irish with fiery tempers can be seen in other expressions, e.g. *paddy* (a common Irish [nick]name) meaning 'a rage, a temper' (see Appendix 5) and in Australian slang to 'throw a mickey' (see *'Irish' mick*) is to have a tantrum (Hughes, 1989). However, the phrase *to get one's Irish up* may have nothing to do with the Irish and be merely a pun on the word 'ire', i.e. anger or rage! Similarly, Green (1998) traces the origin of the nineteenth century phrase 'don't dynamite' (i.e. don't lose your temper) to 'the *Irish Republican* dynamiting attacks of 1880s'. This supposed violent characteristic is also attributed to the Irishmen's Celtic brothers, since 'Scottish' in the nineteenth century also meant 'irritable, easily angered' (Partridge, 1937). See *Irish up, to have one's*. See also *Irish beauty; Irish coat of arms; Irish wedding, to have danced at an*.

Irish up, to have one's In the Mary Jemison's book *A Narrative of the Life of David Crockett* (1834), there is the phrase: 'Her

Irish was up too high to do anything with her' indicating
a bad temper (Rawson, 1991). See also *Irish up, to get one's*.

Irish Uprising As Goddard Lieberson refers to the '*Irish*' *Easter
Rising* and its aftermath in the title of his book. *The Irish
Uprising, 1916–1922* (1966).

V

Irish Valley of the Kings As the Boyne Valley is described where
Irish passage graves and chamber tombs are found (Encycl.
Brit., Vol. 15).

Irish Valuation Act Not an economic Act but the examination
of active soil and subjacent rock in 1827 by Sir Richard John
Griffith, Commissioner of Valuation; also known and published as *Griffith's Valuation*. See also *Irish geology, father of*.

Irish vampire Melton describes the *dearg-dul* as 'the Irish Vampire' (1999). In Irish folklore there is very little written about
this creature – only that to kill it forever, you have to build
'a cairn of stones upon the grave' (according to the website
Vampiric Races). His name comprises two words: *dearg*
(red) and *dul* which may be from *dúil* (desire), i.e. reflecting
his bloodthirsty nature. On similar lines, Eagleton (1999)
alluding to vampire author Bram Stoker, declares: 'Dracula
was Irish. He came from Dublin, not from Transylvania.'
The phrase *Irish vampire* possibly originated from the title
of a sketch (featuring a giant bat hovering over a woman)
by John Tenniel which was shown in *Punch* (1885). See also
Irish Frankenstein.

Irish vegetables Parsnips. The phrase is a translation of the Welsh
llysiau Gwyddelig/Iwerddon (GPC) perhaps coined by analogy
to the (Swedish) swede as opposed to the native British
turnip. See also *Irish cherry*.

Irish velvet A coffee flavoured drink based on *Irish whiskey*. It
is used in some dessert recipes (see Fitzgibbon, 1983). See
also *Irish cream, Irish mist*.

Irish viceroy Formerly the representative of the British monarch
in Ireland. Not all Irish viceroys were hostile to the Irish,
for instance, William Wentworth, second earl of Fitzwilliam,
even supported Henry Grattan's Catholic Relief Bill. He
was so popular that his replacement by the more reactionary Earl Camden, caused widespread unrest – i.e. the Fitz-

william Episode in 1795 (see Brady, 2000).

Irish vine (Ulster) A wild flower: honeysuckle (Macafee, 1996). Not, of course, used for the so-called, *Irish wine*.

'Irish' Virgil In terms of literary greatness, Rumann Mac Colmain (fl. eighth century) was comparable to Virgil (see *'Irish' Homer*). Interestingly, Irish was the first language into which Virgil's *Aeneid* was translated (according to Bord Failte's brochure 'Liberty Ireland'). See also *Irish Hudibras*.

Irish virgin A spinster (Green, 1996).

Irish vocabulary, stage The term is used by Christensen (1996) to apply to the exaggerated artificial vocabulary of the *stage Irishman* (see Appendix 3) as distinct from authentic *Irish English*. It is characterised by expressions which Irish people are supposed to say like 'broth of a boy' and 'top of the morning' as well as 'dear joy'; hence a Dear Joy, for instance, is one nickname for an Irishman (Partridge, 1937).

'Irish' voice Actually it is 'the voice of the Irish' of which St Patrick dreamt in the form of a letter. This voice persuaded him to go back to Ireland. See *Irish patron saint*.

Irish Voltaire George Augustus Moore (1852–1933), novelist: 'He was encouraged by George Russell, who declared that he had always thought Moore's real mission was to be an Irish Voltaire and expose hypocrisy and pomposity' (Welch, 1996). See also *'Irish' Homer*.

Irish (National) Volunteers Militia founded in 1913 who were called to arm themselves to defend *Irish Home Rule* just as the Ulster Volunteer Force were founded (in 1912) to try to prevent it. Their group was founded by members of the *Irish Republican Brotherhood*, Sinn Féin and the Gaelic League. They played a prominent role in the *'Irish' Easter Rising* and afterwards their place was taken by the *Irish Republican Army*. This is not to be confused with The Volunteers, a part-time military force (1778–9) whose role was to deter invasion. In Ulster, there was also Kenneth Gibson's short-lived ultra-loyalist Volunteer Political Party (1974).

Irish voodoo A secretly guarded form of Jasker power system (seems to be a machine that generates energy) created in Ireland with 'a motor that is said to replenish its own energy source' (see www.aps.ory).

W

Irish wager A 'rump of beef and a dozen (bottles of claret)' (Partridge, 1937). It also means 'buttock and trimmings'.

Irish wake 1 In its literal sense a vigil for the dead (Ir. *fair* – to look out for). In *Irish Travellers' Cant* it is called *sory* and refers particularly to the Irish style 'celebration' of this event with an *Irish clay pipe* (dudeen) and *Irish whiskey* offered to visitors who would gather around the deceased to talk and also to play games. By allusion to this, an American wake was a farewell party given to an Irish person leaving to emigrate to America, as they were unlikely to return. See also *Irish cry*, *Irish funeral howl*. **2** 'Any boisterous, noisy event' (Green, 1996). The same as *Paddy's funeral* (see Appendix 5). Even the Irish themselves acknowledge the potential revelry that was often involved in the traditional wake with a host of jokes like: 'What is the difference between an Irish wake and an Irish wedding?' Answer: 'One less drunk!' **3** Irish wake is also a cocktail of *Irish whiskey*, *Irish mist* and *Irish cream* (www.bardrinks.com).

Irish wake amusements The phrase refers to the particular categories of games that were traditionally played at an *Irish wake*. Also the title of Ó Suilleabháin's book (1967).

Irish wake games An alternative term for *Irish wake amusements*. Interestingly, in Irish, *cluiche caointe* can mean either funeral rites or games.

Irish wake house (Ir. *teach faire*). Term used, e.g. by Ó Crualaoich (1998) and refers to the house of the deceased where the *Irish wake* took place.

Irish Walking Patch Cap A cap made with different patches of *Irish tweed* and with a feather at the side. (for picture see www.Irishop.com). See also *Irish Kerby*, *Irish topper*.

Irish Walter Scott John Eglington said '[William] Carleton [the novelist, 1794–1869] was a man sent by God in response to the general clamour for an Irish Walter Scott' (quoted by MacHale, nd). With reference to nineteenth century novelists, many of whom catered for British readers, Connolly writes that for Irish historical fiction 'there were frequent calls for "an Irish Scott"' (1998). Here he echoes Morton's wish that 'The time cannot be far off ... when the Walter

Scott whom Ireland deserves ... will take her heroes from Sarsfield to Collins' (1930) and later adds in relation to Grace O'Malley (see the *'Irish' Rob Roy*) that she is 'waiting for the Irish Walter Scott'.

Irish War, Anglo- See *Irish War of Independence*.

Irish war goddess As Briggs (1976) calls Badb, an incorporation of three goddesses: Neman, Macha and Morrigan. Green (1992) also uses this epithet and Jones (1995) applies it to Badb's aspect, Morrigan. Her name denotes 'crow' and indeed the crow (as a carrion bird) was associated with her.

Irish warm blood A synonym of *Irish sporthorse* (Mason, 1951).

Irish War of Independence (1919–21). Also called the Tan War (Christensen, 1996) as a major part of the struggle was against the hated Black and Tans (so named after their motley black and khaki uniform resembling the Co. Limerick dog breed of the same name). The war began in January 1919 with an ambush at Soloheadbeg, Co. Tipperary; after that episode, attacks against Crown forces intensified. A truce was worked out in July 1921 and a treaty (see *Irish Treaty, Anglo-*) was signed that December. This treaty was to lead to the *Irish Civil War*.

Irish war pipe A synonym of the *Irish pipes* used by some writers (e.g. Baines, 1992) since the *Irish piper* was often present in battle. See next entry.

Irish war piper One who played the *Irish war pipe* (see also *Irish pipes*) in battle (Vallely uses the term, 1999).

Irish warrior and bird goddess So Estiu is called.

'Irish' Warwick castle Or rather 'The Warwick Castle of Ireland' as Morton (1930) dubs the castle of Lismore since he believes, 'The mind immediately connects them, both majestic, both throned on wooded rocks, both reflected in water'.

Irish wash 1 Changing clothes instead of washing. **2** In Ireland 'wash' is the name given to the alcoholic mix prior to it becoming *Irish poteen* (*Irish News*, 8.11.99). See *Irish moonshiner* and *Irish shave*.

Irish Washerwoman A dance tune. In Irish, the *bean-nighe* (or 'washing woman') who washes blood-stained clothes of those about to die, is a guise of the banshee (see *Irish death messenger*).

Irish Washerwoman outfit Innovative design of Welsh-born

Sybil Connolly in 1952 consisting of 'a gilted skirt in red flannel like the petticoats worn in the west of Ireland, with a white cambric blouse and black shawl' (Brady, 2000). See also *Irish dancing costume*.

Irish Washerwoman's Reel (Encycl. Amer., Vol. 28) A dance in 4/4 tempo, the steps of which include the march and gallop. Participants dance in circular fashion with men and women forming separate lines and moving in figures of eight. See also *Irish reel*.

Irish water beings As Jones refers to the merrows (1995), for which see *Irish mermaid*.

Irish water horse The *each/capall uisce* (sometimes with the anglicised spelling *aughisky* – see Briggs, 1976) is a horse that often drowns its rider by taking it into the sea. Joyce calls it a pooka horse (1910) since the *Irish Pooka* 'generally appears in the form of a horse' but will only leave its victims in marshes without killing them. Ireland's Celtic cousins have very similar versions of water horses (e.g. the Welsh *ceffyl y dwr*, the Scottish *each uisage* or *kelpie*, the Manx *cabbyl-ushtey* as well as in the islands off Scotland – the Shetland *shoopiltee* or *njuggle*, the Orkney *tang(ie)* and the Faeroese *nukur*). The distinct *Irish water horse* will drown sometimes out of justice rather than mere spite – e.g. like the horse who was hit by the man it had saved (Ó hÓgáin, 1990).

Irish water spaniel (Ir. *spáinnéar uisce*). The tallest breed of spaniel, bred in Ireland for retrieving. See also *Irish Glen of Imaal terrier* for other Irish dog breeds.

Irish Way, the The route the Irish traders and drovers used through Wales to the English border – from Aberystwyth to Machynlleth (*Country Quest*, April 1999). See also *Irish Road*.

Irish weasel A synonym of the Irish stoat, but whereas 'English' English distinguishes between a weasel, a stoat (which is larger) and a ferret, in *Irish English* the terms stoat and weasel are often interchangeable, hence some writers prefer the latter. Lady Wilde said that 'a purse made from a weasel's skin will never want for money; but the purse must be found, not given or made'. She said it is also unlucky to kill one. O'Sullivan says that it even conducted funerals (1991). The word 'weasel' is also found in Irish fisherman's taboo language (i.e. the special words used at sea for land objects and animals – since the use of their actual names was unlucky). St Clair writes that one type of 'fish was a ling, commonly called a 'weasel' by the fisherman' (1971). See also *Irish hare*.

Irish weave Kinmouth refers to 'the traditional Irish weave of twisted out straw rope' (1993). In the Irish weave the straw rope or *súgán* was pulled from front to back and not in four triangles like the 'English weave'.

Irish wedding 1 A brawl (Green, 1996). See the phrases with Irish wedding in the entries below. **2** The emptying of a cesspool (Partridge, 1937). It seems likely that this particular meaning of Irish wedding (and probably the next) were coined by adding the word 'Irish' as a racist afterthought. Partridge records the unprefixed word 'wedding' which, by the late eighteenth century already meant 'emptying a necessary house [a toilet]'. **3** Onanism (Green 1996; Share 1997). See also *Irish bank, Irish promotion*.

Irish wedding, to dance at an Green prefers this infinitive form (1996) for which see *Irish wedding, to have danced at an*.

Irish wedding, have been to Said of someone who has one black eye (Partridge, 1937). See also following entry.

Irish wedding, to have danced at an 'To have two black eyes' (Partridge, 1937). See also *Irish beauty, Irish coat of arms*. And on the subject of weddings, see the related terms *Irish bouquet* and *Irish confetti*.

Irish wedge tombs An ancient type of Irish tomb (Killanin, 1962) uses the term with reference to the tombs at Labbacallee, Co. Cork – with Neolithic/Early Bronze Age pottery and animal bones etc. See also *Irish passage graves*.

Irish Week Any week of Irish cultural events, usually held outside Ireland, e.g. in Davis and Elkins College, West Virginia (Vallely, 1999).

Irish welcome An invitation to come at any time (Partridge, 1937).

Irish wet fly See *Irish lough wet fly*.

'Irish werewolf' Giraldus Cambrensis had allegedly discovered an Irish werewolf couple (1182–3). Moreover, like Romulus and Remus, the founders of Rome, the Irish saint Albeus was believed to have been suckled by a she-wolf (as was

Cormac Mac Art – see *Irish Solomon)* but no lycanthropic tendencies are recorded. According to Kavanagh (1959) 'the people of Ossory could turn themselves into wolves'. *The Irish Werewolf* is also, of course, the name of the 1970 bootleg Rory Gallagher (alias *Irish rock 'n' roller, the first*) CD recorded at Basel. The *'were'* prefix is from Old English *'wer'* – man – a cognate of the Latin *'vir'* – hence virile – i.e. manly. See also *Irish wolf, Irish wolfhound. See also Irish Frankenstein, Irish vampire.*

Irish wheaten bread Brown soda bread (Connery, 1997). See also *Irish soda bread.*

Irish wheaten terrier (Ir. *brocaire buí*) Soft-coated wheaten terrier. See also *Irish terrier.* See *Irish Glen of Imaal terrier* for other Irish dog breeds.

Irish wheel (*Cym. Sunray X*) A rare variety of orchid.

Irish Whiggery The particular form of whiggery (Liberalism) in Ireland, distinct from that in Britain: 'Irish Whiggery was seen as trimming, latudinarian, soft on Catholics, and too pro-English for its own good' (Foster, 1989). See also *Irish Toryism.*

Irish whin Sometimes used as a synonym of *Irish furze.* A. B. [*sic*] from Co. Down writes: 'There were two types of furze or whin ... the Irish whin and the Scotch whin. The Irish whin was tall and fine; it was moreover a good grower ... of the two the Irish whin was the most valuable as it had plenty of nature in it ... the Irish whin was of great value as horse-food and it gave the horse a very fine and shining coat' (*Ulster Folklife*, Vol. 5, 1959).

Irish whip A cocktail of vodka, pernod, rum, crème de menthe, lemon, lime, soda and orange juice.

'Irish' whiskeries Or rather just whiskeries or whiskyries, a late nineteenth century allusion to the Irish Exhibition in London 1888 (Green, 1998). See also *Irish Industrial Exhibition* and *Irish International Exhibition.*

Irish whiskey 1 Whiskey is one of the *Irish loanwords* in English and derives from the Irish *uisce beatha* which, like the *aqua vitae* means literally 'water of life'. In *Irish Travellers' Cant* it is called *skaihop* (Macalister, 1937) and in *Irish Masonic speech* it is *doun caucha*. In the special tradesman's jargon of *Bearlogair na Saer*, it is called *triompalan*. In slang, the Irish (not Scotch) whiskey is called fish-hooks (Partridge, 1950) or 'grapple the rails' in Cant (cited by Share, 1997). Apart from the spelling (*Irish whiskey* is spelt with a penultimate 'e' as opposed to the Scotch whisky – yet see *Irish whisky*), the Irish drink is unique. It is distilled three times, takes an average of 5–12 years to mature and has a distinct herby mossy taste while the Scotch version is distilled only twice and has a pungent peaty taste. See also *Irish poteen, Irish pot still* and even *Irish Home Rule.* **2** Irish whiskey is also the name of a cocktail containing not only *Irish whiskey* but Triple Sec, Anis, Maraschino, bitters and olive.

Irish Whiskey, Headquarters of As Hughes (2000), calls Midleton, the market town in Co. Cork which is the main centre of *Irish whiskey* distilling.

Irish Whiskey, Home of Another epithet of Midleton (used by Hughes, 2000). See *Irish Whiskey, Headquarters of.*

Irish Whiskey Act (1960) Apart from the obvious triple distillation and use of moss (not peat) in *Irish whiskey,* this Act stated that: 'In order to qualify for the title of Irish whiskey the spirit must be distilled in the State from a mash of malt and cereal grains' (see Magee, 1980).

Irish whiskey and ginger cream A dessert recipe of *Irish whiskey*, ginger marmalade, grated lemon rind, egg whites and heavy cream (see website *Irish Dessert Recipes*). The combination of both whiskey and ginger was recorded by Blake who referred to an interesting custom at a wedding settlement in the west of Ireland in which 'the whiskey is mixed ... with wine coloured ginger beer' (1907).

Irish whiskey butter Made with *Irish whiskey*, castor sugar and butter (Blake, 1971). This is to accompany Christmas pudding made with stout, e.g. Guinness.

Irish whiskey cake With reference to the *Irish whiskey cake* which was used as a wedding (or Christmas) cake, Johnson writes: 'A traditional wedding cake would have three tiers of whiskey cake, the top tier being stored away for the christening of the first child' (1995). With the word 'Irish' prefixed, this recipe seems to be in almost every Irish cookbook (e.g. see Campbell, 1997, Fitzgibbon, 1983; Sheridan, 1966; Thomson, 1982).

Irish Whiskey Frauds Refers to the adulteration of true *Irish* *whiskey* by blending it with Scotch whiskey, done allegedly by Belfast dealers for sale in England. The phrase derives from the headlines of a series of articles written for the Dublin *Evening Mail* by an anonymous author posing as a government official in the early 1900s (Magee, 1980).

Irish whiskey houses As distilleries of *Irish whiskey* are often called (e.g. Magee 1980).

Irish whiskey jug A collectible item which is an attractive porcelain or clay jug for *Irish whiskey*, invariably bearing the name of a particular brand.

Irish whiskey punch This punch is made with boiling water, *Irish whiskey* , three cloves and a slice of lemon (Sheridan, 1966). It is good for flu. It is also called scalteen (Ir. *scailtín*); while the nineteenth century name for it was 'Materials' (Partridge, 1937) yet Share uses this name for the ingredients, not the drink itself (1997).

Irish whisky A misspelling of Irish *whiskey* which should be used only for the Scotch whisky. However, in the past this spelling was used, e.g. by *Paddy Whisky* of the Cork Distilleries Company until 1979 (see Booth, 1995). Likewise there was Allman's *Irish Whisky* (of the Bandon distillery, which ceased production in the 1920s – see Magee, 1980). Yet, by contrast, Magee (one of the foremost experts on Irish whiskey) sometimes uses the Irish spelling for the Scotch version, i.e. referring to 'Scotch whiskey' rather than whisky (1980). With this spelling a whisky mick (see *'Irish' mick*) is also a nickname for an Irishman (Green, 1996).

Irish Whisky Drinker, The The misspelled (i.e. for whiskey) eponym of John Sheehan, who, with Everard Clive, wrote a series of pasquinades for *Bentley's Miscellany*, 1846 (see website *Brewer's Readers Handbook*).

Irish whisper A shout. Also called a 'Mitcham whisper' (Partridge, 1937). See also *Irish hint*, *Paddy's whisper* (Appendix 5).

Irish whist 1 Irish variation of whist 'where the jack takes the ace' (Partridge, 1937). See also *Irish loo*. **2** Sexual intercourse Green interprets the jack and the ace as representing the private parts of the man and woman respectively (1996).

Irish whist, play To have sex (Green, 1998). See also previous entry.

Irish whistle Synonym of the *Irish tin whistle* used by some, e.g. Tom Maguire in his teaching volume: *Irish Whistle Book*.

Irish whitebeam (*Sorbus hibernica*) A species of tree endemic to Ireland. In 1984, the tree was featured on the 22p stamps (belonging to the series of 'Irish Trees' which also featured the *Irish yew* 26p, the *Irish willow* 29p and the birch 44p). (For pictures of these beautiful stamps see www.irishstamps online.com). See also *Irish dwarf pine, Irish juniper, Irish mahogany, Irish willow, Irish yew*.

Irish whitefish As Cochrane calls the pollan found in Lough Neagh (1988) (from Ir. *poll* - lake; see also W. *pwll*). See also *Irish lord, Irish trout*.

Irish White House, the The Áras an Uachtaráin (House of the President) in Phoenix Park, Dublin has been so called. It was built in 1751 and was originally called the Viceregal Lodge, as the *Irish viceroy* stayed there in summer. Duchal (1999) informs us that the White House in Washington DC was designed by Irishman James Hoban (1762–1831) and was modelled on Leinster House in Dublin.

Irish white potato A synonym of the *Irish potato* as opposed to the sweet potato (www.sunspiced.com). See *Irish potato, the birthplace of the*.

'Irish' Wigan Pier Skibbereen has been dubbed 'The Wigan Pier of Ireland' (Ó Faoláin, 1941) since 'all the farcical stories of provincial Ireland that ever were are fathered on this town'. Wigan Pier is not a real pier but is a jocular name for the chutes that tipped coal into the barges of the Leeds and Liverpool Canal in Wigan, England.

'Irish' Wild Geese (Ir. *Na Géanna Fiáine*). Usually simply *Wild Geese* but some writers (e.g. Ó hAllmhuráin, 1998) prefix the word Irish. These were the soldiers often from prominent Irish families who left Ireland for the continent after the *Irish Williamite War*. Many continued their anti-British struggle in the service of foreign European powers. In Irish folklore, 'Wild geese are people who have been enchanted' (Kavanagh, 1959). See also *Irish chateaux*.

Irish Williamite War The Williamite war in Ireland (1688–91) was fought between Irish Jacobites (supporters of the deposed Catholic, King James II) and the Protestant, William of Orange (William III). The most famous battle was the

Boyne (1690) on 1 July (not 12 July as is commemorated because of the calendar change). Losing the battle James fled
to France on his white horse. Henceforth the phrase 'white
horse' refers to cowardice (Green, 1998).

Irish willow (*Sallix hibernica*) A native species of Irish tree. See
also *Irish dwarf pine, Irish juniper, Irish mahogany, Irish whitebeam, Irish yew.*

Irish Windsor chair Similar to the English Windsor chair with
sticks (wooden rod-type parts) but with two stretchers (thin
strips of wood placed across seat) instead of one. Kinmouth
says 'the misnomer Irish Windsor has accordingly been
attached to such chairs' (1993); she believes that the Irish
chair evolved separately without being influenced by the
English Windsor chair.

Irish wine 1 *Irish whiskey* about which 'Peter the Great of Russia
... declared: 'of all wine, Irish wine is the best' (Booth, 1995).
Confusingly, in Ulster slang a 'jenny-wine' is a teetotaler!
(Share, 1997). **2** Guinness – called by James Joyce 'The wine
of Ireland' (quoted by Johnson, 1995; Kearns, 1996). Morton
calls it 'Dublin's black wine' (1930). No relation to *Irish vine.*

Irish wog This pejorative term is used as a synonym for bogwog
(see *Irish bog-trotters*) and combines racist slurs against
both the Irish and the black people (McArthur, 1992). Paule
Dunne records a similar British army slang term for Irishmen as 'wogs from the bog' (see website *A History of Ireland
in Song*). Not the same as *Black Irish* (see Appendix 4) but
corresponds with *smoked Irishman* (see Appendix 3). Similarly, another pejorative word for a black person, i.e. 'nigger'
has been used (in certain combinations) to label the Irishman. Etymologically the word 'nigger' means simply 'black',
(see also 'negro' in Spanish) – hence Nigeria etc. An Irishman has been called Spud nigger (see www.rsdb.org) as
well as green nigger (Green, 1996) and also white nigger
(see www.rsdb.org, according to which 'Blacks called Irish
Americans this during the 1800s in retaliation to being called 'Nagurs'). Black Americans also called the Irish *White
Paddy* (see Appendix 5 section v). White nigger has also
been used for a Jewish person, as opposed to a 'sand nigger',
i.e. an Arab (for which, see the serious and unprejudiced
online article about racist epithets *Nigger and Caricatures* by

David Pilgrim and Philip Middleton). Jay P. Nolan records that pseudo scientists of the nineteenth century even tried to contrive physical 'similarities' between Irish and black people to justify the exploitation of both: 'The Irish, often referred to as the "white negro", occupied a branch closer to the Negro than the Anglo Saxon' (see his online article *Anti-Irish Racism in the United States*). The black person has also been 'insulted' by being dubbed 'Irish' – see *sunburnt Irishman* (Appendix 3). See also *Irish coon, Irishmen of Islam, Irish of South-Western and Western America, Black Irish* (Appendix 4) and *Paddy* and *Paddy Roll* (Appendix 5).

Irish wolf It is unlikely that the wolf in Ireland was really a distinct subspecies like the *Irish hare* or the *Irish stoat/weasel*. Yet Giraldus Cambrensis in 1185 implied unique gestation periods: 'wolves in Ireland generally have their young in December, either because of the extreme mildness of the climate, or rather as a symbol of the evils of treachery and plunder which here blossom before their season' (Killen, 1985). Some writers refer to the so-called *Irish wolf*, e.g. O'Farrell says 'Like Irish wolves, Irish women bark at their own shadows' (1980). Interestingly, according to Partridge, one nickname for Ireland in late seventeenth and early eighteenth century was Wolfland (1937). Shakespeare also refers to 'the howling of Irish wolves against the moon' (*As You Like It*, Act V, Scene II, line 53; the phrase, said by Rosalind, refers to something futile). See *Irish werewolf, Irish wolfhound*.

Irish wolfdog A synonym of the *Irish wolfhound* used, for example, by Fr E. Hogan, SJ, as the title of his book about the breed.

Irish wolfhound (Ir. *cú faoil*) A breed unique to Ireland, also called the *Irish wolfdog* or *Irish hound* which is stronger and larger then the common wolfhound, possibly so called as he was more formidable than the *Irish wolf*. See also *Irish Glen of Imaal terrier* for other Irish dog breeds.

Irish wolfhound breed, saviour of the As the *Irish wolfhound* breeder, Capt. George Augustus Graham, is called (Bremner, 1998). Capt. Graham was a Scot living in England who purchased his first *Irish wolfhound* in 1859 when the breed was on the verge of extinction. In the next few decades he reestablished the breed by crossing it with the very similar but slightly smaller, Scottish deerhound. Yet writing in 1908, Graham stated that there were still *Irish wolfhound* strains 'which may be traced ... to the original breed'.

Irish wolfhound goddess So Tu(i)reann is called (CGG). She was turned into an *Irish wolfhound* by the druidess mistress of her husband. As a wolfhound bitch she bore Bran and Sceolan (Fionn's hounds).

Irish wonder A variety of rose.

Irish wonder tale A term for a category of Irish myth in which magic and the supernatural element prevails, used, e.g. by E. B. Gose, *The World of the Irish Wonder Tale* (University of Toronto, 1984).

Irish work As *Irish crochet* was termed, especially embroidery done in white thread on a white ground (Boyle, 1964).

Irish Workers' League A Marxist organisation that was established by James Larkin in 1924 to replace the Communist Party. It represented Ireland at the *Comintern* in 1924 and 1928 in Moscow. Larkin was disqualified from the seat he won in the 1927 election and generally the party had little support. There was also another Irish Workers' League that revived the Communist Party in 1948.

Irish wrenboys (Ir. *lucht an dreoilín*) The 'Irish wren boys' (see Evans, 1957 and Lawrence, 1997). These are the men who participate in the hunting of the wren on St Stephen's Day (Ir. *Lá an Dreoilín* – Wren's Day). The Irish is often prefixed to distinguish them from the corresponding Welsh and Manx wrenboys. They are also called 'droluns' (Lawrence, 1997) – from Ir. *dreoilin* – or wren – hence *drooleen* – (Joyce, 1910) and *droleen* (Share, 1997); see also W. *dryw*. They would kill a little wren (this bird had allegedly warned Cromwell of an Irish attack and was also used in druid auguries – Kavanagh, 1959). They then carry the wren on a stick and beat an *Irish tambourine*. See also *Irish hobby horse*.

Irish wren hunt As the hunt for the wren by the *Irish wrenboys* is called (e.g. by Hutton, 1996). To take part in this is called to 'go in with the wren' (see website *The O'Byrne Files Dublin Slang Dictionary and Phrasebook*).

Irish wren hunters As the *Irish wrenboys* are sometimes called (e.g. Lawrence, 1997).

Irish wrestling See *Irish collar and elbow method.*

Y

Irishy As distinct from 'Irish' proper, 'Irishy' has the connotations of that which is in an Irish style, but most probably
exaggerated and not authentic. See also *Irishness* and *stage
Irish* in Appendix 4.

'Irish' yard For measuring a yard of wool: 'there was a unit
called the bandle (*bannlaimh*) which was officially 30 inches.
This unit was used in the woollen markets in Co. Galway;
in Kilkenny bandle cloth was only 24 inches wide; and in
Co. Limerick it was 21 inches wide' (Logan, 1986). Similarly, a Welsh yard was 40 inches (Edwards, 1998), a Manx
yard was 37.5 inches (Moore, 1924) and a Scottish yard was
37 inches (Robinson, 1985). See also *Irish acre, Irish mile,
Irish perch.*

'Irish' Yeomanry The word 'Irish' is sometimes inappropriately
prefixed, e.g. by Allan Blackstaff in his *An Ascendancy Army:
The Irish Yeomanry, 1796–1834* (Four Courts, 1998). They
were Irish only in so far as they existed in Ireland. In effect
they were against the Irish cause, being used to control Defenders and *United Irishmen.* They were mostly Protestants
and became closely associated with Orange sectarian violence. See also *Irish Constabularly, Royal.* See also *Irish clubhouse* for some jocular allusions to the police.

Irish yew (Ir. *iúr Éireannach*, Lat. *Taxus baccata 'fastigiata'*) A
synonym of the Florence Court Yew (*taxus baccata stricta*),
a Eurasian and North African variety of yew. See also *Irish
dwarf pine, Irish juniper, Irish lace, Irish mahogany, 'Irish' palm,
Irish whitebeam* and *Irish willow.* However, it is no relation
to the so-called *Irish tree.*

Z

'Irish' Zorro Well, I tried hard to find an entry beginning with
'Z'. From the internet here are two Irish 'connections' with
the famous Mexican bandit-hero (whose name in Spanish
means 'fox'): **1** In her article 'Zorro was Irish', Linda Merle
postulates that 'Zorro … was in fact a bloke from Wexford
called William Lamport' b. 1615 who was banished for his
anti-English activities and travelled to Spain, had connec-

tions with pirates and then went to Mexico where he freed the slaves. So really Zorro should be called 'The Mexican Lamport'. **2** In the video game 'Bushido Blade 2' we are told that 'from the first game ... only Black Lotus, the overly melodramatic Irish Zorro, is missing ...' (www.members. tripod.com).

Appendix 1
The word 'Irish' and its nuances.

The word 'Irish' is extremely rich in connotations. Apart from being an adjective in the sense of that which pertains to Ireland, it also refers to the *Irish language* or *Irish Gaelic* (OED) and even *Irish English* (McArthur, 1992). One internet source states that the term 'Irish' refers not only to 'the aboriginal Celtic-speaking people of Ireland' but by extension, all 'the inhabitants of Ireland and their descendants elsewhere' (www.infoplease.com). Moreover, in history the name 'Irish' has sometimes been used to mean a Scot and vice versa (see *Irish Gaelic, Irish Scot* and *Scots Irish* – Appendix 4 and see also *Irish porridge*).

In cookery, the prefix 'Irish' can have several meanings. Apart from a recipe created by Irish people, it may denote cooking with butter and herbs; and as a prefix to recipes may have the meaning traditional or homemade (see also Ir. *Gaelach* – Irish, homely, pleasant or ordinary). It may also denote the inclusion of *Irish whiskey* perhaps (as do many cocktails with the word 'Irish'). Similarly, an obvious meaning of 'Irish' is *Irish whiskey*, the word 'whiskey' being unnecessary (Partridge, 1937). J. K. Jerome wrote 'He had found a place ... where you could get a drop of Irish worth drinking' (OED). 'Irish' is also a cocktail of vodka, kahlua, coke and Guinness (see Appendix 6 for list of Irish cocktails).

'Irish' can be a temper (see *Irish up, get one's*) as well as something ridiculous or illogical (OED), hence phrases like *You're Irish* (Appendix 4) not to mention *Irish joke* and *Irish logic* etc. 'Irish' can be used synonymously with *Irish bull* (Green, 1996). On similar lines, another negative meaning (as inferred from *weep Irish* – Appendix 4) is insincerity.

In various rhyming slang combinations, e.g. *Irish jig*, the final element can be dropped and just 'Irish' is sufficient (see websites *The Probert Encyclopaedia of Slang* and *Roger's Profanisaurus*). Similarly *Irish stew* (when it means 'true') can be shortened to *too Irish* (Appendix 4). Likewise American newspaper headlines when referring to sports teams representing the *Fighting Irish* (Appendix 4) often use just the name, the 'Irish'.

There is a seemingly infinite range of miscellaneous meanings which have been coined over time for the word 'Irish': an

Irish goat (Mason, 1951); 'a horse bred in Ireland' (Peel, 1978); *Irish linen* (see *Webster's*); 'a tap-dance step consisting of a shuffle, hop, and step' (*Webster's*); a 'choker mouse trap' (for which see *Irish mouse trap*); 'an old game, similar to backgammon, but more complicated' (Halliwell, 1847) and many more.

Perhaps though the most important acquired connotation of the word 'Irish' for centuries has been 'Catholic' (see Connolly, 1998). Indeed, Catholicism has been such a vital part of the Irishman's cultural identity that even several nicknames of the Irishman mean Catholic, e.g. rock chopper (see *'Irish' rock chopper*), *Paddy* (see Appendix 5), and mick (see *'Irish' mick*) as does 'doolan' in New Zealand slang (Green, 1998). Furthermore, other nuances of the word 'Irish' can be gleaned from most of the entries in this dictionary – many of which reflect both the actual and stereotypical characteristics of the Irish.

Appendix 2
Meanings of the word 'Irishman'

Apart from the obvious definition of an 'Irishman' as 'of Irish birth or descent', the word has several other meanings. One of these is an Irish pure bred horse. As Redmond (1979) observes: 'The horse is so identified with Ireland that it was used on the first coins of the new state in the late 1920s and some foreigners still seem to think an Irishman is a horse with red hair'. Indeed, the word 'Irish' can also mean a horse (see Appendix 1).

Another meaning of 'Irishman' is 'a boiled dinner' (Green, 1996); see also *Irish boiled dinner*. Moreover, in underworld slang the 'Irishman' was 'a species of the confidence trick' (Partridge, 1950); see also *Irish toyle*. 'The Irishman' was also an express train which operated from Glasgow to Larne (see Jackson, 1997); see also *Irish Mail*. This is not to be confused with the *Wild Irishman* which is the mail train between London and Holyhead. Talking of the *'Wild Irishman'*, in its other sense it means an indigenous New Zealand plant (Orsman, 1997). Furthermore, in New Zealand English, 'Irishman' also means 'a Maori Catholic' (Orsman, 1997); see also *Irish Maori* again equating the Irishman with his Catholic heritage.

As we have seen, the word 'Irish' can refer to a Scot (see Appendix 1), so in the Scots tongue an Irishman (also spelled Irichman) can also mean a Scot (particularly a Gaelic-speaking Highlander). This meaning is mirrored in the Irish word *'Gael'* which, apart from an Irishman, also means a '(Scottish) high-lander' (*Gearrfhocloir Gaeilge-Bearla*, An Roinn Oideachais, 1981). In view of the common ancestry of the Irish and Scots (and Manx), this identification is to be expected. In addition to the aforementioned meanings of 'Irishman', other meanings can be evinced through some of the following phrases with 'Irishman' in Appendix 3.

Appendix 3
Phrases with 'Irishman'

The following Appendix is subdivided into two sections:

i) phrases which begin with the word 'Irishman's'
ii) Those phrases in which the word 'Irishman' is the second or final element.

For phrases with '*Irishmen*' and '*Irishmen's*' see the main section of this dictionary.

(i)

Irishman's cutting (In both English and Scots usage) 'a cutting taken from a plant with a portion of the root attached' (Robinson 1985). This definition reminds me of the Kerryman gardener's advice to distinguish seedlings from weeds – 'The only sure way is to pull them all out and if they come up again they're weeds' (MacHale, 1979).

Irishman's dinner A fast (Green, 1996; Share, 1997). Interestingly, the word 'Irishman' itself (see Appendix 2) also means 'boiled dinner' (Green, 1996). Talking of food, in English rhyming slang, the Irish-sounding 'Tommy O'Rann' means food ('scan' = food) (Green, 1998). See also *Irish boiled dinner, Irish breakfast, Irish dinner, Irish seven-course meal.*

Irishman's fart See *Irish fart.*

Irishman's fire See *Irish fire.*

Irishman's four-course meal Four pints of Guinness (see www. potters.org). See also *Irish seven-course meal.*

Irishman's friend The potato – so called in the nineteenth century ballad 'The Irish Potato' (Donnelly, 1987). See also *Irish potato* and, for other synonyms, see *Irish apple.*

Irishman's giraffe Baron (1934) uses an unusual expression with reference to an English West Country town: 'Fortune's Well is like the Irishman's giraffe; it can't be true – but it is and I never saw a town which better advertised its own products.'

Irishman's harvest The orange season (Partridge 1937) in the jargon of nineteenth century London fruit sellers. Not connected with the term 'bog oranges' which means potatoes. See also *Irish lemon* and *Irish orange.*

Irishman's hurricane See *Irish hurricane*. (Share records both forms 1997).

Irishman's knife (W. *cyllell wyddel*) Welsh phrase for a spring clasp knife or bowie knife (GPC).

Irishman's necktie A rope in late nineteenth century American slang (see Green, 1998). Rather than refer to any uncouth mode of dress, it probably hints at the hangman's rope round the neck of the *Irish rebel* and is thus comparable to the other American slang terms 'necktie sociable/party', i.e. a lynching (*Webster's*). See also the Columbian necktie, i.e. slitting the throat (Green, 1998).

Irishman's nightingale Green's form (1998) of *Irish nightingale*.

Irishman's obligation 'Like an *Irishman's obligation*, all on one side' - obviously an old English saying coined no doubt by analogy to *Irish evidence* (see the website *Insults and Insulting Quotes about Ireland*).

Irishman's pocket (US slang) 'One that is both capacious and empty' (Share, 1997).

Irishman's promotion See *Irish promotion* (OED gives both forms). See also *Irish rise*.

Irishman's reef Sail tied only at the top (Partridge, 1937). See also *Irish pennant*.

Irishman's ride (Tasmania) 'Bicycle trip in which children take it in turns to ride' (Share, 1997). See also *Irish tandem drive*.

Irishman's stomach Mark Twain once said 'Give an Irishman lager for a month and he's a dead man. An Irishman's stomach is lined with copper, and the beer corrodes it. But whiskey polishes the copper and is the saving of him' (www.all aboutbooze.com). See also *Irish whiskey*.

(ii)

For the sake of brevity it is not possible to contain all proverbs and sayings here with the word 'Irishman', e.g. the nineteenth century US saying 'an Irishman was buried under every tie' with reference to the building of bridges, canals and railroads behind which there was always Irish labour (www.kinsella. org). There are also stereotypes of the Irishman's supposedly violent temperament like the English saying 'The Irishman is never at peace except when he is fighting' (Green, 1996). Moreover the Scots simile 'as loveless as an Irishman' (Morton, 1930), relates to the frequent tradition of the rural Irish of the past to marry not out of love but out of convenience, i.e. *cleamhnas* or matchmaking. Hence, the following list contains mainly two/three-word phrases or collocations rather than sayings.

black Irishman Normally the collective term *Black Irish* (see Appendix 4) is used, yet occasionally this individual form is seen (for instance, see website www.phrases.shu.ac.uk). No relation to *Black Paddy* (see Appendix 5).

broth-of-a-boy Irishman With reference to the *stage Irishman*, Behan says: 'The famed British reserve is as much a myth as the idea of a *broth-of-a-boy Irishman*, he of the ready wit and the warm heart and the great love of a fight' (cited by Christensen, 1996).

Calvinistic Irishman This phrase seems to be a contradiction in terms – yet this is how Morton dubbed the 'typical' Belfast man (1930).

first stage Irishman, the As Crotty (1992) calls Shakespeare's MacMorris, the mercenary soldier in *Henry V* who is 'noisy, quick to take offence, wholly defined by this inferiority complex'. See also *stage Irishman*.

potato-fingered Irishman No relation to 'green fingers', i.e. skill at gardening (which for the *Irish national colour* would be appropriate), but the phrase *potato-fingered Irishman* is applied to somebody (not necessarily Irish) who is 'clumsy and maladroit' (Green, 1996) almost like the phrase 'butter fingers' said to someone who drops (or can't catch) something. See also *Irish potato*.

red-headed Irishman A variety of cactus (*spinosissima*) which is red spined on top (see website www.cactusmuseum.com). The so-called 'Irish cactus' however, is not a cactus, but a cocktail! See also *Irish red*.

smoked Irishman 1 Synonym of *sunburnt Irishman*. **2** In Liverpudlian slang the term has become generalised to refer to any 'person of colour' not just black people. Similarly a 'smoked Yankee' is a 'newly freed black slave' and a 'smoked ham' is 'a native American' (Green, 1996).

stage Irishman A stereotyped/caricature role (not necessarily played by a real Irishman) with an exaggerated *Irishy* (as distinct from authentic Irish) accent, often playing the buffoon with *Irish logic* and speaking a pseudo form of *Irish English* (for which see *Irish vocabulary, stage*). He could wear something green (possibly a hat decorated with an *Irish shamrock*) or brandish – in place of a walking stick – an *Irish shillelagh* etc.

sunburnt Irishman Or *smoked Irishman*. A nickname for African-Americans (Green, 1996) indicating the common Irish/African-American subservient status in America. Conversely, the Irishmen were dubbed 'green niggers' (for which see *Irish wog*).

United Irishman See *Irishmen, United*.

Wild Irishman 1 The term refers to the fiery temperament of the stereotyped Irishman. Apparently in Dutch, the phrase *'De wilde Ier'* or *Wild Irishman* is used to describe a hysterical child (Green, 1996). **2** The *Irish Mail* train between London and Holyhead. **3** A nickname of the *Irish terrier*.

Appendix 4
Phrases in which the word 'Irish' is the second or final element

It would be difficult to record all the compound words where Irish is the suffix, such as anti-Irish, neo-Irish, pseudo-Irish, quasi-Irish, pro-Irish or unIrish etc. However, this list contains perhaps the most colourful expressions ending with the word 'Irish'. I have omitted most hybrid terms such as Dutch-Irish, yet I have included *Anglo-Irish* and *Franco-Irish* which have some historical significance. Moreover, in this relatively brief supplement it was not possible to include the various regional mixtures like Ulster-Irish or Munster-Irish which can refer to dialects of the *Irish language* among other things.

Achill Irish Among Irish Americans (in Cleveland) 'an especially insulting term was "Achill Irish", which alluded to the supposed traitorous conduct of the people who inhabited that island off the coast of Mayo during the bad days' (See www.clevelandmemory.org).

Angle Irish Not the same as *Anglo-Irish* but a separate category of Irish immigrants (especially in Cleveland) who were distinct from both the so-called *shanty Irish* and *lace curtain Irish* (as they called each other). We are told 'Of all the Irish who settled here, the most self-conscious were those who lived hard by St Malachi's spire. Taunted by the more affluent Irish, that is the ones who could afford curtains in the windows ... the Angle-Irish became the most chauvinistic in Cleveland' (www.clevelandmemory.org).

Anglo-Irish 1 The *English Irish* or Palesmen: 'Scholars tend to call them "Anglo-Irish"' (Connolly, 1998). **2** That which refers to both England and Ireland, e.g. *Anglo-Irish Agreement*.

bit Irish, a (Of a statement) rather illogical and similar to the reasoning of *Irish logic* or *Irish bull*.

Black Irish 1 Or as Kipling wrote the 'Black Oirish' (*Soldiers Three*, 1890), i.e. those Irish people with black hair. Apart from the possibility of some being the offspring of Spaniards who came to Ireland, many dark haired Irish people are from pure Celtic stock. Many Welsh cousins, for instance, also have dark hair (but usually with brown eyes) yet blue is more common for dark haired Irish people). **2** It was also a nickname like 'Redlegs' for those Irishmen transported by Cromwell to the Barbadoes (McArthur, 1992). For this reason the verb 'barbadoes' meant to transport people to the West Indies (Green, 1998). **3** The offspring of the Irishmen and their black wives on Montserrat (McArthur, 1992). By coincidence, apart from Guadeloupe (see *Orbis Atlas of the World*), Montserrat is the other island that shares Ireland's epithet as the 'Emerald Isle' (McArthur, 1992). For other connections between the Irish and black people see *Irish coon, Irish wog* and *sunburnt Irishman* (Appendix 3). **4** *Black Irish* is also a cocktail of *Irish whiskey*, kahlua, maraschino cherry and ice cubes (see the website www.webtender.com). **5** The colour 'black' also confusingly (like 'Orange') refers to Unionist orders in Ireland, e.g. the Black Men (see Macafee, 1996). Moreover, I have also seen reference to the 'real black Dubs' who live in Dublin's northside as opposed to the southside 'where the Protestants, academics, teetotalers and foreigners live' (see website *The O'Byrne Files Dublin Slang Dictionary and Phrasebook*). Not to be confused with the cattle *Irish Blacks* and see also *Black Paddy* (Appendix 5).

Bog Irish 'Perceived qualities of those working on peat bogs or living in proximity thereto' (Share, 1997). Such a derogatory phrase was not used only by British people in the past but is sometimes used even by fellow Irishmen in the sense of 'culchie' (see *Irish bog-trotters*).

Castle Irish Or more commonly 'Castle Catholics', where 'Catholic' is used as synonymous with 'Irish' (see Appendix 1). The phrases refer to those Irish people who went to Dublin Castle (when it was the British HQ). It is similar to the phrase 'Castle hack' (Share, 1997). Such people were mostly *shoneens* (Irishmen who aped English ways). A few were actually traitors – hence the term 'castle money' for money paid to informers (Share, 1997), i.e. those 'in the pay of the castle' (Wall, 1995). See also *Irish fine lady's delirium*.

Country 'n Irish See *Irish and Country*.

de-Irishisation 1 The process of de-irishing. **2** The opposite of *Irishisation* in its particular sense with reference to the *Irish theme bar*.

Double Irish A double *Irish whiskey*. Also according to Partridge (1950) 'a double drink of any spirit' is given the Irish
name 'Mickey Flinn' from a nineteenth century Chicago
saloon-keeper (yet the term also refers to a laced drink or
a laxative). Similarly, Brian O'Flynn/O'Lynn is rhyming
slang for gin (Green, 1998). See also *'Irish' mick* and *three
cold Irish* (in this Appendix).

English Irish As distinct from *Irish English*, this was the term
used by Fynes Moryson (1617) as synonymous with *Anglo-
Irish*, 'Old English' or 'Palesmen' (i.e. Seán Ghall) – the de-
scendents of Anglo-Norman conquerors. By contrast, the
'New English' (*Nua Ghaill*) were the later Elizabethan/
Jacobean settlers (see *'Irish' plantations*) (Connolly, 1998).

Faux Irish Phil Hoad's term which is a synonym of 'pseudo-
Irish' (which he also uses) and is applied specifically to the
fake Irish style of many a so-called *Irish pub* (See his online
article *Irish Theme Pubs*).

Fighting Irish 1 A trite label for the Irish similar to *Wild Irish* to
reflect the Irishman's supposed belligerent spirit. **2** a) A
college fraternity – 'The *Fighting Irish* of Notre Dame University' (Dickson, 1997). b) The (American) football or base-
ball team of this fraternity. **3** '*Fighting Irish* was originally
the nickname of New York's heavily Irish 69th Regiment'
(Dickson, 1997). **4** A cocktail of cassis, midori and *Irish
cream* (see website www.orangetree.co.uk). **5** The phrase
Fighting Irish also means 'a boast' (Green, 1998). See also
Irish assurance.

Franco-Irish That which pertains to both France and Ireland.
The French and Irish have had many connections throughout history and sometimes shared a common enemy, i.e.
the English. Interestingly, in nineteenth century tailor's
slang a 'patent-Frenchman' meant an Irishman! (Partridge,
1937). See also *Irish Brigade, Irish chateaux, Irish Legion* and
Irish stew pie for other Irish-French connections.

Gaelic Irish The Irish people of Gaelic (i.e. non English) stock
as opposed to *Irish Gaelic* which is the *Irish language*.

Galeonic Irish One of the three original dialects of the *Irish language* (Connolly, 1998). It was spoken in Connaught, West-
meath, South Longford across to Dublin and as far south
as Wexford. The other two dialects were the Ulster dialect

and the southern dialect (spoken in south Munster, south Clare, Kilkenny and part of Co. Laois).

get one's Irish up See *Irish up, get one's*.

half Irish A person of half Irish blood – and, by extension, a half measure of *Irish whiskey*. See also *Double Irish* and *Irish spirits measure*.

Hisperic Irish According to Macalister (1937), the early Christian scholars in Ireland devised two secret jargons: *Hisperic Irish* and Hisperic Latin, 'based upon Irish and Latin respectively'. See also *Irish Masonic Speech, Irish Travellers' Cant* and *Turkey Irish* (this Appendix).

Hit him again, he's Irish Manx saying (Green, 1996) in the context of the Irishman's supposed readiness to fight (and so needs to be hit to be controlled, perhaps).

lace–curtain Irish The 'genteel and petit-bourgeois' Irish (Green, 1996) as opposed to the *shanty Irish*. Not to be confused with *Irish curtain* or *Irish lace*; however, the latter term may have some association since the *lace-curtain Irish* were wealthy enough to afford genuine *Irish lace* furnishings. Rarely the 'Irish' is dropped and the plain term 'Lace Curtain' is used (www.clevelandmemory.org). See also *parlour Irish*.

Liverpool Irish With reference to Liverpudlian English, Crosby writes, 'the dialect and accent known as Scouse is in fact, "Liverpool Irish" and ... within the city there are other local accents' (2000).

Luck of the Irish See *Irish luck*.

Mediterranean Irish Italians, especially Italian immigrants in America (Green, 1996). Here the phrase may derive from their common Catholic heritage as well as the Irishman's alleged 'Latin' connections (for which see *Black Irish*). The English writer Morton wrote that 'the real Irishman is as different from us as a Spaniard or an Italian' (1930). Indeed, because of his relaxed 'laid-back' yet sometimes volatile character, the often dark-haired Catholic Irishman seems indeed more akin to those races than to the Saxon. See also *Irish Gang, The; 'Irish' Maffia; Irish Mussolini*.

mere Irish Term used by Joseph Th. Leerssen in his work *Mere Irish and Fior-Ghael* (1987) referring to those Irish people who spoke Irish, were Catholic and not loyal to the English crown. See also *Wild Irish*.

Middle Irish The *Irish language* in its form c.1100–1600. See also *Modern Irish, Old Irish*.

Modern Irish The *Irish language* since 1600. It is called in Irish *Nua-Ghaeilge,* i.e. literally 'new Irish' but not to be confused with the term *New Irish*. See also *Middle Irish, Old Irish*.

Murderin' Irish From the mid-nineteenth to the early twentieth century 'a lower classes' exclamation indicative of a climax' (Partridge, 1937). According to Green it 'goes back to the Fenian dynamite campaign of the late 19th century' (1996). Talking of the Irish and murder, Morton wrote 'other nations commit murder for women, but the Irish commit murder for a potato patch' (1930). See also *three cold Irish*.

New Irish By analogy to the *Old Irish* Patrick O'Farrell uses the term 'new Irish' in the new added chapter 'The New Irish and Beyond' (in the third edition of his *The Irish in Australia, 1788 to the Present Day*, Cork UP, 2001) to refer to the modern generation of *Irish diaspora*. Not to be confused with the inhabitants of New Ireland (Papua, New Guinea) who would be called 'New Irelanders'.

Old Irish 1 The *Irish language* in its form c700–1100. **2** More rarely it can refer to the Irish people of history as opposed to the *New Irish*. **3** An old breed of cow for which see *Irish cow, old*.

Oirish A form of Irish which Share describes as a *Paddyism* 'connoting excessive or exaggerated display of perceived national characteristics'; from this root are the forms 'Oirishness' and 'Oirishry' as well as 'Oirishly' (1997). Perhaps the spelling is intended to resemble Irish orthography in words like *oireachtas*, the Irish legislature. See also *Black Irish*.

Out Irish To be more Irish than. Burns wrote: 'I see her face the first of Ireland's sons, And even out-Irish his Hibernian bronze' (from webpage *Robert Burns Country: Epistle from Esopus to Maria*). See also *Irish than the Irish, more*.

parlour Irish Perhaps to avoid the much more pejorative phrase *pig in the parlour Irish*, Vallely refers thus to 'the "parlour Irish" culture adapted by the new Catholic middle classes of the Republic and Northern Ireland' (1999). See also *lace-curtain Irish*.

pidgin Irish See *Irish pigeon*.

pig in the parlour Irish A derogatory phrase stereotyping the

Irish as uncouth and cohabiting with animals as if the *Irish cabin* were a sty. This phrase derives from an exaggerated perception of the rural Irish home – in which livestock were sometimes kept literally under the same roof, since animal quarters were occasionally built onto the side. Yet an animal would only be taken literally inside the house on rare occasions, e.g. when someone brought a piglet near the fireplace for warmth. Sometimes the insult can even be expanded as in 'pig in the parlour dirty Irish'. See also *Irish hen dresser*.

polled Irish A breed of cattle which Mason records as a synonym of *Irish moiled* (1951).

red Irish lord The popular name for the fish *hemilepidotus* found in Canadian and East Russian water (see www.oz.net). It is most probably a subspecies of (or the same as) the *Irish lord*.

Scotch Irish 'As people of Ulster descent are known in the USA' (*Ulster Folklife,* Vol. 5, 1959); more specifically, the Presbyterian immigrants from Ulster in Pennsylvania and Carolina in the eighteenth century (*Brewer's*). Morgan explains that at the time of the anti-Irish riots (see *Irish riots, anti-*) Irish Protestants used this appellation to avoid the 'stigma' of being an Irish Catholic (1996).

Scots Irish See *Scotch Irish*.

Scottish Irish See *Scotch Irish*.

shanty Irish As opposed to the *lace-curtain Irish*, 'The *shanty Irish* or shanty-micks' (see '*Irish*' *mick*) were 'the lower-class, impoverished Irish whose windows, if their shacks supported such things, were covered in sacking, not lace' (Green, 1996). Interestingly, the word 'shanty' is an example of an *Irish loanword* and is derived from Ir. *sean* + *teach* (i.e. 'old house'). Because of this phrase, the word 'Shant' has been used as a nickname for an Irish person. Also in nineteenth century America 'all major cities had their *Irishtown* or 'Shanty Town' where the Irish clung together' (see online article *Irish immigrants in America during the 19th century*).

stage Irish See *stage Irishman* (Appendix 3) and also *Irish vocabulary, stage*.

three cold Irish Like the word 'Fenian' in the nineteenth century, *three cold Irish* meant 'three pence worth of *Irish whiskey* and water' – supposedly derived from the three Feni-

ans: Allen, Larkin and O'Brien (the Manchester martyrs)
hanged for killing Police Sgt Brett in 1867 (Partridge, 1937).
They were trying to rescue Fenian leaders Kelly and Deasy.
Partridge adds that the 'three Fenians hanged' for the
Phoenix Park Murders (1882) could be another association.
However, this is incorrect since five were executed (Brady,
Kelly, Caffrey, Fagan and Curley) and their fellow-accom-
plice, the informer Carey, was later shot. See also *Irish In-
vincibles, Murderin' Irish* (in this Appendix).

too Irish Often, as in many rhyming slang phrases, the second
element of the phrase is dropped (e.g. *Irish jig*, which can be
abbreviated to just *Irish,* for which see Appendix 1). Hence
too Irish means *Too Irish stew* (i.e. true), also simply *Irish
stew*. The omission is probably to avoid any chance of the
outsider deciphering an obvious rhyme. See also *Irish lasses,
Irish rose*.

Too Irish stew True (Green, 1998). A phrase derived from rhyming slang, for which see *Irish stew*. It also appears as 'two
bloody Irish stew'. See also *too Irish* (in this Appendix).

Turkey Irish No relation to *Irish turkey* as *Turkey Irish* refers to
a secret language once used in New York 'in which "*ab*"
comes before a spoken vowel, so that ... "can you?" ... becomes "*caban yaboo*?"' (McArthur, 1992). See also *Hisperic
Irish*.

Two-hand Irish One of two varieties of the board game 'Irish'
(for which see Appendix 1 and also '*Irish' backgammon*)
about which we know very little. The term was used in the
early seventeenth century and is recorded by Hazlitt (1905).
See also *Irish gambit*.

Wandering Irish Term often used (e.g. by Law, 1998) for the
Irish Travellers.

weep Irish 1 From the late sixteenth to mid eighteenth century,
the phrase meant 'To shed crocodile tears; feign sorrow'
(Partridge, 1937). Rather than slurring the Irish as insin-
cere, this phrase most probably derives from the hired *Irish
keeners* and their 'copious lamentations ... at keening'. See
also *Irish cry, Irish funeral howl, Irish wake*. **2** w*eep Irish* also
means 'to talk nonsense' (Green, 1998).

West side Irish The Irish Americans of Cleveland, Ohio – so
called because the expanding Irish community of the 1880s

stretched 'as far west as West 65th Street' (www.cleveland memory.org).

White Irish Catholic (WIC) See *Irish Catholic, White*.

Wild Irish (OED) As distinct from a *Wild Irishman* (see Appendix 3). 'The word "wild" has been used positively in Ireland: by Lady Morgan in her novel *The Wild Irish Girl* (1806) to mean free, unfettered and natural' (McArthur, 1992). Originally it was used, e.g. by Andrew Boorde in 1547 (who speaks of the 'wyld Irysh') to refer to 'The Irish who lived beyond the Pale' (McArthur, 1992). See *Irish Pale*. See also *mere Irish*.

You're Irish 'You're talking gibberish' (Partridge, 1937). See also Appendix 1.

Appendix 5
Phrases with the word 'Paddy'

Sometimes the name 'Paddy' is used as perhaps the most un-fortunate synonym of 'Irish'. Indeed, in several phrases, e.g. *Paddy's hurricane*, the words 'Irish' and 'Paddy' are interchangeable since *Irish hurricane* also exists. The name 'Paddy' has often been so synonymous with the Irishman that he has even been known by rhyming slang forms of this term, e.g. an Irishman has been called a 'goodie and baddie' (Green, 1998) as well as a 'tea caddy' (see website *Cockney Cowboy*) – both phrases rhyming with 'paddy'. This Appendix is probably the most extensive list of phrases ever written with the word 'Paddy'.

For the Irishmen, the name 'Paddy' is in essence just a play-ful pet name of Patrick (see *Irish patron saint*). It seems illogical why this shortened form (used originally with affection for friends and family) became an insulting term in history (corresponding to the word 'Irish'). Perhaps Irish immigrants were heard using this endearing form to various Patricks and the nickname stuck.

Fortunately, Irish heritage is valued by so many Irish im-migrants and their Irish descendants (for whom the term *Plastic Paddy* is inappropriate) that many of these Irish people will quite happily name their bar Paddy's Irish Pub or Paddy's Grill etc. (whether their name is Patrick or not). As for the foreigner, the name 'Paddy's' is perhaps a means of identification. Even if he does not realise that the décor may not always be authen-tically Irish (see *Irish theme bar* and *Irishisation/Irishification*) at least he can be assured that the establishment will at least serve genuine *Irish whiskey* (not Canadian or Scotch) and *Irish stout*.

Nowadays it is often the Irish themselves who coin many of the new phrases with 'Paddy', e.g. cocktails like Paddy's Charm or exquisite flower varieties such as Paddy's Pride. Such phrases reflect the positive Irish connotations that the word 'Paddy' is reacquiring.

For the sake of space I have not been able to include geo-graphical toponyms such as Paddy Creek; brand names like Paddy Whiskey; race horse names; or nicknames of real people.

The entries have been subdivided into five sections:

i) Meanings of the word 'Paddy'.

ii) Forms, e.g. *Pateen* and derivatives, e.g. *Paddyistic*.

iii) Phrases beginning with 'Paddy'.

iv) Phrases beginning with 'Paddy's'.

v) Phrases in which the word 'Paddy'/'Paddy's' is not the first element.

i) Meanings of the word 'Paddy'.

The word 'paddy' is perhaps even richer in meanings than the word 'Irish' itself! Here are over twenty nuances of the word:

a) An Irishman (OED).

b) Specifically any person (usually, but not necessarily, Irish) called Patrick.

c) A rage, temper (OED).

d) 'Erroneous word for baddy' (Partridge, 1937). See also 'goodie and baddie' in the introduction of this Appendix for an Irishman.

e) The same as *paddywhack* (see section iii of this Appendix), i.e. unlicensed almanac (Partridge, 1937) but not in the other senses of *paddywhack*.

f) A hobby, a fad (Partridge, 1937).

g) Worm-eaten (in Kent dialect – Halliwell, 1847). It is probable that this meaning has no association with Paddy in the Irish sense but may be related to the West Indian paddy-bug which eats away at rice.

h) A Chinese person (Partridge, 1950). This is possibly by allusion to a rice paddy. Similarly, perhaps due to the same pun, one strange nineteenth century name for an Irishman was 'Chinaman'! (Green, 1998).

i) Any white person, not just Irish (US African-American slang) (Major 1971). The derivative *patty* is also used (Green 1998). See also *Paddy-roll* (section iii).

j) A policeman (again US African-American slang) (Green, 1998). See also *Irish clubhouse*.

k) A padlock (Partridge, 1950).

l) The ruddy duck (*Webster's*), also *Paddy bird* or *Paddy whack*. See also *Paddy of the bog* (section iii), *Black paddy* (section v).

m) The *Irish terrier*.

n) In Anglo-Manx, the same as *Irish blarney* (Moore, *et al*, 1924).

o) Brick layer or hod-carrier (Green, 1996).

p) Railway worker.
q) Smacking (of a child) (Green, 1998).

ii) Forms, e.g. *Pateen* and derivatives, e.g. *Paddyistic* of the word.
a)Forms of the word 'Paddy'.

Pad rare abbreviation of Paddy (Partridge, 1937).

Pat 1 An Irishman (Partridge, 1937). **2** A Chinese person (Green, 1998) See also *paddy* (section i).

Pateen Pejorative term with the Irish diminutive suffix (Share, 1997). See also *Podgreen*.

Patess Irish woman (Partridge, 1937).

Patland Ireland (Partridge, 1937) see *Paddy Land* (section iii).

Patlander Irishman (Partridge, 1937) See also *Paddylander* (section iii).

Patsy A fool, dupe or victim (Share, 1997; Green, 1998 believes that this word may derive from the Irish name, Patrick).

Patty One of the African-American slang words for a white person (Green, 1996). See also *Paddy boy* (section iii) and *White Paddy* (section v).

Paudeen A plebeian Irishman. From Pádraig (Patrick) + diminutive suffix, *ín* (Wall, 1995).

Podgreen A term of contempt (from Ir. *Pádraigín* – 'little Patrick') and is synonymous with *Pateen* (Share, 1997).

b) Derivatives of the word 'Paddy'.
Most of the collocations and phrases with the word 'Paddy' (in the other sections of this Appendix) are taken from published literature. However, since more 'serious' published sources seldom provide neologisms by adding a prefix or suffix to the word 'Paddy', the following very brief list has been taken mainly from the internet.

anti-paddy 1 On several webpages it means anti-Irish but used facetiously. **2** A type of herbicide – connected with 'paddy' in the sense of rice-field (see www.yi-nong.com).

paddification 1 The *Irishisation* of English pubs into *Irish theme bars*. **2** The word *paddification* has also been used for the 'transformation (i.e. in Taiwan) of western regions with flooded rice paddies' (www.twcenter.org)

paddify The 'making Irish' of something. See also *Irishisation*.

paddyisation Synonym of *Irishisation*.

paddyish *Irishy* or paddy-like.

paddyism An *Irishism* in a facetious or pejorative sense (as opposed to the more academic terms *Irishism* or *Hibernicism*). Share, for instance, describes the pseudo-Irish (and *stage Irish*) euphemism *'Begor(r)(ah)!'* – supposed to be 'By God!' as a *'paddyism'* (1997).

paddyistic Another *stage Irish* phrase, namely 'Top of the morning', is described as a *'paddyistic* greeting' (see website *The O'Byrne Files Dublin Slang Dictionary*).

iii) Phrases beginning with 'Paddy'.

Paddy and Mick Stupid. From rhyming slang *Paddy and Mick* = Thick (Green, 1998). This corresponds with the US nickname for an Irishman – Thick Mick (recorded on the website *The Racial Slur Database*). See also *'Irish' mick, Paddy and Mike, Paddy quick*.

Paddy and Mick joke A category of *Irish joke* in which there are two Irishmen, often one, or both of whom, do or say something that is ludicrous.

Paddy and Mike Bike. More often it is Pat and Mike (Partridge, 1937) See also *Irish tandem, drive; Irishman's ride* (Appendix 3); *Paddy and Mick*.

Paddy barrow (Scot.) A barrow without sides to carry large stones (possibly used by Irish labourers or *spalpeens* – see Robinson, 1985).

Paddy basher By analogy to the similar sounding phrase 'Paki basher' (i.e. the often violent persecution of Pakistani immigrants). The word 'Paddy basher' has been used even in the *Irish parliament* to denote someone (not necessarily physically violent) who is anti-Irish (see two online sources: *Dáil Éireann*, Vol. 259, 22 March 1972, Vote 43: Defence; and *Scots Independent*, November 1995). It is not to be confused with the *St Paddy's Day Bash* which refers to feasting with music etc. on St Patrick's Day (see www.cooking. com).

Paddy bashing Fanatic prejudice against Irish people, for which see *Paddy basher*.

Paddy bird 1 The Java sparrow. **2** As a synonym of *Paddy* or *Paddy whack* it refers to the ruddy duck (*Webster's*).

Paddy boat 'A fishing cutter: first built in the late eighteen fifties by Irish immigrants, being modelled after the Galway "hookers" ... Towards the end of the century the Paddy boats faced strong competition from ... "Guinnie boats", manned by rugged Italian immigrants' (Rawson, 1989). It is almost certain that this vessel is the same as the *Irish boat*.

Paddy boy Also 'paddy-boy' or 'Patty (boy)'; African-American slang referring to any white man, not just an Irishman (Green, 1996). See also *Paddy Roll* and *White Paddy*.

Paddy Brophy See also *Colour of Paddy Brophy, the* (section v).

Paddy Bros One of the two teams (descendants of the Irish) who played in the traditional football game in Llanwennog, Wales, after the Christmas morning service. The other team was the *Blaenaus* (Hole, 1978).

Paddy cake, playing When applied to politicians etc. it means pussy-footing around rather than dealing with a problem seriously. It is a corruption of the children's rhyme, 'Pat a cake, pat a cake, baker's man ...'

Paddy Doyle 1 a) In late nineteenth/twentieth century military slang to 'do Paddy Doyle' means 'to be a defaulter' (one who doesn't pay a debt) (Partridge, 1937). b) Moreover, in British army slang, to 'do Paddy Doyle' also means 'to serve time in the punishment cells' (Green, 1996). See also *Irish theatre*. **2** The phrase 'We'll pay Paddy Doyle for his boots' appears in the popular sea shanty of the same name each line of which begins 'To me Way-ay-ay-yah!', indicating the fact that the song was sung by sailors to keep rhythm when raising the sails or tying off the bunting (see www.speakeasy.org). See also *Irish pennant*.

Paddy frog (Ulster) A frog (Macafee, 1996). Despite the fact that this term is used in the north of Ireland, it may well be derived not from the name *Paddy* in the sense of Irishman but from the English (and Scots) *paddock* from the Old English *pad(d)e* meaning toad. See also cognates in German *Padde*, Dutch *Pad* and South African English *padda* (see Brandford, J. and Brandford, W., *A Dictionary of South African English*, 1991). The phrase corresponds with *Irish nightingale*. See also *Paddy hat*.

Paddy funeral Form used by Green (1996) for the more common *Paddy's funeral*.

Paddy hat (Ulster) toadstool (Macafee, 1996). Again, as with *Paddy frog*, although this phrase is used in northern Irish English, it is probably derived from *paddock-stool* i.e. toadstool, rather than any reference to the Irish name 'paddy'. See also the Old English North Country dialect word *pad-stool* – toadstool (Halliwell, 1847). See also *Irishette, paddy-straw*.

Paddy Irishman A cocktail.

Paddy Kelly In Liverpudlian dialect, this is the docks' police officer (see website *Merseytalk4*). See also *Irish clubhouse* for Irish-related synonyms of policeman.

Paddy kraayll (A.Mx) In the English of the Isle of Man (as opposed to the Manx Gaelic proper) this refers to: **1** A variety of *Manx Codlin*, i.e. an apple also called pursemouth. **2** A variety of potato called pink-eyes. Both terms are derived from the noted agriculturalist, Juan Mooar Pherick Robin y Kraayl, i.e. Big John son of Patrick son of Robert Kreale (Moore, *et al*, 1924).

Paddy ladle (Scot.) A tadpole (Robinson, 1985). See *Paddy frog*.

Paddy Land Also Paddyland or *Paddy's Land,* i.e. Ireland (Partridge, 1937). Green provides us with the form *Patland* (1996). Other names for Ireland which derive from Irish names are *Mickey land* (see '*Irish' mick*) and *Murphyland* (see *Irish potato*), not to mention *Teagueland* (see *Irish Teague*). However, the term is not to be confused with 'Pad-Land' which was Devonshire dialect for 'a parish pound' (Halliwell, 1847).

Paddylander An Irishman (Green, 1996).

Paddy last One who comes last in something, e.g. in a race.

Paddy malone Or more commonly Pat Malone, which is Australian rhyming slang for 'alone' and is sometimes lengthened to 'Pat Maloney' (Green, 1998).

Paddy man 'One of the rank and file of the old BWL Regiment' (Frank A. Collymore, *Barbadian Dialect*, the Barbados National Trust: 1955). Perhaps so called from the Irish presence in the West Indies. See also *Black Irish* (Appendix 4).

Paddy market A synonym of *Paddy's market* when it means 'flea market' (see website *Openair Market Search Words and Phrases*).

Paddy martins Sharkey recalls that traditional Irish clothes were accompanied by Paddy martins, which were 'footless stockings known as *troighín*' (1985)

Paddy McGinty's goat (Also popular in NZ slang) Everyone: 'Tom, Dick and Harry' (Green, 1998). See also *Up goes Paddy McGinty's goat* (section v).

Paddy melon Also 'Paddymelon' which, in Australian English refers to 1 A type of Wallaby. 2 A type of shrub that grows in the Australian bush (Hughes, 1989). Due to the strong Irish presence in Australia (which has probably contributed more to Australian culture and history than any other group, save the aborigines) the association of the word with the Irishman is not improbable.

Paddy melon hole (Aust.) Or simply 'melon hole'. A natural depression in the ground of the Australian outback (Hughes, 1989). Perhaps so named as made from an imprint of a *paddymelon stick*?

Paddymelon stick (Aust.) 'An aboriginal weapon used as a missile in hunting small game' (Hughes, 1989). Hughes is unspecific as to whether or not this weapon is a (form of) boomerang. See also *Irish boomerang*.

Paddy-noddy Embarrassment (Halliwell, 1847).

Paddy of the bog The heron (Share, 1997). See also *Irish bogtrotters, Black Paddy* (section v).

Paddy print A fingerprint (Partridge, 1950). Despite the fact that some slang terms depict the Irish as police (*Irish clubhouse*) or even as criminals (*Paddy wagon*), this word may not be related to Paddy, meaning an Irishman, but possibly the pad of ink on which one presses one's finger before making the print, i.e. 'paw print' (See also Sp. *Pata*).

Paddy quick 1 A stick. **2** Thick (See also *Paddy and Mick*). **3** A kick. All three meanings are examples of rhyming slang (Partridge, 1937).

Paddy Racsyn (W. *Padi Racsyn*) A Welsh 'children's' game in which the boy acts the part of a drunken father and thrashes any of the other children he catches (GPC). In Welsh, 'padi' means 'an Irishman' or 'tantrum'.

Paddy rammer A hammer (rhyming slang – see Partridge, 1937). See also *Irish screwdriver*.

Paddy Roll Henry Turner writes with reference to men who guarded the slave plantations, 'such men were known then as *Paddy Rolls* by the Negroes ... punishment was often administered by them, and the very mention of the name was sufficient to cause stark fear'. Hence, the slaves even sang a song 'Run nigger run, the Paddy Roll will get you' (see website http://newdeal.feri.org/asn/). These plantation guards may not necessarily have been mostly Irish since in US African-American slang *Paddy* (see section i) has always been used as a generic insult for all whites.

Paddy roller A synonym of *Paddy Roll*. According to Richard Schaeffer, 'the term *Paddy roller* seems to be derived from a folk pronunciation of "patroller"' since they would patrol the black slaves (www.afrigeneas.com).

Paddy-row 'More jackets off than blows struck, where sticks supply the place of fists' (Partridge, 1937). See also *Irish shillelagh, Irish stick-fighting*.

paddy someone (A.Mx) To use *Irish blarney* on someone, e.g. 'She can paddy him nice' (see Moore, *et al*, 1991).

Paddy-straw 1 The poisonous mushroom – 'the death cap' in North America. See also *Paddy hat*. **2** The Chinese 'straw mushroom'.

Paddy-tang In Orkney, a type of seaweed used to feed pigs (Lamb, 1998). Perhaps the phrase is not due to the fact that the Irish (like the Welsh) eat seaweed, e.g. *dulse*, but it may relate to the Orkney word *tang(ie)* (see *Irish water horse*).

Paddy train The train 'used to take the men in and out of the mines', perhaps so called since some Irish immigrants worked in British mines. A train of this type is still in operation to give rides to visitors in the National Coal Mining Museum for England at Caphouse Colliery, Yorkshire Coal Fields (for a picture of it see www.ncm.org).

Paddy wagon 1 A police car or van, from the period when the Irish dominated American police forces (Rawson, 1989). This is the most probable derivation, Partridge (who also records it as 'Patty wagon') says it may be so-called 'Because its driver and the company are pretty sure to be Irish' (1950). **2** The website *The Racial Slur Database* implies that by extension the term *Paddy wagon* was used to refer to an Irishman himself as well as the vehicle. In Irish slang the word 'wagon' by itself is an insult for a woman (Share, 1997).

Paddy Ward's pig A person who is lazy and forever relaxing (from eighteenth century slang – see Share, 1997).

Paddy Webb (NZ) The train at Rewanui – named after Labour government minister Patrick (Paddy) Charles Webb (1884–1950), a former miner. Webb, who may well have been of Irish extraction, arranged this service to help miners who worked late shifts (Orsman, 1997). See also *Paddy train*.

Paddy wester Also paddywester 1 'a bogus seaman carrying a dead man's discharge papers' (Partridge, 1937). 2 An incompetent sailor (*ibid*). For other 'Irish' nautical phrases see *Irish hurricane, Irish pennant* and *Irishman's reef* (Appendix 3).

Paddywhack 1 An Irishman (especially a strong and stout one (Rawson 1989) See also the traditional song 'I'm Paddy Whack from Ballyhack'. 2 A rage or temper. Indeed the word 'Paddy' is redundant since irrespective of the anti-Irish slur, the word 'whack' by itself means 'a rage, bad temper' (Green, 1998). Green believes 'whack' to be an abbreviation of *paddywhack* – but *paddywhack* is probably a later elaboration of 'whack'. 3 The same as *Paddywhack almanac* (Partridge, 1937). 4 A smacking (Aust. children's slang) (Partridge, 1937). Once again, the word 'whack' alone also means beat. 5 By extension to the previous meaning it can be a thrashing (Rawson, 1989). 6 As a verb, to beat severely (Green, 1998). 7 A *stage Irishman* (see Appendix 3) (Green, 1998). 8 (Amer.) The ruddy duck (*Webster's*). See also *Paddy bird*. 9 The gristle on meat (*Brewer's*).

Paddywhack almanac Or simply *Paddywhack* or *Paddy's watch*. An unlicensed (bogus/fake) almanac (type of calendar indicating astrology and festivals) – so called according to Green as 'such an almanac "*Comes the Paddy over*"', i.e. confuses its user (Green, 1998).

Paddywhacker An Irishman (synonym of *Paddywhack*). In fact the word 'whacker' on its own is a 'generic nickname for anyone with first name "Paddy"' (Share, 1997).

Paddywhackery The abstract noun of *Paddywhack* (Share, 1997).

Paddywhacking A beating (see *Paddywhack*).

Paddywhack the drumstick A 'partly echoic, partly rhyming' elaboration of *Paddywhack* (Partridge, 1937). See also *What Paddy gave the drum* (section v).

Paddywood The booming Irish film industry (the term is quite recent and used, e.g. by Eagleton, 1999). It is coined perhaps by analogy to Bollywood (i.e. Bombay Hollywood to refer to the Indian cinema industry). See also '*Irish*' *Hollywood.*

iv) Phrases that begin with 'Paddy's'

Paddy's apple (NZ) A potato (Orsman, 1997). See also *Irish apple* for more synonyms and *Irish potato.*

Paddy's Blackguards A nickname of the 18th (Royal Irish) Foot Regiment in the British army – so called as they were Irish. They served from 1863–70). See webpage http://hicketypip. tripod.com/history.htm). See also *Irish Brigade, 'Irish' greenfinch* and *Irish Guards.*

Paddy's Day Or *St Paddy's Day*. A term used affectionately, especially by Irish Americans, for St Patrick's Day. See also *Irish national day.*

Paddy's Eve The eve of St Patrick's Day when the Irish are cooking special Irish recipes and making big preparations.

Paddy's eyewater Or more rarely *Irish eye-water*. Illicit whiskey, poteen (Share, 1997). See also *Irish poteen.*

Paddy's funeral Also *Paddy funeral* – 'any boisterous occasion' (Share, 1997). See also *Irish wake.*

Paddy's Goose No relation to *Irish goose*. *Paddy's Goose* was the White Swan pub in High Street, Shadwell in nineteenth century London, the landlord of which may have been Irish (see Green, 1998). Many seamen were recruited here.

Paddy's hurricane Nineteenth century nautical term recorded by *Webster's* and Partridge (1937) for which see the synonym *Irish hurricane*. More rarely it is *Irishman's hurricane* (Share, 1997).

Paddy's lamp (Ulster) A simple oil lamp (Macafee, 1996).

Paddy's land Phrase used by Partridge (1937) as synonymous with *Paddy Land.*

Paddy's lantern The moon (late nineteenth century nautical slang – see Partridge, 1937). The association of this phrase with the Irish may be recent, since Halliwell recorded that the moon was once called 'parish lantern' (1847). So it is possible that 'Paddy's' is a corruption of 'parish'. See also *Irish lantern.*

Paddy's Lucerne A type of Australian shrub (Hughes, 1989). It may or may not be the same plant as that for which the Latin name is *Sida rhonbifolium* or *commonsida* (see website www.growinglifestyle.com).

Paddy's mare On foot, 'for Paddy is too poor to afford a horse' (Radford and Smith, 1945). The same as 'Shank's pony'. (See also It. *il cavallo di San Francesco*).

Paddy's Market 1 'A market for the sale of secondhand goods, especially clothes' (nineteenth/twentieth century slang, Partridge, 1937). Synomym of 'fair'. As Morton observed, 'it is always market day somewhere in Ireland' (1930). **2** 'any kind of cheap market' (Green, 1998) – more specifically a flea market (see *Paddy market* section iii). **3** (Scot.) A confused scene or untidy room (Robinson, 1985). This meaning may well derive from actual markets. **4** A market in Glasgow (Robinson, 1985). **5** (Nineteenth century) a market in Haymarket Square, Melbourne (Green, 1998).

Paddy's Milestone A nickname for the island of Ailsa Craig in *the Irish Sea*. The phrase is also used in Scotland (see Robinson, 1985).

Paddy's Opera As Thackeray called the choral service at St Patrick's Cathedral, Dublin in 1843 (quoted by Share, 1997). See also *Paddy's Wigwam*.

Paddy's pig There are two phrases New Zealanders use: 'as ignorant as Paddy's pig' and 'as Irish as Paddy's pig' (Orsman, 1997). See *Irish as Paddy Murphy's pig, as*.

Paddy's poke In card playing, cutting a deck by 'pushing out the middle section ... and placing those cards on top' (see website *Macguarie Dictionary Book of Slang*). See also *What paddy shot at* (section v of this Appendix).

Paddy's rhubarb (Scot.) The plant butter burr (Robinson, 1985).

Paddy's shuttle A commuter service that serves mainly Irish passengers in the US. See also *Irish Channel, Paddy train, Paddy Webb*.

Paddy's stope (Ulster) A large wooden bucket with a pole passed through the holes in two staves to be carried by two people (Macafee, 1996).

Paddy's surprise A cocktail of *Irish poteen*, cointreau and vodka – topped up with orange juice, bitters and blackcurrant (see Poteen Cocktails in www.irish-poteen.com).

Paddy's toothache A synonym recorded by Share (1997) for *Irish toothache*.

Paddy's watch A synonym of *Paddywhack almanac* recorded by Green (1998).

Paddy's Well In Scotland, a 'spring in Fardoun Parish is locally known as Paddy's Well, and an annual market goes by the name of … Paddy's Fair' (Macinlay, 1893)

Paddy's whisper (A.Mx) 'A stage whisper' (that all can hear) (Moore, *et al*, 1924). Almost identical to an *Irish whisper*.

Paddy's Wigwam The Catholic Church in Ipswich (www.ipswichaway.co.uk). See also *Paddy's Opera*.

v) Phrases in which the word 'Paddy' is the middle or final element

all behind like Paddy with the rent Phrase said of someone who cannot keep to a schedule (Radford and Smith, 1945).

anti-paddy See section ii of this Appendix.

As ignorant as Paddy's pig An equivalent form of *Irish as Paddy Murphy's pig, as*.

As Irish as Paddy's pig Nineteenth century equivalent of *Irish as Paddy Murphy's pig, as*.

Black Paddy Ulster name for the bird called the shag; also known in Ulster as the 'black hag' (Macafee, 1996). No relation to *White Paddy*. See also *Paddy of the bog* (section iii).

Colour of Paddy Brophy, the (In Waterford) a pale, unhealthy colour (Share, 1997).

Come the Paddy over 'To bamboozle' (Partridge, 1937). By the same token 'to come the blarney over' is to flatter (Green, 1998) See also *Irish blarney*.

Do Paddy Doyle See *Paddy Doyle* (section iii of this Appendix).

Having a paddy In a temper or having a tantrum (see website http://phrases.shu.ac.uk/).

In a paddy In a temper (see *Having a paddy*).

Like Paddy with the rent See *all behind like Paddy with the rent*.

Pay Paddy Doyle See *Paddy Doyle* (section iii of this Appendix).

Plastic Paddy Often in plural 'plastic Paddies' referring to 'Children of first-generation Irish immigrants in Britain' (Share, 1997, see also Arrowsmith, 2000).

Put the Paddy on A.Mx expression which is synonymous with to *paddy someone* (Moore, *et al*, 1991).

St Paddy's Day As St Patrick's Day is sometimes affectionately called.

Simian Paddy A caricature of the Irishman with a crouching body and ape-like face (See also Italian '*scimmia*' – monkey). Obnoxious sketches of this genre appeared in *Punch* magazine in the nineteenth century. Through the propaganda of Goebbels (see also also *Irish Goebbels*), Hitler used the same racist technique against the Jews by portraying them not as apes but as vermin.

Simianised Paddy Synonym of *Simian Paddy*.

Stand Paddy (Of a pedlar) 'to sell from a stationary position' (Partridge, 1937). Also 'stand pad' (not to be confused with 'stand pat': underworld slang for not giving information to the police [Partridge, 1950; see also *Irish evidence*]). Partridge derives the phrase 'Stand Paddy' from an old word 'pad'– i.e. road. Alternatively, the phrase 'Stand Paddy' may derive from a 'pad' (of cardboard etc.) on which a beggar sits (see also the phrase 'sit pad' – to beg in a sitting position which Partridge gives as a synonym of 'Stand Paddy', 1937).

We'll pay Paddy Doyle for his boots See *Paddy Doyle* (section iii of this Appendix).

Up goes Paddy McGinty's goat Or simply 'up goes McGinty's goat' – a New Zealand phrase indicating that the excitement begins (Orsman, 1997). See also *Paddy McGinty's goat* (section iii).

What Paddy gave the drum (Mid nineteenth century military slang) A beating (Allsopp, 1996; Green, 1998). See also *Paddywhack* (section iii of this Appendix) and section i 'Paddy' meaning 'to beat'. See also *Irish frame drum* and *Irish tambourine*.

What Paddy shot at (Formerly used in Nova Scotia) 'the term for a useless hand in cribbage which scores zero' (http://phrases.shu.ac.uk/). See also *Irish loo*.

White Paddy US Black Slang for any white person (Green, 1996); others are *Paddy boy*, *Patty* and patty-boy (*ibid*). Also simply *Paddy* is used (see section i of this Appendix). See also *Paddy roller* (section iii). For the similar phrase 'white nigger' also used by Black Americans to refer to the Irish, see *Irish wog*. It is distinct from *Black Paddy*.

Appendix 6

List of cocktails with the words 'Irish', 'Irishman('s)' and 'Paddy('s)'

Owing to lack of space, it was not possible to list all these cocktails and their recipes within the main section of the dictionary. Most are either the creation of the Irish themselves or contain an authentic Irish drink – usually either *Irish whiskey* or *Irish cream*. Many of the recipes can be found on the internet.

i) Irish, Irish Alexander, Irish Almond, Irish Angel, Irish Ayes Cocktail, Irish Banana, Irish Bitch, Irish Blackthorn, Irish Blessing, Irish Bloody Mary, Irish Bluebull, Irish Blue Shock, Irish Brogue, Irish Buck, Irish Bulldog, Irish Cactus, Irish Canadian Sangaree, Irish Cappuccino, Irish Car Bomb, Irish Car Bomber, Irish Charlie, Irish Cheer, Irish Chocolate Martini, Irish Cocktail, Irish Coconut, Irish Colada, Irish Colorado, Irish Comfort, Irish Cooler, Irish Cow, Irish Cresta, Irish Cup o'Joe, Irish Curdling Cow, Irish Dawg, Irish Delight, Irish Down Under, Irish Dream, Irish Egg Nog, Irish Enema, Irish Eyes, Irish Fix, Irish Fizz, Irish Flag, Irish Float, Irish Fool, Irish 49, Irish Freeze, Irish Frog, Irish German Nut, Irish Gold, Irish Griep, Irish Gun Runner, Irish Haemorrhage, Irish Hammer, Irish Handshake, Irish Headlock, Irish Heather, Irish Horseman, Irish Ice, Irish Italian, Irish Keg Bomb, Irish Kilt, Irish Kiss, Irish Knight, Irish Lady, Irish Long, Irish Magic, Irish Maria, Irish Martini, Irish Mexican bull, Irish Mint, Irish Mist, Irish Mist Kiss, Irish Mixer, Irish Monastery Fizz, Irish Monk, Irish Monkey, Irish Mounty, Irish Mudslide, Irish Mystery, Irish Night, Irish Nut, Irish Orange Margarita, Irish Orgasm, Irish Pancake, Irish Pirate, Irish Platinum Margarita, Irish Pride, Irish Quaalude, Irish Rainbow, Irish Raspberry, Irish Red Fizz, IRA, IRA/Letter Bomb, Irish Rickey, Irish Rose, Irish Rover, Irish Russian, Irish Sangaree, Irish Sanka, Irish Schnappa Bull, Irish Scott, Irish Shillelagh, Irish Shitkicker, Irish Shock, Irish Shockwave, Irish Sleeper, Irish Sling, Irish Slut, Irish Smoothie, Irish Sombrero, Irish Special, Irish Spring, Irish Sting, Irish Stinger, Irish Stirisch, Irish Sunrise, Irish Sunset, Irish Surfer, Irish Thunderbird, Irish Toad, Irish Toboggan, Irish Triple Coffee, Irish Velvet, Irish Whip, Irish Whiskey, Irish Whiskey Highball, Irish Widow, Irish Wings, Irish Winter.

ii) Black Irish, Bubbling Irish Nut, Bucking Irish, Erins Irish, Espresso Irish, Everyone's Irish, Fighting Irish, Sweaty Irish, Wild Irish Rose.

iii) Irishman's Deep Throat, Chilly Irishman, Extra Nutty Irishman, Flaming Irishman, Fruity Irishman, Fullblooded Irishman (FBI), Green Irishman, Nutty Irishman, Paddy Irishman, Randy Irishman, Red hot Irishman, Shitfaced Irishman, Silly Irishman.

iv) Paddy, Paddy('s) Night, Paddy's Brainstorm, Paddy's Caffeine, Paddy's Charm, Paddy's Paralyser, Paddy's Smacker, Paddy's Surprise.

Adams, J. R. R. (1998) 'Swine-Tax and Eat-Him-All Magee: The Hedge Schools and Popular Education in Ireland' in Donnelly Jr., J-S. and Miller, Kerby A. (eds) *Irish Popular Culture: 1650–1850* (Irish Academic Press: Dublin), pp. 97–117.

Alexander, Marc (2002) *A Companion to the Folklore, Myths and Customs of Britain* (Sutton Publishing: Bath).

Alford, Violet (1962) *Sword Dance and Drama* (Merlin: London).

Allen, Darina (1994) *Irish Traditional Cooking* (Kyle Cathe: London).

Allsopp, Richard (1996) *Dictionary of Caribbean English* (Oxford University Press: Oxford).

Anon (1978) 'Ainmneacha Plandaí agus Ainmhithe (Flora and Fauna Nomenclature)', (An Roinn Oideachais: Dublin).

Arrowsmith, Aidan (2000) 'Plastic Paddy: Negotiating Identity in Second-Generation "Irish Writing in English"' in *Irish Studies Review*, Vol. 8, No. 1, pp. 35–43.

Ayto, John (1994) *A Gourmet's Guide: Food and Drink from A to Z* (Oxford University Press: Oxford).

Baines, Anthony (1992) *The Oxford Companion to Musical Instruments* (Oxford University Press: Oxford).

Ballard, Linda (a) (no date) *Ulster Needlework: A Continuing Tradition* (Ulster Folk and Transport Museum).

Ballard, Linda (b) (no date) *Tying the Knot: Marriage Traditions in the North of Ireland* (Ulster Folk and Transport Museum).

Ballard, Linda (1998) *Forgetting Frolic: Marriage Traditions of Ireland* (Institute of Irish Studies: Belfast/Folklore Society: London).

Barber, Katherine (ed.) (1998) *The Canadian Oxford Dictionary* (Oxford University Press: Oxford).

Baron, Stanley R. (1934) *Westward Ho! From Cambria to Cornwall* (Jarrold: London).

Bennett, Douglas (1991) *Encyclopaedia of Dublin* (Gill and Macmillan: Dublin, rep. 1994).

Berlitz, Charles (1983) *Native Tongues* (Granada: London).

Bernstein, Ken (1980) *Ireland* (Berlitz Travel Guides: Lausanne, 9th edn. 1991).

Blake, Carla (1971) *The Irish Cookbook* (Mercier: Cork, rep. 1992).

Blake, T. P. U. (1907) 'Matrimonial Customs in the West of Ireland' in *Folklore*, Vol. 18, pp. 77–82.

Blevins, Winfred (1993) *The Wordsworth Dictionary of the American West* (Wordsworth Reference: Hertfordshire).

Bluett, Anthony (1994) *Things Irish* (Mercier: Cork).

Bonthrone, Grace C. (1960) 'Childhood Memories of County Antrim' in *Ulster Folklife*, Vol. 6, pp. 32–42.

Booth, Hohn (1995) *A Toast to Ireland: A Celebration of Traditional Irish Drinks* (Blackstaff: Belfast).

Boyce, Charles (1985) *The Wordsworth Dictionary of Furniture* (Wordsworth Editions, 1996: Hertfordshire).

Boylan, Henry (ed.) (1998) *A Dictionary of Irish Biography* (Gill and Macmillan: Dublin).

Boyle, Elizabeth (1964) 'Embroidery and Lacemaking in Ulster' in *Ulster Folklife*, Vol. 10, pp. 5–22.

Brady, Ciaran (2000) *The Hutchinson Encyclopaedia of Ireland* (Helicon: Oxford).

Breathnach, Breandan (1971) *Folk Music and Dances of Ireland* (Mercier: Cork, rep. 1989).

Bremner, Muriel Monsell (1998) *The Wolfhound Guide to the Irish Wolfhound* (Wolfhound Press: Dublin).

Brett, Walter (ed.) (no date) *The Rose Encyclopaedia* (C. Arthur Pearson Ltd: London).

Brewer, Ebenezer Cobham (1870) *Brewer's Dictionary of Phrase and Fable* (Cassell:

London, rev. edn. 1981).

Briggs, Katherine (1976) *A Dictionary of Fairies* (Penguin: Middlesex, rep. 1979).

Buchanan, Ronald H. (1961) 'Folklife in the Highlands' in *Ulster Folklife*, Vol. 7, pp. 51–62.

Campbell, Georgina (1996) *The Best of Irish Breads and Baking* (Wolfhound Press: Dublin, rep. 1997).

Canny, Nicholas (1989) 'Early Modern Ireland, c.1500–1700' in Foster, R. F. (ed.) *The Oxford Illustrated History of Ireland* (Oxford University Press: Oxford).

Cartier-Bresson, Henri (1994) *Irish Crochet Lace* (Dover Publishing Co.: New York).

Christensen, Lis (1996) *A First Glossary of Hiberno-English* (Odense University Press: Denmark).

Clark, Thomas L. (1996) *Western Lore and Language* (University of Utah Press: Salt Lake City).

Cochrane, James (1988) *Dictionary Game Dictionary* (W and R Chambers: Edinburgh).

Cole, Rosalind (1973) *Of Soda Bread and Guinness* (Bobbs-Merril Co. Inc.: Indianapolis, New York).

Connery, Clare (1997) *Irish Food and Folklore* (Hamlyn: London).

Connolly, Sean (1998) 'Ag Déanamh Commanding: Elite Responses to Popular Culture' in Donnelly Jr., J-S. and Kerby, A. Miller (eds) *Irish Popular Culture, 1650–1850* (Irish Academic Press: Dublin).

Connolly, S. J. (ed.) (1998) *The Oxford Companion to Irish History* (Oxford University Press: Oxford).

Crawford, W. H. (no date) *The Irish Linen Industry* (Ulster Folk and Transport Museum/The Irish Linen Guild).

Cregeen, Archibald (1835) *A Dictionary of the Manks Language* (J. Quiggin: North Quay, rep. Yn Cheshaght Ghailckagh: Braddan, Isle of Man, 1969).

Crosby, Alan (2000) *The Lancashire Dictionary of Dialect, Tradition and Folklore* (Smith Settle: Otley, W. Yorkshire)

Crossley-Holland, P. (1997) *Telyn Teirtu: Myth and Magic in Medieval Wales* (Centre for Advanced Welsh Music Studies: Bangor).

Crotty, Patrick (1992) 'Fathers and Sons' in *The New Welsh Review*, No. 17, pp. 104–60.

Curran, Bob (2000) *The Truth about the Leprechaun* (Wolfhound Press: Dublin).

Danaher, Kevin (1964) *In Ireland Long Ago* (Mercier: Cork).

Danaher, Kevin (1972) *The Year in Ireland* (Mercier: Cork).

D'Arcy, Frank (1999) *The Story of Irish Emigration* (Mercier: Cork).

Day, Brian (2000) *Chronicle of Celtic Folk Customs* (Hamlyn: London).

Dickson, David (1995) 'The Other Great Irish Famine' in Pórtéir, Cathal (ed.) *The Great Irish Famine* (RTE/Mercier: Cork).

Dickson, Paul (1997) *Labels for Locals: What to call people from Abilene to Zimbabwe* (Merriam Webster: Springfield, Massachusetts).

Dixon-Kennedy, Mike (1996) *Celtic Myth and Legend: An A–Z of People and Places* (Blandford, Cassell: London, rep. 1997).

Dodd, A. H. (1972) *A Short History of Wales* (Batsford: London, rep. 1984).

Donnelly, Nell (1987) *Pot Luck: Potato Recipes from Ireland* (Wolfhound: Dublin, rep. 1998).

Douglas, Andrew (ed.) (1995) *The Premier Guide to the Isle of Man* (Lidy Publications: Kilgetty).

Douglas, Ronald Macdonald (1936) *The Irish Book* (Talbot Press: Dublin).

Drummond, David (1996–97) 'Irish Mouse Traps' in *Folk Life*, Vol. 35, pp. 54–62.

Duchal, Alicia (1999) *An A–Z of Modern America* (Routledge: New York).

Dwelly, E. (1988) *The Illustrated Gaelic English Dictionary* (Gairm: Glasgow).

Eagleton, Terry (1999) *The Truth About the Irish* (New Island Books: Dublin).

Edwards, Anthony (1995) 'Footprints of St Patrick in Wales' in *The Celtic History Review*, Vol. 1, Issue 2, pp. 5–8.

Edwards, T. B. (1998) *Welsh Nots, Welsh Notes and Welsh Nuts: A Dictionary of Phrases Using the Word 'Welsh'* (Gwasg Carreg Gwalch: Llanrwst, Wales).

Ellis, Peter Berresford (1985) *The Celtic Revolution* (Y Lolfa: Talybont, Wales, 2nd rep. 1988).

Ellis, Peter Berresford (1987) *A Dictionary of Irish Mythology* (Constable: London, rep. Oxford University Press: Oxford, 1991).

Ellis, Peter Berresford (1992) *Dictionary of Celtic Mythology* (Constable: London).

Encyclopaedia Britannica (1929 edn).

Encyclopedia Americana (1963 edn).

Encyclopaedia of Sports, Games and Pastimes (1988) (Sri Satguru Publications: Delhi).

Evans, E. Estyn (1942) *Irish Heritage: The Landscape, The People and Their Work* (W. Tempest, Dundalgan Press: Dundalk, 9th rep. 1967).

Evans, E. Estyn (1957) *Irish Folk Ways* (Routledge and Kegan Paul: London, 6th rep. 1976).

Evans, E. Estyn (1959) 'A Pennsylvanian Folk Festival' in *Ulster Folklife*, Vol. 5, pp. 14–19.

Fitzgibbon, Theodora (1983) *Irish Traditional Food* (Gill and Macmillan: Dublin, rep. 1991).

Fleming, John, Honour, Hugh and Persner, Nikolaus (1966) *The Penguin Dictionary of Architecture* (Penguin Books: Middlesex, rep. 1980)

Floyd, Michael (1937) *The Face of Ireland* (B. T. Batsford: London, 2nd edn 1947–8).

Foster, R. F. (1989) 'Ascendancy and Union' in R. F. Foster (ed.) *The Oxford Illustrated History of Ireland* (Oxford University Press: Oxford).

Geiriadur Prifysgol Cymru: A Dictionary of the Welsh Language (University of Wales Press: Cardiff).

Gmelch, George (1977) *The Irish Tinkers: The Urbanization of an Itinerant People* (Cummings: New York, 2nd edn. Waveland Press: Illinois, 1985).

Gove, Philip Babcock and Merriam-Webster (eds) *Websters Third New International Dictionary Unabridged* (Merriam-Webster: Springfield, Massachusetts).

Gray, Peter (1995) 'Ideology and the Famine' from Pórtéir, Cathal (ed.) *The Great Irish Famine* (RTE/Mercier: Cork).

Green, Jonathan (1996) *Words Apart: The Language of Prejudice* (Kyle Cathe: London).

Green, Jonathan (1998) *Cassell's Dictionary of Slang* (Cassell: London, pbk edn. 2000).

Green, Miranda J. (1992) *Dictionary of Celtic Myth and Legend* (Thames and Hudson: London).

Grimes, Dorothy A. (1991) *Like Dew Before the Sun* (Grimes: Rushden, Northamptonshire).

Halley, Ned (1996) *The Wordsworth Dictionary of Drink* (Wordsworth Editions: Ware, Herts.)

Halliwell, J. O. (1847) *Dictionary of Archaic and Provincial Words* (George Routledge: New York, 7th edn 1924).

Hawkins, R. E. (1984) *Common Indian Words in English* (Oxford University Press: Oxford).

Hazlitt, W. C. (1905) *Dictionary of Faiths and Folklore* (Reeves and Turner: London, rep. Bracken Books, London, 1995).

Healy, Paul (1998) *Gaelic Games and the Gaelic Athletic Association* (Mercier: Cork).

Hickey, D. J. and Doherty, J. E. (1980) *A Dictionary of Irish History 1800– 1980* (Gill and Macmillan: Dublin, rep. 1987).

Hilliard, Richard (1962) 'Biddies and Straw Boys' in *Ulster Folklife*, Vol. 8, pp. 100–2.

Hole, Christina (1978) *A Dictionary of British Folk Customs* (Hutchinson and Co. Ltd: London/Granada: St Alban's, Herts.).

Hughes, Joan (ed.) (1989) *Australian Words and Their Origins* (Oxford University Press: Melbourne).

Hughes, Martin (2000) *World Food: Ireland* (Lonely Planet: Victoria, Australia).

Hutton, Ronald (1996) *The Stations of the Sun* (Oxford University Press: Oxford).

Jackson, Alan A. (1997) *The Wordsworth Railway Dictionary* (Wordsworth: Ware, Herts.).

Jarman, A. O. H. and Jarman, Eldra (1991) *The Welsh Gypsies: Children of Abram Wood* (University of Wales Press: Cardiff).

Jeans, Peter D. (1993) *Ship to Shore* (ABC–Clio: Oxford/Santa Barbara, rep. 1998).

Jeffery, P. H. (no date) *Ghosts, Legends and Lore of Wales* (Old Orchard Press: Foxton).

Jenkins, J. Geraint (1962) *Agricultural Transport in Wales* (Welsh Folk Museum: Cardiff).

Johnson, Margaret (1995) *Cooking with Irish Spirits* (Wolfhound: Dublin, 2nd rev. ed. 1998).

Jones, Alison (1995) *Larousse Dictionary of World Folklore* (Larousse: Edinburgh/New York).

Jones, Noragh (1993) *Living in Wales* (Gomer: Llandysul).

Joyce, P. W. (1910) *English As We Speak it in Ireland* (Wolfhound Press: Dublin, rep. 1991).

Kane, J. N. and Alexander, G. L. (1899) *Nicknames and Sobriquets of US Cities, States and Counties* (Scarecrow: London, rep. 1979).

Kavanagh, Peter (1959) *Irish Mythology: A Dictionary* (Goldsmith: Newbridge, Co. Kildare, rep. 1988).

Kearns, Kevin C. (1996) *Dublin Pub Life and Lore: An Oral History* (Gill and Macmillan: Dublin).

Kee, Robert (1980) *Ireland: A History* (The book of the BBC/RTÉ tv series, Weidenfeld and Nicolson: London, rep. 1981).

Kelly, John (1866) Dictionary of Manks (The Manx Society: Douglas, rep. Scolar Press, Yorkshire, 1977).

Kemp, Peter (ed.) (1976) *The Oxford Companion to Ships and the Sea* (OUP: Oxford, rep. 1992).

Kennedy, Michael (1980) *The Concise Oxford Dictionary of Music* (Oxford University Press: Oxford).

Kiberd, Declan (1991) 'Irish Literature and Irish History' in Foster, R. F. (ed.) *The Oxford Illustrated History of Ireland* (Oxford University Press: Oxford).

Kiely, Kevin (1999) 'Heaney and Other Noblemen' in *Books Ireland*, March 1999, pp. 55–6.

Killanin, Lord and Duignan, Michael V. (1962) *The Shell Guide to Ireland* (Macmillan: London, rep. 1989).

Killen, John (ed.) (1985) *The Irish Christmas Book* (Blackstaff: Belfast).

Kinealy, Christine (1995) 'The Role of the Poor Law During the Famine' in Pórtéir, Cathal (ed.) *The Great Irish Famine* (RTE/Mercier: Cork).

Kinmouth, Claudia (1993) *Irish Country Furniture 1700–1950* (Yale University Press: New Haven/London).

Knowles, Elizabeth (ed.) (2000) *The Oxford Dictionary of Phrase and Fable* (OUP: Oxford).

Kohn, George C. (1995) *The Wordsworth Encyclopaedia of Plague and Pestilence* (Wordsworth: Ware, Herts.).

Lamb, Gregory (1988) *Orkney Wordbook* (Lamb: Lerwick).

Law, Gary (1998) *The Cultural Traditions Dictionary* (Blackstaff: Belfast).

Lawrence, Elizabeth Arwood (1997) *Hunting the Wren* (University of Tennessee Press: Knoxville).

Leach, Maria (ed.) (1949) *Funk and Wagnalls Standard Dictionary of Folklore, Mythology and Legend* (Horgenand Row: New York, rep. 1984).

Lenihan, Pádraig (1995) 'Gaelic Warfare' in *The Celtic History Review*, Vol. 2, Issue 1, pp. 9–12.

Livingstone, E. A. (ed.) (1977) *The Concise Oxford Dictionary of the Christian Church* (OUP: Oxford, rep. 1980).

Logan, Patrick (1986) *Fair Day: The story of Irish fairs and markets* (Appletree Press: Belfast).

Loomis, Roger S. (1949) 'Celtic Folklore' in Leach, Maria (ed.) *Funk and Wagnalls Standard Dictionary of Folklore, Mythology and Legend* (Horgenand Row: New York, rep. 1984).

Lover, Samuel and Crofton Croker, Thomas (1995) *Ireland* (Senate: London).

Lysaght, Patricia (1986) *The Banshee: The Irish Supernatural Death Messenger* (O'Brien: Dublin, rep. 1996).

Lysaght, Patricia (1997) 'Caoineadh os Cionn Coirp: The Lament for the Dead in Ireland' in *Folklore*, Vol. 108, pp. 65–82.

Macafee, C. L. (1996) *A Concise Ulster Dictionary* (OUP: Oxford).

Macalister, R. A. Stewart (1937) *The Secret Languages of Ireland* (Cambridge University Press: Cambridge, rep. Craobh Rua Books, Armagh, 1997).

Mac Cullagh, Richard (1992) *The Irish Curragh Folk* (Wolfhound: Dublin).

Macdonald, A. M. (ed.) (1977) *Chambers Twentieth Century Dictionary* (Chambers: Edinburgh, rep. 1981).

MacHale, Des (no date) *Best Irish Humorous Quotations* (Mercier: Cork).

MacHale, Des (1979) *The Official Kerryman Joke Book* (Mercier: Cork).

Macinlay, James M. (1893) *Folklore of Scottish Lochs and Springs* (William Hodge: Glasgow, facsimile rep. Llanerch: Felinfach, Wales.

Mac Lysaght, Edward (1979) 'The 1890s and 1900s in Clare' in Gmelch, Sharon (ed.) *Irish Life and Traditions* (O'Brien: Dublin and Syracuse University Press: New York).

MacManus, Dermot (1959) *The Middle Kingdom: The Faerie World of Ireland* (Colin Smythe: Gerrards Cross, rep. 1993).

McArthur, Tom (ed.) (1992) *The Oxford Companion to the English Language* (OUP: Oxford).

Mc Guire, Kim (2000) *Irish Love and Wedding Customs* (Wolfhound: Dublin).

Mc Mahon, Sean (1997) *The Story of the Claddagh Ring* (Mercier: Cork).

Magee, Malachy (1980) *1000 Years of Irish Whiskey* (O'Brien: Dublin).

Mahon, Brid (1991) *Land of Milk and Honey* (Poolbeg: Dublin, rep. Mercier, Cork, 1998).

Mahon, Brid (2000a.) *Rich and Rare: The Story of Irish Dress* (Mercier: Cork).

Mahon, Brid (2000b.) *Ireland Folklore* (Mercier: Cork).

Major, Clarence (ed.) (1971) *Black Slang: A Dictionary of Afro-American Talk* (Routledge and Kegan Paul: London/New York).

Malcolm, Elizabeth (1998) 'The Rise of the Pub' in Donnelly, J. S. and Miller, Kerby A. (eds) *Irish Popular Culture 1650–1850* (Irish Academic Press: Dublin).

Mason, I. L. (1951) *A World Dictionary of Livestock Breeds, Types and Varieties* (CAB International: Walingford, 4th edn 1996).

Matthews, John and Matthews, Caitlin (1998) *British and Irish Mythology: An Encyclopaedia of Myth and Legend* (The Aquarian Press, Harper Collins: London).

Melton, Gordon I. (1999) *The Vampire Book* (Visible Ink Press, Gale Research: Farmington Hills, MI).

Moore, A. W., Morrison, Sophia and Goodwin, Edmund (1924) *A Vocabulary of The Anglo-Manx Dialect* (OUP: Oxford, rep. Yn Cheshaght Ghailckagh, 1991).

Morgan, John (1996) 'Irish Americans' in Jan Harold Brunvald (ed.) *American Folklore: An Encyclopedia* (Garland Publishing: New York/London).

Morton, H. M. (1961) 'The Magic Road Round Ireland' in *National Geographic*, March 1961, Vol. 119, No. 3, pp. 293–333.

Morton, H. V. (1930) *In Search of Ireland* (20th edn. Methuen: London).

Napier, Christopher (1989) 'Part II: Addresses and Discussion' in Crozier, Maurna (ed.) *Cultural Traditions in Northern Ireland* (Institute of Irish Studies, Queen's

University: Belfast, rep. 1993).

Neaman, Judith and Silver, Carole G. (1983) *A Dictionary of Euphemisms* (Unwin: London).

Newby, Eric (1987) *Round Ireland in Low Gear* (William Collins: Glasgow, rep. Picador: Oxford, 1988).

Newman, Harold (1981) *An Illustrated Dictionary of Jewelry* (Thames and Hudson: London, rep. 1999).

Ó Brógáin, Séamus (1998) *The Wolfhound Guide to the Irish Harp Emblem* (Wolfhound: Dublin).

Ó Ciosáin, Niall (1998) 'The Irish Rogues' in Donnelly Jr., J. S. and Miller, Kerby A. (eds) *Irish Popular Culture 1650–1850* (Irish Academic Press: Dublin).

Ó Crualaoich, Gearóid (1998) 'The "Merry Wake"' in Donnelly Jr., J. S. and Miller, Kerby A. (eds) *Irish Popular Culture 1650–1850* (Irish Academic Press: Dublin).

Ó Dónaill, Niall (ed.) (1978) *Gearrfhocloir Gaeilge-Bearla* (An Roinn Oideachais: Dublin, concise edn 1981).

Ó Faoláin, Sean (1941) *An Irish Journey* (Readers Union with Longmans Green: London).

O'Farrell, Padraic (1980) *How the Irish Speak English* (Mercier: Cork, rep. 1993).

O'Farrell, Padraic (1980) *Irish Proverbs and Sayings* (Mercier: Cork).

Ó Giolláin, Diarmuid (1998) 'The Pattern' in Donnelly Jr., J. S. and Miller, Kerby A. (eds) *Irish Popular Culture 1650–1850* (Irish Academic Press: Dublin).

Ó Giolláin, Diarmuid (2000) *Locating Irish Folklore: Tradition, Modernity, Identity* (Cork University Press: Cork).

Ó hAllmhuráin, Gearoid (1998) *A Pocket History of Irish Traditional Music* (O'Brien: Dublin).

Ó hÓgáin, Dáithí (1990) *Myth, Legend and Romance: An Encyclopaedia of the Irish Folk Tradition* (Ryan Publishing: London).

Ó hÓgáin, Dáithí (1995) *Irish Superstitions* (Gill and Macmillan: Dublin).

Ó Muirithe, Diarmaid (1997) *A Word in Your Ear* (Four Courts Press: Dublin).

Ó Muirithe, Diarmaid (1999) *The Words We Use* (Collection 3) (Four Courts Press: Dublin).

Ó Muirithe, Diarmaid and Nuttall, Deirdre (eds) (1999) *Folklore of County Wexford* (Four Courts Press: Dublin).

Opie, Iona and Opie, Peter (1959) *The Lore and Language of Schoolchildren* (Clarendon Press: Oxford).

Orsman, H. W. (ed.) (1997) *The Dictionary of New Zealand English* (OUP: Oxford/Melbourne/New York).

Ó Suilleabháin, Sean (1967) *Irish Wake Amusements* (Mercier: Cork, rep. 1997).

O'Sullivan, Patrick V. (1991) *Irish Superstitions and Legends of Animals and Birds* (Mercier: Cork).

Parlett, David (1992) *A Dictionary of Card Games* (OUP: Oxford).

Parry-Jones, D. (1964) *Welsh Children's Games and Pastimes* (Gee and Sons: Denbigh).

Partridge, Eric (1937) *The Penguin Dictionary of Historical Slang* (Penguin Books: Middlesex, rep. 1988).

Partridge, Eric (1950) *The Wordsworth Dictionary of the Underworld* (Wordsworth: Ware, Herts., rep. 1995).

Partridge, Eric (2000) (8th ed. edited by Paul Beale) *A Dictionary of Slang and Unconventional English* (Routledge: London)

Pascoe, L. C. (ed.) (1968) *Encyclopaedia of Dates and Events* (Hodder and Stoughton: Sevenoaks, rep. 1974).

Payton, Philip (1996) *Cornwall* (Alexander Associates: Fowey).

Peel, Hazel M. (1978) *Pocket Dictionary of the Horse* (Abson Books: Bristol).

Pennant, Thomas (1778) *A Tour in Wales* (abridged by David Kirk for Gwasg Carreg Gwalch: Llanrwst, 1998).

Pepper, John (1983) *Illustrated Encyclopaedia of Ulster Knowledge* (Appletree: Belfast).

Pickering, David, Isaacs, Alan and Martin, Elizabeth (eds) (1991) *Brewer's Dictionary of 20th Century Phrase and Fable* (Cassell: London, rep. 1994).

Pratt, T. K. (1988) *Dictionary of Prince Edward Island English* (University of Toronto Press: Buffalo, rep. 1996).

Purcell, Deirdre (1991) 'The Role of The Church' in *Insight Guides: Ireland* (APA Publications: Singapore, 3rd edn.).

Radford, Edwin and Smith, Alan (1945) *To Coin a Phrase: A Dictionary of Origins* (Macmillan: London, 1981).

Rawson, Hugh (1989) *A Dictionary of Invective* (Robert Hale: London, rep. 1991).

The Readers Digest Great Encyclopaedic Dictionary (1965) 3 Vols (The Readers Digest Association: London/Montreal/Cape Town).

Redmond, Garry (1979) 'The Sporting Tradition' in Gmelch, Sharon (ed.) *Irish Life and Traditions* (O'Brien: Dublin/Syracuse University Press: New York, rep. 1986).

Rimmer, Joan (1969) *The Irish Harp: Coairseach na hEireann* (Mercier: Cork, 3rd edn 1984).

Robb, Martha (1998) *Irish Dancing Costume* (Country House: Dublin).

Robinson, Mairi (ed.) (1985) *The Concise Scots Dictionary* (Aberdeen University Press: Aberdeen, rep. 1991).

Rose, Carol (1998) *Spirits, Fairies, Gnomes and Goblins: An Encyclopaedia of the Little People* (ABC-CLIO: Santa Barbara/Oxford).

Rosenstock, Gabriel (1993) *The Wasp in the Mug* (Mercier: Cork).

Ross, Ruth Isabel (1997) *Irish Oatmeal Cookbook* (Gill and Macmillan: Dublin).

Rowe, John (1965) 'Cornish Emmigrants in America' in *Folk Life*, Vol. 3, pp. 25–38.

St. Clair, Sheila (1971) *Folklore of the Ulster People* (Mercier: Cork).

Scott, John S. (1958) *Penguin Dictionary of Civil Engineering* (Penguin: Harmondsworth, Middlesex, 4th edn 1995).

Sennet, Bob (ed.) (1977) *Complete World Bartender Guide* (Poorhouse Press: Florida, rep. Bantam Books: Florida, 1988).

Seymour, John (1971) *About Pembrokeshire: Gwlad yr Hud/Land of Enchantment* (T .J. Whalley: Haversfordwest).

Shaffrey, Patrick (1979) 'Five Cities' in Gmelch, Sharon (ed.) *Irish Life and Traditions* (O'Brien: Dublin/Syracuse University Press: New York, rep. 1986).

Share, Bernard (1997) *Slanguage: A Dictionary of Irish Slang* (Gill and Macmillan: Dublin).

Sharkey, Olive (1985) *Old Days, Old Ways* (O'Brien: Dublin/Syracuse University Press: New York, rep. 1987).

Shaw, Carol P. (1996) *Famous Irish Lives* (Collins Gem, Harper Collins: Glasgow).

Shaw-Smith, David (1984) *Ireland's Traditional Crafts* (Thames and Hudson: London, rep. 1986).

Sheridan, Monica (1965) *The Art of Irish Cooking* (Doubleday and Co.: New York, rep. Hippocrene Books: New York, 1996).

Shields, Hugh (1993) *Narrative Singing in Ireland* (Irish Academic Press: Dublin).

Simes, Gary (1993) *A Dictionary of Australian Underworld Slang* (OUP: Oxford).

Simms, Katharine (1989) 'The Norman Invasion and the Gaelic Recovery' in Foster, R. F. (ed.) *The Oxford Illustrated History of Ireland* (OUP: Oxford).

Simpson, J. A., Weiner, Edmund S. (eds) (1989) *Oxford English Dictionary* (OUP: Oxford, 2nd ed., 20 vols).

Smith, Brian (1991) *The Horse in Ireland* (Wolfhound: Dublin).

Smith, D. J. M. (1988) *A Dictionary of Horse-Drawn Vehicles* (J. A. Allen and Co.: London).

Smith, Joanne (1995) *A Multi-ethnic Feast: Cuisine, Texas* (University of Texas Press: Austin).

Smith, M. W. G. (1971) *National Apple Register of the United Kingdom* (H.M.S.O.:

London).

Smith-Twiddy, Helen (1979) *Celtic Cookbook* (Y Lolfa, Talybont: Wales, rep. 1989).

Stalmaszczyk, Piotr (1997a) 'Dinnshenchas – Irish Placename Lore' in *The Celtic Pen*, Issue 12, Spring 1997.

Stalmaszczyk, Piotr (1997b) 'A Note on Celtic Influence in English' in *The Celtic History Review*, Vol. 2, Issue 4, Summer 1997.

Stephens, Meic (ed.) (1986) *The Oxford Companion to the Literature of Wales* (OUP: Oxford).

Swainson, Charles (1886) *The Folklore and Provincial Names of British Birds* (facsimile Llanerch: Felinfach, rep. 1998).

Thomas, Colin and Thomas, Avril (1997) *Historical Dictionary of Ireland* (Scarecrow Press: Lanham, MD/London).

Thomas, David (1939) *Animal Call-words* (Spurrell: Carmarthen).

Thomas, N. L. (1988) *Irish Symbols of 3500 BC* (Mercier: Cork).

Thompson, G. B (1959) 'A Preliminary Report' in *Ulster Folklife*, Vol. 5, pp. 9–13.

Thomson, George L. (1982) *Traditional Irish Recipes* (O'Brien: Dublin).

Thurston, H. A. (1954) *Scotland's Dances* (G. Bell and Sons: Glasgow).

Tucker, E. (1996) 'St Patrick's Day' in Brunvald, Jan Harold (ed.) *American Folklore: An Encyclopedia* (Garland Publishing: New York/London).

Urdang, Lawrence (1991) *A Dictionary of Names and Nicknames* (OUP: Oxford).

Vallely, Fintan (ed.) (1999) *The Companion to Irish Traditional Music* (Cork University Press: Cork).

Voth, Norma Jost (1981) *Festive Cakes of Christmas* (Herald Press: Scottdale, Pennsylvania/Waterloo, Ontario).

Wall, Richard (1986) *An Anglo-Irish Dialect Glossary for Joyce's Works* (Syracuse University Press: New York).

Wall, Richard (1995) *A Dictionary and Glossary for the Irish Literary Revival* (Colin Smythe: Gerrards Cross).

Weatherhill, Craig and Devereux, Paul (1994) *Myths and Legends of Cornwall* (Sigma: Cheshire).

Webber, Christopher (1989) *Bluff Your Way in Racing* (Ravette Books: Horsham).

Webber, David J. V. (1987) *An Illustrated Encyclopaedia of the Isle of Man* (rev. ed. The Manx Experience: Douglas, 1997).

Weiss, Rita (1985) *Favorite Irish Crochet Designs* (Dover Publishing Co.: New York).

Welch, Robert (ed.) (1996) *The Oxford Companion to Irish Literature* (Clarendon Press: Oxford).

White, Carolyn (1976) *A History of Irish Fairies* (Mercier: Cork, 4th edn 1992).

Wilcox, R. Turner (1969) *The Dictionary of Costume* (B. T. Batsford: London, rep. 1989).

Wilde, Lady (1991) *Irish Cures, Mystic Charms and Superstitions* (Sterling: New York).

Wilde, Lady (1996) *Ancient Legends of Ireland* (Sterling: New York).

Wilde, Sir William B. (1852) *Irish Popular Superstitions* (compiled by Mairtin O'Criofa, Sterling Publishing: New York, 1995).

Yates, Dora E. (1953) *My Gypsy Days* (Phoenix House: London).